D0770580

The Selected Works of Mahasweta Devi

Mahasweta Devi (b. 1926) is one of our foremost literary personalities, a prolific and best-selling author in Bengali of short fiction and novels; a deeply political social activist who has been working with and for tribals and marginalized communities like the landless labourers of eastern India for years; the editor of a quarterly, *Bortika*, in which the tribals and marginalized peoples themselves document grassroot level issues and trends; and a socio-political commentator whose articles have appeared regularly in the *Economic and Political Weekly*, *Frontier* and other journals.

Mahasweta Devi has made important contributions to literary and cultural studies in this country. Her empirical research into oral history as it lives in the cultures and memories of tribal communities was a first of its kind. Her powerful, haunting tales of exploitation and struggle have been seen as rich sites of feminist discourse by leading scholars. Her innovative use of language has expanded the conventional borders of Bengali literary expression. Standing as she does at the intersection of vital contemporary questions of politics, gender and class, she is a significant figure in the field of socially committed literature.

Recognizing this, we have conceived a publishing programme which encompasses a representational look at the complete Mahasweta: her novels, her short fiction, her children's stories, her plays, her activist prose writings. The series is an attempt to introduce her impressive body of work to a readership beyond Bengal; it is also an overdue recognition of the importance of her contribution to the literary and cultural history of our country.

The Selected Works of Mahasweta Devi

List of Titles

Mother of 1084
A Novel. Translated and introduced by
Samik Bandyopadhyay.

Breast Stories: Behind the Bodice, Draupadi, Breast-Giver
Translated with introductory essays by
Gayatri Chakravorty Spivak.

Five Plays: Mother of 1084, Aajir, Urvashi and Johnny, Bayen, Water
Adapted from her fiction by the author.
Translated and introduced by
Samik Bandyopadhyay.

Rudali: From Fiction to Performance.
This volume consists of the story by Mahasweta Devi
and the play by Usha Ganguli.
Translated with an introductory essay by Anjum Katyal.

Dust on the Road: The Activist Writings of Mahasweta Devi
A collection of articles published in
Economic and Political Weekly, Frontier, and other journals.
Edited and introduced by Maitreya Ghatak.

DUST ON THE ROAD

The Activist Writings of
Mahasweta Devi

Edited with an introductory essay by
MAITREYA GHATAK

CALCUTTA 1997

Cover image: Chittrovanu Mazumdar
Cover design: Naveen Kishore

ISBN 81 7046 143 X

Published by Naveen Kishore,
Seagull Books Private Limited,
26 Circus Avenue, Calcutta 700 017, India

Printed in India by Laurens & Co
9 Crooked Lane, Calcutta 700 069

CONTENTS

Introduction

The present volume is a collection of articles by Mahasweta Devi, written between 1981 and 1992. The selection covers most of her activist writings in English, published in journals and newspapers including *Economic and Political Weekly, Business Standard, Sunday* and *Frontier,* and a small but significant part of the large volume of her writings in Bengali, published in various newspapers and periodicals. The selection has been careful to include all the important essays and reports on the subjects and areas of concern which have preoccupied her over the years.

The articles deal with a range of issues relating to the deprivation, degradation of life and environment, exploitation and struggles of the labouring poor and the underprivileged, the landless and small peasants, sharecroppers, bonded labour, contract labour, and miners in West Bengal and Bihar. Many of them, but by no means all, are tribals.

For those who know her only through her fiction, the topics would appear familiar, as she has dealt with them in her novels and stories, and the people she writes about appear as characters in her fiction. This drawing directly on her intimate knowledge of ground realities characterizes her creative writing. As a writer, she is on record as saying that her commitment involves documenting the past and the continuing struggles of the people in their historical perspective. But Mahasweta is much more than a narrator of social reality and peoples' struggles.

In fact, creative writing is only one side of Mahasweta. There are several other dimensions to her personality: activities and priorities which are distinct but closely interrelated. So much so that they are practically inseparable and, for an understanding of the one, the totality needs to be taken into account. She cannot be branded by any one conventional label such as writer, social activist, reporter, editor or organizer of peoples' groups at the grassroots level: each is a true, but partial description of her. All these facets of her personality, considered together, sharply distinguish her from her contemporaries, not just in her home state of West Bengal, but in the rest of the country too.

THE MANY FACETS OF MAHASWETA DEVI

Creative Writing

As a creative writer, her contribution is important, both in significance and in volume. Her innovations with language and style have been recognized by critics and contemporaries as important contributions to the history of Bengali literary convention; and her prolific pen makes her one of the most widely published authors in her native tongue, Bengali.

Her first book, *Jhansir Rani* (The Queen of Jhansi), a biography of the woman ruler of a princely state in north India, who fought against the British in 1857, in the first war of independence by the Indian people, was published in 1956. To write this book, in 1954, Mahasweta felt she needed to go to the Bundelkhand area in the then United Provinces, far away from her home state West Bengal, where the legendary rebel queen continues to live in the minds and lore of the common people: not a very easy task given her situation at that point of time. Neither she, who was unemployed, nor her husband—a noted playwright and a card-holding member of the Communist Party of India (CPI), who did not have a job either—had the money. But, through generous support from friends and well-wishers, she was able to raise a total of Rs 400, a princely sum for her in those days, and off she went on her long journey, leaving behind her husband and a 6-year-old son. Both in terms of the choice of the subject—a young princess of a tiny state teaming up with rebel forces in 1857 against the might of the British empire and getting killed in the process—and the meticulous research that went into the writing of the book, drawing not only from all possible conventional archival sources but also from the oral traditions of the people of the area, transmitted through generations of lore and legends—Mahasweta charted a distinct path for herself.

Since then, 94 titles of fiction have been published, till January 1996. This does not include non-fiction works, books edited by her, textbooks she has written for schoolchildren, or translated versions of her books. (In fact, she co-authored an important series of textbooks for schoolchildren who study Bengali as a second language.)

Among Indian languages, her books have been translated into Hindi, Assamese, Telegu, Malayalam, Marathi, Oriya, Punjabi, Gujarati and Ho, a tribal language. She is being translated into Santhali, another tribal language. She has also been translated into English, Italian, Japanese and French.

If we divide her 40 years of creative writing, starting from 1956 as the base year, into 4 10-year phases, we see that in the first 10 years (1956–65), 19 titles were published; in the next 10 years (1966–75), 9; in the following 10 years (1976—85), 27; and in the last 10 years (1986–95), 39. The list, of course, keeps growing.

1966–75 may appear to be a lean period in her creative writing, but only quantitatively so. It is during this period that her creative writings took a sharp turn and she wrote 3 novels of consequence. They were *Kavi Bandyoghoti Gayiner Jivan O Mrityu* (The Life and Death of Poet Bandyoghoti Gayin), depicting the struggle of a lowcaste boy to achieve human rights; *Andharmanik* (lit. Jewel in Darkness, the name of a village), depicting the upheaval in Bengal's social life caused by the Bargi (Maratha cavalry) raids during the mid-18th century, and *Hajar Churashir Ma* (Mother of 1084), dealing with the radical left Naxalite movement of the early 70s in an urban setting. During this phase, she also wrote a few powerful short stories. It was a period of transition in the life of Mahasweta. She was, it would seem in hindsight, driven by a terrible restlessness, preparing for major changes in her life and career, both in terms of creative writing as well as her other activities.

She began her third creative-writing phase (1976–85) with a series of novels depicting the struggles of the people against exploitation, starting with *Aranyer Adhikar* (Right to the Forest). This was based on the life and struggles of Birsa Munda and the famous Munda rebellion against the British in the late 19th century. It was a moving account of the intrusion of non-tribals into the tribal heartland of Singbhum in Bihar under the British administration, the ruthless exploitation of the tribals, the disintegration of their agrarian and social order, and their militant struggle against the intruders under Birsa's leadership, a century ago. She got the state-sponsored Sahitya Akademi award for 1979 for this work.

From then on, the subject of her creative writing has remained the socially marginalized, the poor and the tribals, and their struggles. The tribals, who constitute 8 per cent, and the so-called scheduled castes, who constitute 17 per cent, of India's population, and who belong to the bottom of India's caste hierarchy, along with other depressed communities, meet these criteria as no other social category in this country does. They remain the focal point of her writing. With her intimate knowledge of what happens at the ground level, she depicts their life with brutal accuracy, savagely exposing the mechanics of exploitation and oppression by dominant sections of the society, who have the direct support of the state system—politicians, the police, and the administration; the process through which resources meant for the development of the poor evaporate even before they 'trickle down' to the people for whom they are meant; how the system has a vested interest in keeping the poor in poverty, turning them into beggars for the very resources which should be theirs by right.

Mahasweta has been criticized by literary purists who feel that she is merely a chronicler of social reality. But even a superficial reading of her fiction will establish that this is unjustified. She transcends the boundaries of material concerns, and highlights the value of a universal consciousness of exploitation and the strength to protest against it. Dr Nelson Mandela, handing her the Jnanpith—the highest literary award—in Delhi recently, said that 'she holds a mirror to the conditions of the world as we enter the new millenium.'

Her admiration for those who raise their voice in protest is apparent in her writings, and has remained consistent throughout her writing career, from her very first novel. Whether it is a struggle for political power or more immediate problems like demands for land, a higher share of the crop, minimum wages, roads, schools, drinking water, or for sheer human dignity, these remain the hallmark of her fiction—especially the little known, little lauded struggles which are part of everyday life and don't necessarily find a place in history books or the mainstream media.

One could ask—are the people she writes of at all aware of her creative writings? In 1992, I was doing fieldwork in a tribal village in the Medinipur district of West Bengal, for the National Institute of Adult Literacy. The village had just passed through an intensive literacy campaign and the purpose of the research was to see if any reading habit was retained after the campaign was withdrawn. The general complaint was that there was no reading material. In a village, a young tribal boy brought out a book, an abridged version of Mahasweta's *Birsa Munda,* written specifically for young readers. He said that this book was read by everyone of his community; it was through this book that they had learnt a lot about Birsa Bhagawan. The boy was a Munda. The book was also translated into the Ho language in Bihar.

Reportage

It is during this third phase, more specifically from 1980–81, that several other dimensions of Mahasweta started coming to the fore, almost simultaneously, setting her completely apart from her contemporaries. It was a new phase in her life, a phase of expanding horizons and activities, almost a period of liberation from the narrow, insular confines of her urban middle-class existence and environment, many norms of which she found oppressive and unacceptable.

Though she had been travelling in the tribal areas of Bihar and the countryside of West Bengal for years before this, it is from this period that she felt a desperate urge to communicate to a wider audience about what was happening to the people in the name of development, and their struggles for survival. It was as if she felt she had so much to say and do, in such a short time, that fiction was not an adequate enough medium for her. She wrote for newspapers and journals on a wide range of topics—the deprivation amongst and discrimination against tribals and the rural poor; police atrocities; official crimes of omission and commission; struggles of the poor for survival, identity and dignity; the need for literacy, education, irrigation, drinking water; the non-payment of minimum wages to workers in various unorganized sectors; problems of environment and ecology, and the need for more effective monitoring of government programmes so that they reached their target groups, organizations of the rural poor.

She considered this work to be so important that in 1982 she took leave for two years from the college in Calcutta where she had been teaching English Literature since 1964, and joined *Jugantar*, a Bengali newspaper, as a roving reporter. This gave her greater opportunity to travel in the countryside and she wrote weekly columns regularly for 2 years. It was during this period that she came into contact with a large number of people in the rural areas, common people, activists, even government officials and functionaries at the district, block and village levels, who became a part of her vast network and fan club, and remain so even today. They often provided her with information and leads which she followed up.

In 1984 she resigned from her teaching job and wrote for a Bengali daily, *Dainik Basumati*, for about a year. The following year she joined *Bartaman*, another Bengali daily with a deep penetration in rural areas, for which she wrote a weekly column till 1991. Since 1992 she contributes, from time to time, to another Bengali newspaper, *Aajkal*. Her newspaper writings have made her a household name among many people who may not even suspect that she is also a creative writer.

This volume includes a representative selection of her writings of this period.

Bortika

For a fuller understanding of the contents of this volume, there is another side of Mahasweta Devi that needs to be taken into account. In 1980, she started editing a Bengali quarterly called *Bortika* (torch). *Bortika* was an obscure literary periodical edited by her father from a district town. Once she took charge, after the death of her father in 1979, she changed the journal beyond recognition. Almost overnight it became a forum where small peasants, agricultural labourers, tribals, workers in factories, rickshaw pullers, could write about their life and problems. Many of the Lodha and Kheria tribals of Medinipur and Purulia districts, on whom there is a section in this volume, have written for this journal. For many of them, this was the first time they had written for any publication. Chuni Kotal, on whom there is an article in this volume, wrote for *Bortika* way back in 1982, 10 years before she was driven to commit suicide. In this way, *Bortika* is the first significant effort in alternative literature in Bengali.

Special issues have been published on tribal groups of West
Bengal, brick-kiln workers, the plight of workers in factories that
have closed down, land alienation among tribals, witch-killing,
movements of agricultural labourers, sharecroppers and
peasants, bonded and contract labour, problems of the Muslim
community—in short, the very type of issues which are being
covered in this volume.

Bortika also provided a forum for a number of young middle-
class people, activists, even people working for the government,
to write on a wide range of subjects that concerned the common
people. The editor only insisted that the contributions must be
based on facts, figures, observations and even surveys—only those
actually relevant to an understanding of a problem that affected
the people, or those which provided some directions for change.
She has no patience with abstract, theoretical and academic
research which she considers of little relevance to the real-life
situation.

Without any background of formal research, she meticulously
prepares detailed questionnaires and guides for surveys which are
intelligible for her type of contributors and circulates them
through her journal and her own remarkable network-cum-
courier service. The topics covered in *Bortika* are of a very wide
range, from general socio-economic village surveys to surveys on
problems of agricultural labourers, small peasants, tribal groups,
rickshaw pullers, workers in the unorganized sector, to give a few
examples. People from these backgrounds are invited to write
about their own situation, which they do, in large numbers. A
large number of people who generally remain invisible to the
urban middle class, even to scholars of subaltern studies, started
entering the pages of *Bortika*, as well as Mahasweta's life, straight
from their world, which was light years away for most of her
contemporaries. A unique venture, it is neither a 'project' for
Mahasweta, nor 'funded' by any source. *Bortika* limps ahead,
barely managing to recover its costs from a few advertisements
and its limited circulation.

A Resource Centre

Mahasweta Devi is also a one-person resource centre for
people in distress, a role that started demanding a considerable

part of her time in 1981 and still continues, with no sign of
abating, sometimes leaving her little privacy or time for other
activities, particularly creative writing. A large number of people
from many parts of the state, mostly remote villages, approach
her with their problems, personal or collective. She is always
accessible to them. Every day, a large number of such people
come to her or write to her. Many of them stay with her during
their visits. It can be anything. A daughter has been kidnapped
and the father feels that the police is not doing what it should;
the employment exchange is not forwarding names of those
registered for many years; government norms for reservation
quotas for scheduled castes and tribes are being flouted; tribal
children are not being admitted to school or getting
accommodation in a hostel; police atrocities on tribals and non-
tribals; lack of drinking water in some village; the inability to get
government credit despite fulfilling all norms; the fear of violent
attacks on some small tribal group; a complaint from marginal
farmers over government inaction for irrigation; request for
government recognition to a school; request for admission to
hospitals—practically anything imaginable.

She gives them a patient hearing, asks incisive questions, gives
them a dressing down for vague answers and the lack of proper
documents, methodically extracts all the essential information
and documents, and furiously starts phoning or shooting off
letters to the relevant people, officials, departments and
ministers. She even calls on them if she feels it is necessary. She
writes all the letters herself, by hand, making the requisite
number of carbon copies, and files all the papers carefully. Every
year, she writes several hundred such letters, follows them up,
calls and meets officials and others if necessary, in Calcutta or
even the districts. Sometimes she uses her newspaper columns to
draw the attention of the government to the problems that are
brought to her notice.

Powers that be in her home state are wary of her often
unwelcome intrusion into forbidden territories, sometimes
causing them considerable embarrassment. They are
uncomfortable with someone so fiercely independent, who is not
afraid of taking sides, without toeing the line of any political
party, leftist, rightist or centrist. Yet, at a personal level, she is able
to evoke a prompt response, if not always action, from the

authorities at all levels, including ministers. And it is not always because they want to get her off their backs as quickly as possible. There are many officials at various levels, from secretaries to the Government of India in Delhi down to officials at Block Offices in remote areas, who admire her for her work and do whatever they can. When it comes to seeking the help of the authorities and the administrative machinery at any level, she is very pragmatic in her outlook, and will approach anyone, often with a humility foreign to her personality. A seasoned realist because of her wide experience of ground-level activism amongst those most vulnerable and poverty-stricken, she operates very much through the system, which she recognizes and depicts, in her fiction, as ruthlessly exploitative and anti-people. She feels personally responsible for those whose cause she espouses, and is always conscious that they should not suffer as a result of her intervention.

Though many of the problems brought to her still remain unsolved, it is through no lack of effort on her part and, in a large number of cases, she has been able to move the government machinery into action and achieve positive results. She doesn't give up easily.

Small Groups

Early in this phase, Mahasweta Devi felt the need for organized group action. As early as 1981, she was involved in the formation of an organization of bonded labourers in Palamau district, along with a local journalist, Rameshwaram. Since then, she has been associated with a large number of organizations, most of them tribal and a few of those traditionally considered untouchable by Hindu society. Her belief in organized group action by these sections of the society arises primarily out of a feeling that many basic problems of these people are not addressed by the government or the organized political parties, who are more interested in using the people as voting fodder. She firmly believes that unless people unite in groups, assess their own situation, bring pressure on the authorities in a united manner, and actively participate in whatever needs to be done for them, no meaningful change can come about and that these grassroots-level organizations are best suited for planning and implementing development programmes for their own areas. She has taken up the cause of the voluntary organization—she does not use the term NGO (non-governmental organization)—at different policy-making levels, and has also served as a member of CAPART, a body set up by the Indian Government for funding development projects by voluntary organizations. Not many people know that she was awarded the title Padmasree over 10 years ago (awarded to distinguished citizens by the Government of India) not for her work as a writer, but for her work amongst small tribal groups of the Purulia and Medinipur districts of West Bengal.

Among the organizations she is associated with—she took the initiative in founding a few of them—are Paschim Banga Munda Tribal Samaj Sugar Ganthra; Paschim Banga Lodha Sabar Denotified Tribe Kalyan Samiti; Paschim Banga Bhumij Tribal Samajkalyan Samiti (Medinipur district); Paschim Banga Bhumij Tribal Samajkalyan Samiti (Purulia district); Paschim Banga Oraon Tribal Kalyan Samiti; Paschim Banga Sahis Scheduled Caste Kalyan Samiti; Paschim Banga Harijan Kalyan Samiti (North 24 Parganas district); Bharat Ker Adim Jaati Tribal Samiti (North 24 Parganas district); Adibasi Kalyan Samiti (South 24 Parganas district); Palamau Zilla Bandhua Samiti (Palamau district, Bihar); Adim Jati Aikya Parishad, Berhampur Municipal Sweeper Association (Murshidabad district); Paschim Banga Baul Fakir Sangha (Murshidabad district), and Paschim Banga Kheria Sabar Kalyan Samiti (Purulia).

Though the degree of involvement with individual organizations has varied over time, her involvement is always active rather than nominal, as a mere figurehead. She is as comfortable leading processions of bonded labourers through the streets of Daltonganj in Palamau, Bihar, as she is shouting slogans before the office of the Deputy Commissioner, or marching with the sweepers and scavengers of Berhampur in West Bengal—her family's hometown for many years—or shouting slogans with striking workers or dancing with tribal men and women, in high spirits, at a fair in Purulia district. At one large gathering of tribals in Jhargram, Medinipur, a few minutes before the meeting, Mahasweta was whisked away by a group of tribal youth. The meeting was about to start. There was no sign of her. Then, suddenly the whole atmosphere changed, enlivened with the rhythmic beating of the *dhamsa*, *nagara* and *madal*. It was a real sight for the large gathering that had assembled for the meeting. A group of tribals, dressed in their traditional costume, were approaching in procession, playing their musical instruments, carrying Mahasweta on a *duli* (a kind of palanquin) on their shoulders, with Mahasweta thoroughly enjoying the adulation despite her precarious position. She is willing to make all sorts of concessions for the tribals, to whom she is either ma (mother, amongst the Kheria tribals) or *marang dai* (elder sister, for the Santhals).

Whether it is an organization distributing artificial limbs amongst the physically handicapped in north Bengal, or another mobilizing public opinion against the taking over of agricultural lands for industrial projects in southern Bengal, or another protesting against police atrocities in some remote village, or against the government move to set up a missile-testing range in Chandipur in Orissa—all take her active support for granted and generally get it, even those few who probably do not deserve it.

For the last few years, she has been a regular feature at various handicraft exhibitions and sales in Calcutta, selling handicrafts made by an organization she is associated with.

For over the last 10 years, her involvement with the Paschim Banga Kheria Sabar Kalyan Samiti, a tribal organization, has been very close. She devotes a large part of her time and energy to this organization which is based in Purulia, the most backward district of West Bengal by all parameters. The Kherias of Purulia are a small group of tribals.

As this introduction was being written, a representative of the Paschim Banga Baul Fakir Sangha informed me of how, years ago, Mahasweta's intervention saved a number of members of this group from severe persecution by religious fundamentalists in some villages of Murshidabad district.

No one, not even Mahasweta, who is now 71, can meet the demands of such varied types of activity without her current involvement in any one adversely affecting another. But she keeps on trying, nevertheless. Nowadays, she occasionally laments that her working hours have come down from 18 hours a day to a mere 14, and, at this rate, she must live till the year 2025 to complete the projects she has already undertaken. She still has miles to walk, under the scorching sun and over the barren fields of Purulia, Medinipur, Palamau or Singbhum, oblivious to physical discomfort. For her, life has never meant looking back;

only looking forward. To new ideas, schemes, projects and activities. To motivating and enthusing others to organize themselves for their own development. To taking sides. To speaking up where silence would be a shame. To making trouble where not to do so would be a crime.

THE CONTENTS OF THIS VOLUME

Just as Mahasweta Devi's activist writings cannot be fully understood in isolation from her total range of activities, of which they are an integral part, the different subjects selected for this volume are also linked together integrally, and are facets of a common process of deprivation, exploitation of the vulnerable and marginal sections of the society, distortions in development, as well as the peoples' struggles and search for alternatives.

The issues have not yet reached a point 'where the discontented elements are compelled to organize themselves and the extreme tensions building up within the "complex molecule" that is the Indian village may end in an explosion' ('Causes and Nature of Agrarian Tensions', Ministry of Home Affairs, 1973). The big explosion envisioned by many and feared by some, hasn't taken place yet. But in the last 30 years, a series of outbursts of people's anger and disappointment, as well as a search for alternatives, have taken place and continue to do so. Many issues which have come to the fore in the last 3 decades have to do with areas traditionally ignored by the left, like caste and tribe, gender, ecology and environment, community and ethnicity, for instance. They are welcomed by many as new forms of social movements while others look at them as attempts to fragment the process of class struggle. The issues dealt with by Mahasweta Devi have to be seen in this perspective. They have been arranged in 9 sections, though there is an inevitable overlapping of issues between sections.

The Bonded Labourers of Palamau

This volume starts with a series of articles written between 1981 and 1984, focusing on the bonded labour system in Palamau district of Bihar. Palamau is the least developed district in one of the least developed states, which, incidentally, is also one of the richest in terms of forests, mineral resources and people. During this period, Mahasweta Devi also wrote a book on the bonded labour system, jointly with Nirmal Ghosh, that was published in Hindi, so great was her involvement with the subject. She was associated with the formation of the first association of bonded labourers of Palamau district in 1981, along with Rameshwaram, a journalist-activist of Daltonganj in Palamau district.

Under the bonded labour system, a person loses his status as free labour and virtually becomes serf labour under a person from whom he has taken a loan, the amount of which may appear to be ridiculously small. He forfeits the right to seek employment elsewhere, and the right to sell his labour or the products of his labour in the open market at market value. He or a member of his family has to work under the creditor till the loan is repaid. But the wages are absurdly low and the rate of interest astronomically high. Bonded labourers are not in a position to bargain over their wages and must accept whatever is customary for the landlords to give them. So once someone gets into bondage, he remains so till he dies and very often his son or someone in the family has to continue as a bonded labourer. Inter-generational bondage is a common feature of the system.

The system operates in many parts of India under various local names. According to an estimate made by the Gandhi Peace Foundation and the National Labour Institute in 1980, there were over 2 million bonded labourers in Andhra Pradesh, Bihar, Gujarat, Karnataka, Madhya Pradesh, Rajasthan, Tamil Nadu and Uttar Pradesh. Tribals formed over 18 per cent of the bonded labourers of these states and the scheduled castes 66 per cent. Together they accounted for nearly 85 per cent of those in bondage.

Though the Commissioner for Scheduled Castes and Tribes has been reporting to the parliament about this system since 1951-2, it was only in 1974-76 that the abolition of the system, identification of bonded labourers, and their rehabilitation, started, as part of a package of populist measures by the Government of India. I conducted evaluation studies of the rehabilitation measures in Palamau (Bihar) and Medak district (Andhra Pradesh) in 1980 on behalf of the Public Enterprises Centre for Continuing Education, Delhi, a government sponsored organization, a year before Mahasweta Devi went to Palamau. I visited many of the villages mentioned in this section. I also found, as Mahasweta's reports amply demonstrate, that the rehabilitation measures had, by and large, failed, because they were inadequate, and moreover provided through officials and sometimes the very people who were owners of bonded labourers. The land given was insufficient and unfit for raising any crop. The animals provided by the contractors mostly died within days. Some of the released labourers were getting entrapped into bondage again. Others were being taken away, as far away as the 'green revolution' belts in northern India, as contract labour, on terms which were extremely harsh.

So far, there is little difference between what a so-called professional researcher and Mahasweta Devi, the writer, found the situation to be in Palamau. But the similarity ends there. The researcher came, collected information, went away, submitted his report and started worrying about his next project. For Mahasweta, the bonded labourers of Palamau were not mere subjects for research, nor raw material for her literary writing. So, in the very first year of her visit to Palamau in 1981, she and her local associates had a long discussion with the bonded labourers and landless people. At the end of the discussion, a slate was brought, and Mahasweta, in her wobbly handwriting in the Hindi Devanagari script, wrote 'Semra Bandhua Mukti Morcha', or Semra Bonded Labour Liberation Front. This later became the Palamau District Bonded Labourer Liberation Front or Mukti Morcha. That happened to be on May Day of 1981.

The second article in the section deals with May Day of 1983. I was also present, as an observer. For the first time in the history of the district town of Daltonganj in Palamau, a large number of bonded labourers, men and women, assembled in a 2-day meeting and then marched in procession to the office of the district's administrative head, with Mahasweta, the well-known social activist Swami Agnivesh, Rameshwaram and other associates. The procession was led by 2 tribal women. Here is an eyewitness account:

> They made a round of the town before arriving at the headquarters of the DC of Daltonganj. The DC made a rare appearance to take the memorandum . . . Change is definitely in the air, with hundreds of bonded labourers—men and women—giving full-throated vent to their dreams:
> *Kamanewalah Khayega*
> *Lootnewallah Jayega*

Naya Jamana Ayega
(Those who earn shall eat;
those who exploit shall go;
a new era will come.)
(Mahua Bhattacharya, *Frontier*, 4 June 1983.)

In 1985 Mahasweta Devi visited a conference of the bonded labourers at Palamau. It was well attended by activists and media persons from various parts of the country. Apart from the problems of bonded labourers, the luring of poor children from the district to the carpet factories of Uttar Pradesh, forcing them to work practically as slaves, came to the surface. I was also present and found it to be a big affair, a national seminar replete with the media and leaders from Delhi. Yet, as Mahasweta Devi herself observed, something was amiss—the spontaneous participation of the bonded labourers as in the earlier conferences was not there. They were, almost, passive participants. One came back with a distinct feeling that if the earlier conferences were their own, this time it was held for them.

In the last article of the section, based on reports from a group of activists, Mahasweta Devi underscores the futility of rehabilitation without overall development, which, she feels, is possible only through a mass movement.

Within a few years of her last visit there, radical peasant movements involving issues of landlord exploitation, land, wages, collection of forest products, had taken root and the major CPI(ML) organizations were all present in the district, in growing strength. Pockets of struggle have developed in many parts of Palamau, including the Ranka block mentioned by Mahasweta Devi. This, even if indirectly, helped the bonded labourers, many of whom defied their creditors and refused to continue as bonded labourers. As a result, the owners of land, desperate in their need for labour, are offering sharecropping arrangements (DN, 'Agrarian Movement in Palamau', *Economic and Political Weekly*, 20 August 1988). In fact, some radical groups—Maoist Communist Centre (MCC) and a faction of the Indian Peoples' Front (IPF)—have effectively taken control of the vast reserved forest areas of the district (*The Telegraph*, 18 January 1997) and forest officials do not dare to enter the forests, according to newspaper reports. *Dharumaru*—catching them and beating them into bondage—as Mahasweta saw it and described in these

articles, is, hopefully, a thing of the past, though Palamau
continues to remain the poorest district of Bihar.

Contract Labour

And this leads directly to the second section of this volume
where Mahasweta Devi, in the first article 'Contract Labour or
Bonded Labour?' discusses the problems of thousands of
labourers of Bihar and West Bengal, who are driven by dire
poverty out of their homes, to work on contract, and are often
cheated of the money promised them by shrewd contractors and
recruiters. But that is only part of the story. Young tribal women
are taken away as labourers to the brick kilns of West Bengal or
Bihar, where they are not only ruthlessly cheated of their money,
but are regularly sexually exploited by the brick-kiln owners, their
employees, or those whom the owners want to keep in good
humour. Many do not come back.

West Bengal is a major recruiter of tribal women who come to
work in the brick kilns. In 1984, Mahasweta Devi published a
special number of *Bortika*, based on a survey of a number of brick
kilns of the state, and documented how the tribal women are
exploited. Because they come for about 5 months a year, and do
not vote in the state, no political party is interested in taking up
their cause. Whatever legal protection there is for contract
labourers exists on paper only. Only a few months ago, in January
1997, newspapers reported the rape and molestation of women
brick-kiln workers in a West Bengal district.

In a brick kiln, of the various operations involved, the most
arduous is the task of carrying bricks on the head. Even today,
those who do this work are mostly tribal women from Bihar and
Orissa. According to the *Bortika* survey of 1984, the going rate for
carrying 1000 bricks was Rs 3.30–4.40. And the average daily
earning, if they get the money, would be a mere Rs 4–5 after a
backbreaking day's work. The exploitation is no less ruthless in
brick kilns in Bihar. The rates have improved a little in recent
years but are nowhere near the government-fixed minimum
wages.

Yet, when the call comes, they have to go, for all the mother
may grieve over her daughter, Bali, as Mahasweta quotes from a
moving Ho song. Because, for the migrant labourer, life in the
green-revolution belt of Punjab, Haryana or western Uttar
Pradesh or the brick kilns of West Bengal or Bihar may be tough,

but back home it is impossible. She mentions the appalling situation of health facilities ·and education for children, and wonders what happened to the astronomical sums which have been spent in the name of tribal development in this part of Bihar. There is no work. No education for the children. No treatment for those who become ill.

According to a recent nationwide survey, about half the children in Bihar have not received a single dose of any vaccination and those who have received all doses of all vaccinations would be less than 10 per cent, the worst picture among all the states of India. Among the tribals, the situation is even worse, whether it is Bihar or West Bengal (Maitreya Ghatak, 'Red Eye of the Needle', *The Telegraph*, 14 February 1996).

Deprived of their land, with growing restrictions on their access to the forests, with little scope of employment even in areas where big industrial projects have come up on what was once tribal land, totally marginalized in their homeland, they have to migrate even in the best of years.

But is it only the tribals from Bihar or other states who migrate? The answer is provided by the other article of this section 'An Eastside Story'. Nearer home, right in the city of Calcutta, thousands of migrant labourers, both tribals and non-tribals, have over the years worked on such government projects as the Metro Railway, the Eastern Metropolitan Bypass, and the second Hooghly Bridge. Here also, poor landless people from surrounding districts of West Bengal have been recruited by contractors through a chain of agents and sub-agents. They are not paid the money they are promised and sometimes return, defeated, after working 12 hours a day, for months together, for food alone. For Mahasweta, the system of contract labour is a vicious form of labour exploitation that has come up all over the country and it is, virtually, a new form of bondage.

No Escape

The articles in this section deal with the degradation of the eco-system and the lop-sided afforestation policy of the government. The first article, 'Witch Sabbath at Singbhum' also shows how there is a systematic attempt, under the sponsorship of Hindu fundamentalists, to create a divide among tribals, so that the exploitation of tribals and their natural resources can continue unabated.

In fact, this article deals with a range of issues that tells the whole story of exploitation of the tribals in Singbhum, Bihar. Migration, because the local economy does not sustain them—not because it cannot, but because the tribals have lost all control over it; police atrocity; vicious communal politics by Hindu fundamentalists and their attempts to break tribal unity and create tension between Christian and non-Christian tribals so that the plunder of the natural resources by industrialists, politicians, traders, contractors, officials can continue; ravaging the environment in the name of industrialization and forcing poorly paid tribals to work in asbestos and cement mines without any protective measures, leading inexorably to severe illness—and even death—from asbestosis and silicosis.

This she reported in 1981. She went there again in 1983 and saw the ecological devastation that was being perpetrated by open cast mining and cement and asbestos factories and how, under the excuse of industrialization, the tribal land was continuing to be grabbed. She discusses these issues in the second article of this section, 'A Countryside Slowly Dying'.

For the tribals, it is not only wolves on the prowl, but tigers, bears and snakes which are blocking all the escape routes. There is no escape, as Mahasweta quotes from a song in the Ho language about a cowherd who has lost his way.

Are Mahasweta Devi's concerns about asbestosis and silicosis unfounded or exaggerated? Hardly, if one goes by facts available nearer home. In West Bengal, there is a stone-crushing unit at Chichurgeria in Jhargram, a tribal area of Medinipur district. In only 3 years, as recently as 1992–95, 20 workers—all of them tribals and 7 of them women—have died of silicosis and 12 others are waiting for death. The situation prevailing here is the same as Mahasweta Devi saw at Jhikpani and Roro of Singbhum, though on a much smaller scale. The matter was brought to the notice of the Supreme Court on 20 March 1996 by a non-government organization and Justice Kuldip Singh and Justice G. P. Patnaik have, in their recent judgement, ordered payment of compensation to the affected families and people (*Shram Bulletin*, vol. 2, October 1996). This was the first such case, probably, where compensation was ordered by the apex court of the country. But, one wonders, apart from these 20 in West Bengal, how many thousands are dying every year in all parts of the country in the stone-crushing, cement and asbestos industries? And how many more are going to die with the spurt in these industries under globalization of the economy? Protective measures just add to the cost of production and make you less competitive.

The third article in this section, 'Eucalyptus: Why?' deals with a question that has been a matter of major controversy among environmentalists, officials and experts—that of largescale plantation of eucalyptus under the social forestry programmes sponsored by the World Bank throughout the 80s and 90s. Those supporting eucalyptus emphasize its quick growth, and hardiness, as it is not destroyed by cattle. Those against eucalyptus—Mahasweta is one of them—criticize it on various grounds, the main one being the high consumption of water, which affects the underground water table. Experts on both sides present conclusive evidence in support of their respective arguments. But all agree that the water consumption rate of certain species of eucalyptus is very high and does affect the water table.

But Mahasweta's other criticisms against eucalyptus are irrefutable. For her, whether it is eucalyptus or anything else, the acid test is whose purpose it serves. Eucalyptus does not bear fruit, does not encourage undergrowth and wild life, and can help only certain types of industry with raw material, for instance, paper, matchstick or rayon. Whose interest are they going to serve? Surely not those of the people who live near the forests, the tribals, whose sustenance, traditionally, comes from the forests.

Like the celebrated environmentalist Sundarlal Bahuguna, she strongly supports the planting of a diverse range of trees that can provide food, fuel, fodder, and other means of sustenance. For years she has been arguing the case for planting a balanced forest of diverse varieties of plants, including fruit-bearing trees, and the need for a strong movement against eucalyptus plantation. Only recently, in a major departure from the policy followed so far, the Government of West Bengal has announced that henceforth, fruit-bearing trees would form half of all trees planted under the social forestry programme. If implemented, it would vindicate Mahasweta's years of campaigning.

Land and Employment

The displacement of tribals from their land—a historical process—has increased significantly over the last few years in the tribal heartland of Bihar, Madhya Pradesh, Orissa, Maharashtra, Gujarat and elsewhere, thanks to the massive expansion in so-called development projects under the various 5-year plans. And now there is a further spurt in such projects with the globalization of the economy and availability of generous credit from the World Bank for big industrial, irrigation and mining projects. But even before the World Bank came into the picture, right from the beginning of the 5-year plans in the early 50s, thousands of tribals have been uprooted and dams, factories and townships stand on what was tribal habitat even a few years ago. According to an estimate made in 1989, since independence, 1,65,00,000 people, many of them tribals, have been uprooted by various development projects in the country. Of them, only 39,50,000 (or less than a quarter) have been rehabilitated (Walter Fernandes, J. C. Das and Sam Rao, *Displacement and Rehabilitation—An Estimate of Extent and Prospects,* Delhi, 1989).

According to a more recent estimate, over 20 per cent or 13.5 million tribals have become victims of development. Out of the 1.7 million displaced by only 119 central and state projects for which data is available, over half are tribals. Mines have displaced 1.4 million tribals. Dams have displaced 5.3 million tribals. Industries, sanctuaries and national parks and other projects have displaced nearly another million tribals. Even though tribals constitute only about 8 per cent of the country's population, we see that they usually constitute about half of those displaced by development projects. There is no uniform rehabilitation policy for them ('Indigenous Peoples in India,' Sarini Occasional Paper, no. 1, Bhubaneshwar, 1997).

In the last 3 years, I have visited coal mine areas in Madhya Pradesh and Orissa and have seen how the tribals are being evicted, some for a second or third time in their lives, so that more aluminium or steel can be produced. It is another matter that the steel or the aluminium will not improve the quality of life for the tribal in any manner. The compensation, based on the amount of landholding, means almost nothing for many tribals, as they may not technically own any land. Neither the central nor the state governments have accepted the norm of 'land for land' as a basis for compensation. Not that this would have benefited those tribals who have no land at all. Even when a job is offered by way of compensation, the tribals who get the jobs promptly separate from their parents, leaving them to fend for themselves.

But the alienation of tribal land is an ongoing process even in West Bengal, despite the existence of stringent laws to protect the interests of the tribals, as Mahasweta shows. Sometimes it happens through the exercise of sheer musclepower, in brazen defiance of laws, with the administration and the law enforcement authorities looking the other way or even providing support. Those who dare to protest are harassed by the administration in every possible way. Agnu Panna, a tribal who had enough faith in the system to do everything possible under the existing laws for years, struggled in vain to get back his land, as Mahasweta found out. Sometimes it happens clandestinely, through devious means, taking advantage of the economic vulnerability of the tribal and his ignorance of the laws that exist to protect him. Mahasweta also points to the recent practice of starting new tea gardens in erstwhile West Dinajpur district, which is accelerating the alienation of tribal land in the area. According to the existing laws, no tea garden can be started on forest land, Teesta Command Area land, land given to landless people by the government, tribal land or agricultural land. Yet, flouting all government regulations, in the last 5 years, over 300 tea gardens have been set up in north Dinajpur, Jalpaiguri and Coochbehar districts. Of them, over 120 have been started in a single subdivision of north Dinajpur district, according to a recent press report (*Anandabazar Patrika*, 13 February 1997). The same report indicates that thanks to obliging panchayats and officials, getting a 'no objection certificate' is not difficult.

Exporting more tea is very important for some people, but why should tribals and poor peasants be systematically deprived of their only means of livelihood and that, too, in a state like West Bengal? As Mahasweta points out, among those who are grabbing tribal land for tea gardens are some who have the highest political connections in the state and the total support of the administration. Though the administration has extensive powers to provide redress to the tribals under law, it often pretends to be ignorant of these provisions. Thus the whole system is loaded against the poor and often illiterate tribal whose land is being taken away. He does not stand a chance against the formidable combine of land grabbers, local panchayats, politicians, the police, the administration and crafty lawyers. In surveys conducted by the Government of West Bengal in the 70s and early 80s on indebtedness and alienation of land among tribals, it was found that both went together, and that they existed on a very wide scale in the state.

Another article in this section, 'The Call Never Comes', deals with the problem of unemployment among tribals in West Bengal. There are constitutional provisions regarding reservation in recruitment and promotion for scheduled castes and tribes in India. It is a common experience, all over the country, that the quotas reserved for these categories are never filled, with manipulation and violation of rules subverting these regulations. But here Mahasweta deals with another side of the problem. Scheduled caste and tribe youth, registered with employment exchanges for years, do not get even a single 'call' for an interview through these exchanges. True, the problem of unemployment among educated youth is a general problem in the country. In West Bengal alone, there were 5 million job aspirants registered with the employment exchanges of the state in 1994 (Statistical Abstract, Government of West Bengal, 1994–95). In the same year, only 9893 were placed through the exchanges. In 1980, there were 2.5 million youth registered and 13,831 were placed. Things have, apparently, worsened in the last decade and a half. While this is a general problem, the tribal youth are in a specially disadvantaged situation as they lack the influence or connections to get even a single call, despite being registered for years. Mahasweta raises questions about obvious cases of discrimination where Lodhas are 'not found to be fit' for employment as forest guards, or tribals are systematically kept out of thousands of posts of primary teachers even in tribal areas. Only recently I found that in the tea-garden area of Dooars in Jalpaiguri district, primary schools in predominantly tribal areas have recruited non-tribals as teachers. They just come and go, as their language is not understood by the tribal children. Mahasweta also points to cases where those who are neither from a scheduled caste nor tribe manage to illegally procure such certificates to secure jobs in reserved posts. As things stand, tribals are not getting any special benefits, and they are being systematically denied the opportunity of getting even the jobs reserved for them. The growing resentment over these issues is alienating the tribal youth from the mainstream all over the country. The consequences are there for everyone to see: increased political separatism and revolutionary activity.

Political and Cultural Dimensions of Discrimination

The first article in this section deals with the Jharkhand movement, a movement for a separate homeland for the tribals. Historically speaking, the movement has its origin in the struggles of Tilka Majhi, 1784; the Ho revolt, 1820; the Kol insurrection, 1832; the Santhal rebellion, 1855; and the Birsa movement, 1895–1900. The formal demand for Jharkhand was raised by the tribal leader Jaipal Singh after independence. The demand was rejected by the State Reorganisation Committee in 1955. For an understanding of the demand for a separate Jharkhand state, some basic idea about the tribal population is necessary. At the last head count (1991 census), India had a total tribal population of 67,758,390, accounting for about 8 per cent of the country's population. But the tribal population is unevenly distributed among states and zones. The central and eastern regions are numerically the tribal heartland of the country, accounting for nearly 55 per cent of the country's tribal population. Here Madhya Pradesh accounts for about 23 per cent of the country's tribals, followed by Orissa (10.38 per cent), Bihar (9.77 per cent), Andhra Pradesh (6.20 per cent) and West Bengal (5.62 per cent). The other zone accounting for over 28 per cent of the country's tribals is the western zone. Here Maharashtra tops the list with 10.80 per cent, followed by Gujarat (9.09 per cent) and Rajasthan (8.08 per cent). These 2 zones account for nearly 83 per cent of the country's tribals. The north-east accounts for 12.15 per cent, and the southern zone, consisting of Karnataka, Kerala and Tamil Nadu, accounts for only 4.15 per cent.

If we take a map of India, plot all the districts and show those which have a high (35–75 per cent) to moderately high (15–35 per cent) concentration of tribal population, we would see that there is a countrywide contiguous tribal corridor starting from Maharashtra–Gujarat–Rajasthan that extends through Madhya Pradesh, Bihar, Orissa and parts of West Bengal. Then there is the north-east, which has the highest concentration of tribals among the Indian states.

If you look at such a map, an interesting picture emerges, a picture of not one, but 3 distinct Indias. The tribal corridor, running roughly across and through the centre of the country, forms a divide between north and south India. It also contains India's richest deposits of minerals and forest produce. In the post-independence period, the people of Jharkhand demanded a separate state comprising 18 districts of Bihar, 3 districts of West Bengal, 4 districts of Orissa and 2 districts of Madhya Pradesh. The area has an overall population of 4 crores, with about 30 per cent tribals. The demand has historical roots in the South-West Frontier Agency formed by the British in 1833, when all these areas were a single unit with Chhotanagpur having its headquarters at Hazaribagh; later distributed among the 4 states when the agency was dissolved (A. K.Roy, 'Jharkhand Area Autonomous Council,' *Economic and Political Weekly*, 3 December 1994).

After years of agitation, the movement received an impetus from a situation that is directly linked to the employment of tribals. Before the coal mines were nationalized in 1972, a large number of tribals used to work in the mines. With nationalization, the mainstream people saw the opportunity for an expanded work force, paid at lucrative public-sector rates. Overnight all the records were manipulated, the names of genuine tribal workers deleted and thousands of fictitious names of non-tribals inserted. It is they who finally got most of the jobs—yet another example of criminal discrimination against tribals who had been working for years at meagre private-sector wage rates. At this time, the tribals' struggles became a point of convergence for left trade union movements in the coalfields and the agrarian movements of the Santhals, also heavily influenced by the Marxist Coordination Committee. As the movement began to gain momentum, an unsympathetic mainstream society did not hesitate to brand it secessionist.

Big industry considered the Jharkhand movement a threat to its continuing exploitation of resources, and unleashed all sorts of divisive forces, encouraging communalism, casteism and ethnic violence, all of which were previously almost unknown in these areas. As is clear from the earlier section on ecological degradation in tribal areas, these issues did not escape Mahasweta's keen attention; she also sharply pointed out how the vicious forces of communalism were being systematically used to destroy tribal unity.

Mahasweta's article on Jharkhand, written 15 years ago, refutes this premise of divisiveness and unequivocally supports the demand for a separate state of Jharkhand. Even today, the issue is far from being resolved, even though the Government of Bihar has formed a Jharkhand Area Autonomous Council comprising the tribal areas of Bihar. The Council has been given little power and meagre resources. It has failed to meet the aspirations of the tribals of even Bihar alone. One wonders, if India today can have 26 states out of the 14 we had at the time of independence, why can't we have a few more that meet the legitimate aspirations of large sections of the people? Mahasweta's article on Jharkhand has to be seen in this perspective.

The next article in this section is a passionate plea for according tribals their rightful place in the history of the country, as well as a demand for recognition of tribal languages and identity. It is true that the struggles of the tribals in British and even pre-British days have been neglected in books of history by both British and Indian historians. Only recently does one see some signs of change in this respect.

The question of tribal identity is closely linked with tribal languages. Most tribals live in close proximity to non-tribals. Inevitably, a large section tends to adopt the surrounding non-tribal language as its mother tongue, or to retain both the languages in home environments. The situation becomes more complex when a particular tribal language-speaking group is scattered over several states. But it is also true that practically nothing has been done in independent India to sustain and develop the tribal languages. As Mahasweta points out, if Sindhi and Kashmiri can be recognized, why not Santhali, as there are many more people speaking Santhali than Kashmiri? There are quite a few tribal languages spoken by more people than those who speak Sindhi. Yet Sindhi has been recognized, but not the tribal languages. Not a single national-level literary award for work by a tribal on tribals in his/her own tribal language or in the language of his/her state has been declared even 50 years after the independence of the country.

For centuries forces in this country have worked to absorb,

assimilate and even destroy tribal identity. The dominant Hindu society has already co-opted, through the process of Sanskritization, many tribal groups and ways which are today indistinguishable from the dominant culture. The wave of assault from the process of missionization under colonial patronage (Lachman Khubchandani, *Tribal Identity*, Delhi, 1992), posited alternate religions and values of life against indigenous beliefs and customs. And now, in independent India, forces have been unleashed by the development process in the form of mining, deforestation, construction of high dams, steel plants, and townships affecting tribal areas, accelerating the destitution and marginalization of the tribals. Add to this the continuous onslaught in the media and on cultural fronts which attack all indigenous cultures of the country, but more so tribal culture because of its vulnerability. In such a situation, Mahasweta's pleas for recognition to some tribal languages, declaration of national-level awards for works by tribals and recognition of the role of the tribals in the anti-imperialist movements, gain importance.

Lodhas and Kherias of West Bengal

The next section deals with smaller tribal groups of West Bengal, the Lodhas of Medinipur district and the Kherias of Purulia district. In the census, both are recorded as Savaras. The census does not publish the numbers of Lodhas and Kherias separately. According to available estimates, the Lodha–Savaras of Medinipur would be just over 40,000 in number. The Kheria–Savaras are a much smaller group, numbering today around 15,000. Most of the Lodhas and Kherias do not have any land of their own and work either as agricultural labourers or are engaged in food gathering, fishing, and hunting to the extent possible in the current situation (this is more prevalent among the Kherias). Numerically and otherwise, the Lodhas are somewhat more advanced than the Kherias. Not only are these tribes the poorest of the poor in their respective districts— Santhals and Mundas would be considered much more 'advanced' than them—they are seriously handicapped on another count. Under the colonial regime, several tribes in various parts of the country were officially notified as 'criminal' tribes. Lodhas and Kherias fall into this category. The implication is that whenever a crime is committed anywhere in the vicinity, not only the police, but even the society at large takes it for granted that the criminals are these tribals. And retribution follows. After independence, in the 50s, these tribes were officially 'denotified' but the stigma continues. For many years, even after independence, the only Kheria one saw in the town of Purulia was in chains, being escorted by the police to the courts. For years after the denotification, throughout the 60s and 70s, all sorts of atrocities were committed on these tribes not only by the non-tribal Hindus, but by advanced tribal groups as well. On some pretext or the other, hundreds of Lodhas have been cruelly killed by these people.

In the early 80s, Mahasweta came into contact with them and took up their cause in her own way. In 1982 she published a special number of *Bortika* on the Lodha–Kherias and their problems. Many Lodhas wrote about the problems they have to face, the lack of development in their areas and their abject poverty, with no opportunity of livelihood. Whenever there was any incident of atrocity against the Lodhas, Mahasweta took it up with the administration. There have been quite a few occasions when news reached her about possible attacks on the Lodhas, and she moved the administration to take pre-emptive action. But, above all, she tackled the issue of lack of development among these groups. How far their material condition has changed over the years as a result of these efforts is debatable, but the administration today is irrefutably more sensitive to incidents of atrocity, which have reduced in frequency; and above all there is much more awareness and confidence in these groups and they have become more assertive about their rights.

Included in this section is the story of Chuni Kotal, a girl belonging to a poor Lodha family of Medinipur. For months together every year, her family could not afford rice; they had to survive on food collected from the jungles. Starvation was a regular feature. In the 1982 Lodha–Kheria number of *Bortika*, Chuni wrote her own life-story, in which she described how, under circumstances many would consider impossible, she took her Higher Secondary (school-leaving) examination. For a tribal girl in West Bengal, this was a truly difficult feat. Consider the statistics published by the Government of West Bengal, based on the 1991 census (Statistical Handbooks of West Bengal, 1994). In West Bengal, the literacy rate among all categories of men is 68 per cent (rounded off). Among women it is 47 per cent. Among scheduled-caste men and women it is 34 per cent and 14 per cent respectively. But among the scheduled tribes, it is as low as 21 per cent for men and 5 per cent for women. For Lodhas and Kherias, it is even lower. Chuni Kotal became the first female graduate amongst the Lodhas. Then she got a job. Later she gained admission into Medinipur University for her Masters in Anthropology. There she became the butt of ridicule among a section of the students and faculty, and got caught in the crossfire in a battle for power amongst the faculty. Even in her place of work, life was made miserable for her by her immediate bosses. Unable to bear the pressure, she committed suicide in 1992. Of course, inquiry committees were set up, and, of course, no one was found guilty. Chuni's sin was that she had dared to forget her origins and her rightful place.

Organizations of the Rural Poor

The articles in this section deal with organizations of the rural poor. Both were published in the mid-80s when there was increasing awareness among the planners and policy makers that without the participation of the people, development remains incomplete. This was also the period when there was a substantial growth in the number of NGOs working in Third World countries, including India. Multilateral, bilateral and other funding bodies had started channelizing development funds through the NGOs. Today, there is a massive growth in the number of NGOs all over the country. However, most of them are based in urban areas and managed and controlled by the middle class. Many of the NGOs are organizations set up and run for the so-called target groups and not really controlled or managed by them. Generous funds are available to these NGOs, with very little actual accountability to the people for whom these funds are procured. And there is very little voluntarism left, most of the work being executed by poorly paid project staff. Mahasweta is a strong believer in voluntary action and voluntary organizations. But her type of voluntarism is somewhat different.

Strangely, Mahasweta's initial inspiration over grassroots-level organizations came from seeing the good work done among the poor Kherias of Purulia by the District Science Centre, very much a government organization. But the way in which the person in charge of the Centre, Amalendu Roy, mobilized people at the grassroots level, and got development projects executed by the people themselves, was an eye-opener for Mahasweta. She doesn't believe in grandiose schemes, but in those which the people themselves can manage; which need not cost a lot but can solve some of the people's basic problems through their own initiative. She also feels that the massive leakage that takes place in government development programmes can be eliminated when people manage their own projects. She herself is associated with a number of such organizations and deeply involved with the Paschim Banga Kheria Sabar Kalyan Samiti based in Purulia, where a number of development schemes have been implemented by the people through grassroots-level initiatives. Over the last decade she has been deeply involved in the affairs of this organization, which has really made an impact on the condition of the Kheria tribals. Not only have new avenues of income been created for this small tribal group, but, more importantly, the Kherias, who are still at the hunting and food-gathering stage (with almost nothing to hunt and gather in the dwindling forests), have found a new identity, as well as the collective strength to protest against their oppression by dominant communities, the police and the administration, merely because they were once classified as a criminal tribe by the British. The relentless efforts of Mahasweta and this organization have led to a perceptible change of attitude in the police and administration. So involved is Mahasweta with this group that she calls it 'the last bus stop' in her life.

Superstition, Casteism and Communalism

The articles in this section deal with issues of superstition, casteism and communalism—both among tribals and in mainstream society—and document some commendable efforts to counter this menace. Amongst the tribals, belief in the 'witch' has been there for a long time. Mahasweta tries to analyse the reasons why it persists even today, and how the superstitious beliefs of the ignorant are being used by some people for material benefit or to settle personal scores. She also discusses instances where it was possible to prevent killings, mostly (though not always) of women, after branding them as witches, through the sincere efforts of the administration. In this connection she also pays tribute to the late Santhali poet and writer Saradaprasad Kisku, who was a crusader against the custom of witch-hunting in his own community and bravely fought the system at considerable risk to himself, also inspiring a large number of youth of his own community to take up the cause. Mahasweta rightly points out that till there is an improvement in the availability of medical facilities and education—till overall development takes place—such age-old beliefs cannot be eliminated easily. Mahasweta also discusses such superstitious beliefs among people in mainstream urban society, who are supposed to be both educated and enlightened.

In other articles she discusses the problems of untouchability and communalism. What she saw in the *domtolis* (the doms are the untouchables who service the cremation grounds; their ghettoes are shunned by other inhabitants of the area) of Daltonganj, in Bihar, makes her question the very basis of independence of the country. She also points out how untouchability exists in West Bengal as well, and how a section of the administration turns a blind eye to cases of blatant casteism and communalism.

A Tribute

The last article in this volume, 'Remembering Asoke Bose', was written jointly by Mahasweta and me in early 1984, soon after we heard that Prakash Roy, the veteran CPI trade-union leader in Madhya Pradesh, had died. The article is not a history of the peasants' movement in the Kakdwip area of West Bengal, but our tribute to one of the key leaders of the movement. In Madhya Pradesh, where Prakash Roy chose to live after 1952, and also in his own political party, the CPI, few knew that the man known as Prakash Roy was actually Asoke Bose and that he was living in Madhya Pradesh under a fictitious name, as a fugitive from the law. Nor did many people know that the name Asoke Bose and its aliases, Bidyut or Nikunja, once used to strike terror in the minds of landlords, their employees and the police, in the Kakdwip area of West Bengal in 1948–51; or that there was a large financial reward declared for his arrest. He left West Bengal not only to save himself from the capital punishment which seemed certain, but also to save a few of his associates from the same fate.

In the mid-70s, both Mahasweta and I were interested, for our own separate fields, in understanding the nature and causes of agrarian movements in various parts of the country, particularly West Bengal. Around that time, I was involved in a research project that tried, among other things, to reconstruct some of the movements of the past not only from archival materials but also from the memories and experiences of some of the participants, both leaders and common peasants. It was during this time that I came into contact wih a number of such activists. Mahasweta took a strong interest in the work and also met quite a few of them. It was through her enthusiasm that, later, special issues of *Bortika* were brought out in 1986–87, documenting the well-known Tebhaga movement in Kakdwip, as well as in the rest of Bengal.

In 1980, under somewhat dramatic circumstances, I came upon Dr Purnendu Ghosh in Bilaspur, Madhya Pradesh—the same man who has been mentioned as the 'Ranga Doctor' in the article. In 1948–49, Dr Ghosh was in charge of a medical squad treating peasant activists injured in action. After the collapse of the Kakdwip movement, he spent a few months in prison. After his release, he settled down in Bilaspur, little knowing that his former leader Asoke was just a few hundred kilometres away in Rajnandgaon. Dr Purnendu Ghosh became a very successful doctor in Bilaspur.

Yet, when radical movemens started spreading in Madhya Pradesh and Bihar in the early 70s, Purnendu established links with some of the radical groups and started training them in 'last-aid', like he had done in Kakdwip years before. Last-aid, because injured peasant activists had nowhere else to go for treatment. In the 70s he was arrested twice and spent 2 years in jail.

After years of living in nearby towns, only a few years before I met Purnendu, he came to know that the famous trade-union leader of the CPI, Prakash Roy, was none other than his one-time leader Asoke Bose. They met once. By then there was an invisible barrier between the two. The latter now believed in parliamentary democracy, while Purnendu remained an incorrigible believer in more radical alternatives. Yet his respect for the Asoke Bose of 1948–50 remained undiminished.

In January 1983 we received news from Purnendu that Asoke Bose was unwell. Both Mahasweta and I wanted to meet Asoke Bose in person; so off we went to Bilaspur. Accompanied by Purnendu, we met Prakash Roy alias Asoke Bose alias Bidyut alias Nikunja, and spent two days with him.

It was a memorable experience for all of us. For Mahasweta, it was part of her relentless search for heroes, a search that had started decades ago with the queen of Jhansi; Purnendu was revisiting a leader who had inspired him over 32 years ago; as for me, I was tracing the most important missing link in the Kakdwip movement.

Due to a cerebral attack some years before, Asoke had a problem with speech. He could speak, but slowly. There was a time when his speeches could rouse sharecroppers and agricultural labourers, inspiring them to confront armed forces at the risk of their own lives, as Purnendu repeatedly reminded us. Now, when he was asked a question, he took some time before responding, and spoke very slowly. Yet, on two occasions he spoke with lightning speed, surprising all of us.

The first time was when Purnendu casually asked which peasants had been killed in the first major confrontation in Chandanpinri village. Almost in one breath, Asoke mentioned all the 8 names correctly.

I am specifically mentioning this because, on 9 May 1997, there was a meeting in Chandanpinri to pay homage to the Kakdwip heroes, living and dead. I was in Chandanpinri after many, many years. A monument has been erected at the exact spot where the police killed 4 women and 4 men in November 1948. The monument, I was told, has been erected under the patronage of the state's major communist party and its peasant wing. It was erected over 10 years ago. The name of one peasant activist, Adhar, who was killed that day, was missing from the list of martyrs engraved on the monument. For the last 10 years the villagers of Chandanpinri have been repeatedly drawing the attention of the powers that be to the matter, to no avail. But the names were deeply imprinted on the mind of Asoke, even after 32 years.

The second question was asked by Mahasweta and myself. What, according to him, were the most significant mistakes of the Kakdwip movement? Again, Asoke spoke at lightning speed, and mentioned what he considered to be the three most important mistakes. These were: that peasant activists, who were practically unarmed, were asked to confront armed forces—instead, guerrilla warfare techniques should have been adopted; that the issues about which peasants were conscious and prepared to fight were often mixed up with issues about which they were not aware, such as the capture of state power, and yet they were asked to fight for them; that terrorism by individuals, groups or even armed squads cannot replace peoples' participation.

These were not new points to us—he had mentioned them in the document he submitted to the CPI in 1951. What is important is the priority he gave them, over many others. They remain relevant for radical peasant movements even today.

With hindsight, one could ask today if the Kakdwip movement was really a failure. Kakdwip was a continuation of the earlier Tebhaga movement, when the sharecroppers demanded a two-third share of the crops. In Kakdwip, it reached a new level—a demand for land was also raised. It is because of the militancy of the movements that in 1949 an ordinance was issued virtually accepting the demands of the sharecroppers. Thus, the Tebhaga and Kakdwip movements paved the way for the land reform measures of subsequent periods, and also inspired the radical Naxalite movement in the late 60s.

On our return from Rajnandgaon, Mahasweta Devi contacted Kangsari Haldar, a veteran leader of the Kakdwip area before Asoke went there. (He has been mentioned in the article.) Kangsari kept in touch with Asoke in later years, even supporting him financially. Kangsari Haldar, who is 87 today, helps run a local school for girls in South 24 Parganas. For years he had been trying to upgrade the school and recruit new teachers: in vain, as the government recognition would not come. Mahasweta Devi intervened and the recognition came promptly.

Recently, when Mahasweta Devi was handed the wellknown jnanpith literary award by Dr Nelson Mandela, she said in her acceptance speech that as we are about to enter the new millenium, a curtain hangs before us. A curtain of all-pervading darkness. A darkness that separates the people from mainstream society. What is necessary is to tear apart that curtain, see what lies on the other side, and, in the process see our own, true face.

As this volume shows, she did try. Albeit in her very own way.

Maitreya Ghatak, August 1997, Calcutta.

The Bonded
Labourers of
Palamau

Back to Bondage

Rameshwaram was my host at Daltonganj. This remarkable man has his own press in an outer room. A freelance journalist, he dreams of starting a weekly newspaper, a wish which has little chance of fulfilment. It does not dampen his spirits at all.

He collects data and statistics on Palamau, covers hundreds of miles on foot visiting one bonded-labour village after another, plays willing host to all the visitors interested in the real Palamau, with the help of an even more remarkable family unit and some faithful friends. His wife, who is a teacher, bears the heavier burden most cheerfully. I was really struck by his children. His schoolgoing sons and college-going daughter cook, sweep the house, draw water from the well, water the garden, look after the guests. All of them share the sympathy of their father and mother for the exploited lower castes and·the *bandhua majdoors* or bonded labourers. I do not see such co-ordination between preaching and practising in the so-called politicized households of West Bengal.

After a quiet night on the open terrace, Rameshwaram woke us up in the early morning. Our team of 5—Rameshwaram, myself, Mahadeb Topo, an Oraon bank employee, Shashi the photographer and Sravan Kumar, a Hindi poet and bank employee from West Bengal—ran towards the banks of the River Koel and mounted a truck. The truck took us to Chainpur. Our destination was Semra, a bonded-labour village some miles away. We walked along the dusty road.

Semra village came into the limelight when, in 1976, a camp

for freed bonded labourers was conducted there from March 20 to March 26. The National Labour Institute, Delhi, union and state Labour Ministries and the district administration collaborated in holding the camp. Baliram Bhagat, Speaker of the Lok Sabha, inaugurated the camp. The collaborators were further helped by resource persons from the A. N. Sinha Institute of Social Studies, Patna; Ranchi University, Bihar Tribal Research Institute, Ranchi; Indian Institute of Public Administration, New Delhi; the Commissioner, Patna Division, and a number of his colleagues, and Dr Philip Herbst of the ILO. Junior officers in the district administration also collaborated in holding the camp.

The camp, referred to by the villagers as the *shivir*, was inaugurated by the Lok Sabha Speaker and aroused great enthusiasm. The participants, ex-*kamias* in 1976, said that they needed Rs 6 a day for a family of 4. To tide over the lean months, they wanted freedom to collect *mahua* and other edible jungle fruits. They wanted a minimum of 10 acres of cultivable land, the necessary agricultural equipment, seeds and a well. Some had already been given 2 acres of *tanr*—or rocky land—by the Deputy Commissioner. The Deputy Commissioner instructed the soil conservation department to give priority to such lands and to employ only those persons as labourers who would be the ultimate beneficiaries. The forest and other departments employing labour had been issued similar instructions to give priority in matters of employment to ex-bonded labourers. This was necessary because the former bonded labourers were being boycotted by their erstwhile masters in matters of employment (R. N. Maharaj, 'Freed Bonded Labour Camp in Palamau', *NLI Bulletin*, October 1976).

The same article mentions that 'in addition to these measures, the Deputy Commissioner had also distributed among them some poultry, Yorkshire pigs, and milch cattle. Our participants could testify to the correctness of all this. From our side we also gave them some feedback.' They were told of the minimum wages fixed by the Government of Bihar and other measures planned for them. 'With the help of a pair of scales, paddy and standard metric weights we could clearly demonstrate to them how much they had been cheated in the matter of payment of wages.'

In all, 60 freed bonded labourers participated in the camp

and 8 were from Semra.

Gradually we neared Semra. A big pond on the left of the road was a great relief to our eyes. But the water was green, unfit for drinking. Buffaloes wallowed in the mud. An old woman washed clothes. The *mouja* Semra is actually composed of 3 villages. Semra on the roadside, Kharo and Bahera further up in the hills. Towards the west is Loharsimi. Semra is big, the other 3 villages smaller and situated at a distance from one another. The first thing we noticed was the receding forest line. The entire vast stretch was bare, barren, without trees. The first house we stopped at belonged to the village *hajam*. A youth gave us drinking water. Rameshwaram asked him to accompany us. The boy talked. We wanted to go to Kharo and Bahera, not Semra. Semra was a brahmin-dominated village, the village of *maliks* or owners of bonded labourers. According to a government report, 84 bonded labourers were identified at Semra and 43 were freed, given land and agricultural equipment, houses for the homeless, bullocks and milch cows.

The grandfather of this boy, Raghunandan Hajam, had 12 acres of good cultivated land. Rameshwar Pande, Ayodhya Pande's father, somehow implicated him in a legal matter and took away the land. A civil case was started. Aliyar, Kismat and Chaon were 3 militant sons of Raghunandan, and they did not allow Pande's men to come near the land. Then the 3 died, under mysterious circumstances, after a puja at the brahmin's house, vomiting blood, all on the same day.

'Had they eaten *prasad* there?'

'How do I know?'

All the boy knows is that the curse of the gods had fallen on the Hajam family. The 3 fighters died, the old man is both heart-broken and terror-stricken. Now they have a single acre, purchased from someone. As we talked, one or two persons joined us. Baliram Bhuiya, a freed bonded labourer, was digging chunks of earth to repair his home. Then came Mangru Mian, another freed bonded labourer, to meet us. And brahmins Suman Pande and Suresh Pande. We said, 'We have come to see how the freed bonded labourers are faring. So please let us be with them. They won't feel free if you are with us.' They left.

Gradually our group grew to 30 or 40, and we moved from one village to another. They knew Rameshwaram very well and trusted him. Why wouldn't they? He was not one of those who came and raised their hopes and then let them down. This dark, honest-faced, *khaini*-chewing man was '*thik 'hai*'. Why, Rameshwaram's visit was overdue. He had promised them such a visit in January this year. Rameshwaram said, 'Didi, we are observing May Day most sincerely, celebrating it with the bonded labourers.'

Mangru was a young man of 30 or so, but the inside of his mouth was all twisted. Gums broken, teeth broken, it was shocking when he opened his mouth. Yes, he was freed. Was given 80 decimals of barren rocky land far away from the village, on the slope of a hill, where it would be impossible to attempt soil reclamation even with good irrigation facilities. In any case, there was nothing by way of irrigation. Not a well, nor a tubewell. The Dhonra river was dry throughout the year, except during the monsoon months. Mangru's question was everyone's question. Why was a *shivir* held when nothing followed the holy resolutions and promises? Why were the freed ones mostly given barren, rocky and uncultivable land far away from their homesteads? And why 80 decimals? How could 80 decimals solve the problem of an increasing family? 'That is why we are going back to bondage,' one of them said.

Mangru had bravely tried to do without the ex-masters. Then Ayodhya Pande had him brought to him, and asked him to work in bondage. When Mangru refused, he was tied up and cruelly beaten. Ayodhya crushed his face repeatedly with his shoes. Mangru vomited blood and prayed for water. Ayodhya's son Ramaballav urinated on his face. Then the other bonded labourers took Mangru to Daltonganj Hospital and got him treated.

The *shivir* gave them nothing. Yet the *shivir* was good. Why ? Because before the *shivir*, the *maliks* practised the *dharumaru* system. Under the system, the *malik* is under no obligation to give an advance to the *dharumaru*. He or his henchman could get hold of anyone and force him to give free labour. Not that everyone was a *dharumaru begar* (farm labourer), but anyone could become one at any time. It was safer to enter debt bondage.

I came to know of the *dharumaru* system from the account of the 'maneater' of Jogikhura, known as J.P., who enjoyed the privilege of being a very high-up official of Bihar State Lac

Marketing Cooperative Federation. He monopolized the lac
industry, the irrigation department, controlled the teachers'
union through a relative of his and published a weekly to
publicize his name. He also usurped all the *bhoodan, khodkar,
rayati* and *adhibhokta* land from the poor (these are various
sources of land and tenure systems, e.g. *bhoodan* is land
voluntarily given up to the government, who then redistributes it
amongst the poor); and kept not *kamias* but *dharumarus*. His son
and nephew had allegedly murdered 2 tribals in 1974. He looted,
plundered, and let loose a reign of terror over his subjects while
his son and nephew killed men and raped women, according to
the report in the *NLI Bulletin* of October 1976; and surprisingly
for us, though naturally enough for Palamau, remained a big
government official and an elected member of the legislative
council of the state.

Palamau is, in reality, a mirror of true India. J. P. is not that
powerful now because of a temporary loss of political patronage.
But he has never been put before a judicial commission to
account for his crimes, involving so many violations of the penal
code. J. P.'s immunity to the law encourages the brahmins of
Semra. Is not J. P. a great man ? And is he not a brahmin? What
impact it may have on the harijans and poor tribals may be easily
guessed. And when a J. P., a Mauar, gets support from the 'big
ones', the lower grade officials who actually implement the laws
and do the work realize that it is futile to work honestly. They
become oppressors within their own spheres of power and
exploit and oppress the poor to their hearts' content. See
Palamau with an outsider's eye and you will feel that the district
machinery, the landholders, the contractors, all think that the
poor are born to serve them. It is as natural to the exploiters as
the sky and the hills they see.

We went to another village and entered an adivasi home.
These people were not bonded labourers. They gave us cold
water and *sattu-pani. Sattu,* soaked in water, is a good protection
against the heat of the sun. There was *sattu* in plenty and all of us
drank liberally. Then we went to see the houses built for 7
homeless persons. These 7 had never had any home; they had
stayed at their *malik's* while in bondage. They were allotted land
for homes on a distant elevated barren spot opposite Loharsimi,
quite far away from Semra. The *tanr* or rocky land given to them

lay not less than 3 miles away. We saw 7 rooms built on the barrack pattern, one adjoining the other, in the depths of the wilderness, mud walls raised and unthatched. The area is totally devoid of water, too. The *sarpanch*, Baleshwar Pande, and the *karamchari* asked the 7 men to gather wood to thatch the roof, and as soon as they did so, Kunj Sahay, the forest babu, had them brought in and harassed. Then, to appease the babu, these 7 unfortunates went to the *sarpanch*, who said that they must pay Rs 983. They sold the bullocks received for their rehabilitation, plus 70 quintals of wheat lying with the *sarpanch* issued as their share for working in the Food for Work Programme. In fact, the *sarpanch* told them that he would arrange the sale on their behalf. The bullocks were bought by Paras Pande, the wheat by the other Pande and the forest babu was appeased.

There in the wilderness we saw the hut of Bikhan Mochi, a bonded labourer of Muneshwar Saha of Loharsimi, owner of 50 acres of land. He had borrowed Rs 55 about 10 or 12 years ago and still owes the *malik* Rs 18 or 19. Bikhan was very uncomplaining about the affair. It is all in the order of things: the rocky barrenness, the *malik*-owned cultivated fields, the arrogance of the brahmins, the helplessness of the poor lower castes and tribals. The Bikhans never stand up and want to know their rights because the effort would lead them nowhere. Bikhan also said that his *malik* was a good man. Others nodded their heads in assent. He is a *charwaha*. He gets a meal a day when he works for his *malik*. When the *malik* has no work for him, he collects firewood and sells it. Father of 2 sons and a daughter, he also said that he would have to borrow Rs 800–900 when the daughter came of marriageable age. '*Aisa to hotai hai*—that's the way it is.'

While we talked, Suresh Pande came up again. He insisted that we go to his house for some rest and refreshment. Rameshwaram asked him to run home and wait for us. Someone commented, '*Khufia pulis hai*—he is a police informer, and acts like one, always trying to spy on people.'

Then, after a mile-and-a-half of walking over rocky paths in the blazing heat, we reached Kharo village and entered the house of Rameshwaram's friend. He surprised us by offering us hot tea. '*Kya tajjub*,' Rameshwaram said. How amazing! No, no *tajjub*. Had not Rameshwaram promised to come one day? Had not the villagers been looking forward to that day, keeping apart a packet of tea-dust, sugar and milk powder? They braved the sun and went to the shop at Semra to buy *paan* for me. Then, after a few songs by Sravan Kumar, they too sang songs, beating a *dholak*, songs depicting their miserable lives. And then came the greatest surprise when they said that lunch was ready. Yes, they knew that we were carrying a tiffin carrier with us, but we would have to eat their *khana*. They had prepared *puris* and potato and brinjal curry, and there was sugar. We ate what they gave us and they ate our lunch. Then the talks began. Their talk centred on the *shivir* or NLI camp of 1976. They gave us the names of some of the Semra brahmins—rich landowners, almost all of them. Rajuram, Ayodhya, Bhola, Ganesh and his 7 sons, Sudarshan, Baleshwar, Baldeo, Brijdeo, Lava, Girja, Shankar, Jwala, Mangal, Dharamjit, Manmohan, Sumer, Dharamraj, Raghab, Suresh, all bear the surname Pande and are all brahmins. Apart from brahmins, there are Muneshwar, Jeetan, Bela and Narayan Sahu among the wealthy. The Sahus lend money at 6 per cent per Rs 100 per month.

Not only have these landowners usurped the land of the harijans, Muslims and adivasis, they have deprived them of the land given to them after their liberation from bondage. In Semra 84 bonded labourers were identified and 43 were set free. Mangru Mian had been given, like many others, rocky *tanr* land unfit for cultivation, and nothing had been done to provide irrigation. Now Ayodhya holds the *parcha* held by Mangru's grandmother, one of 12 bhuiyas who were allotted comparatively better land near the villages Bahera, Chatur, Makar, Sudan, Durjan, Parbhu, Jhori, Banwari, Raghuni, Kail, Ramdas, Dwarika and Garju. Daroga Saha of village Salatua, block Chainpur, tills and enjoys the benefit of the land though the bhuiyas are *parcha*-holders. Tax is paid in their names. On paper they are owners of the land but in reality they are not. Of these 12 freed bhuiyas, Sudan has gone back to bondage under Raghab, Raghuni and Kail under Vyas, Ramdas under Ayodhya and Dwarika under Sakchan Majhi.

That May Day, in 1981, we met about 30 bonded labourers at Semra village. Almost all of them had been freed but were now back in bondage, out of the necessity for sheer survival. Among them were people who had borrowed as little as Rs 80 and were serving their *maliks* for over 3 to 4 years. There was Sitaram, a

young boy of 18 who was still under bondage for Rs 500 borrowed
by his father 38 years ago. The owners were all upper-caste—
brahmins—and one of them was also the *sarpanch* or head of the
local panchayat. Vyas Pandey keeps 7 bhuiyas—Harwaha Kirit,
Raghuni, Kail with his wife and children, Sumaru, Deodhari,
Lochan and Arjun. The wages of a *harwaha* are two-and-a-half *seers*
of *kutcha* paddy a day, 5 'cottahs of *palhatu* land after 1 year.
Palhatu land is given to a *harwaha* as long as he is in service. With
the termination of the service, the land reverts back to the *maliks*.
When husband and wife both work, the *malik* gives foodgrain for
1 person only. I have made special reference to Vyas Pande
because he is the village *mukhia* and Baleshwar is the *sarpanch*.

I have referred to Vyas and Baleshwar Pande and now I want
to refer to Jwala Pande. Jwala was the *mukhia* of the village when
bonded labourers were freed at Semra; some were freed from his
bondage, too. The camp had given them hope that their life
would take a new turn. But the land *parcha*, agricultural
equipment, domestic and agricultural cattle, all came through
these *mukhias* and *sarpanchs*. Only 43 were freed and 41 remained
in bondage. The soil was never reclaimed, provision for water
never made, forest officials never offered them employment.
They found themselves stranded and forsaken by all, as much at
the mercy of their *maliks* as before. In fact, the situation was
worse, as the *maliks* would not give them work on a wage basis,
and they could never use the land. In order to survive, they first
sold the agricultural tools, fertilizer and paddy seeds, then the
cattle. Then those who were ready to go back to bondage did so.
But this time the terms were more stringent. So, bonded labourer
or no bonded labourer, all go to the forest to gather firewood to
sell in the open market. If they collect *mowa* fruit the *maliks* take
half the share. Those once freed are now the laughing stock of
the *maliks*, forest officials, block *karamcharis*, police, everyone. Has
not the government, at their cost, provided the *ilaka* with the
greatest *tamasha* ever? Are they not worse off than before? Their
children never go to Semra Middle School. Are there not 2
schools for the bonded labourers at Ramkanda and Koriatho?

I have some questions. Why was it not stated in the report I
have mentioned that Jwala Pande was the *mukhia*? Why are once-
freed bonded labourers going back into bondage one by one?
Why were these people given a shortlived experience of being set

free from bondage, and made to participate in such a
hypocritical 'help and succour' farce when it was well known that
the *mukhia* and the *sarpanch*, themselves bonded-labourer owners,
would handle all the relief measures? Why could not
arrangements be made for soil reclamation and irrigation? Why
were they allowed only 80 decimals of barren and rocky land per
family? This only shows that the government cared little whether
freed labourers went back to bondage or not. How much money
was allotted for building houses for the homeless? How much
money has been granted and spent for rehabilitation of the freed
ones and where has that money gone ? It is as clear as daylight
that the persons concerned have not seen any of it. And, last of
all, why make a publicity stunt out of Semra when all is chaos and
despondency and misery there ? I think that a cruel joke has been
played upon the *bandhua majdoors* of Semra. The sooner it is
remedied, the better.

If this be the lot of Semra, then what is happening to other
bonded-labour villages? Only the forest sustains these
unfortunates. One old man quietly said, '*Jab jangal giya, hum log
bhi mara*—When the jungle goes, it's the end of us.'

From *Business Standard,* 27 May 1981.

The Slaves of Palamau

They came from 50 villages in the district of Palamau, Bihar—men, women and children, some of them in their mother's arms—trudging into the district town of Daltonganj. All of them shared a common bond; they were all *bandhuas* or bonded labourers. There were 2000 of them who have not yet been officially identified by the district administration for, it seems, the administration has one of its eyes shut. The official figure put out is 1014. In private conversation, however, district officials themselves consider the official figure an absurdity. The administration depends upon the *sarpanchs* and the *mukhias* of the villages, and in Palamau these village chiefs are those to whom the labourers are bonded.

It is totally inconceivable that a *bandhua* can actually come forward and declare himself to the district administration, defying the near-almighty Rajput or brahmin who has, over centuries, exploited and used him as a slave. To unite the bonded labourers and urge them to come forward jointly and fight against exploitation, needs courage. Such a task is best achieved by individuals or organizations with dedication. Palamau is fortunate to have the editor of *Ishumaan*, Rameshwaram, a true friend of the bonded labourers. It was through his efforts that Mughal Bhuiya, a *bandhua* from Semra, participated in the Bandhua Choupal organized by Swami Agnivesh in Delhi in 1981. This year, on 1 May 1983, Rameshwaram took a step forward by organizing a meeting of the bonded labourers in Daltonganj under the aegis of *Ishumaan* and the Palamau (Bihar) Bandhua Mukti Morcha (PBMM).

The PBMM is often referred to as 'our *samiti*' by the bonded labourers. In 1981, I saw with my own eyes what it is to be a *bandhua* when I hitch-hiked to Semra, a predominantly *bandhua* village, along with Rameshwaram and a few other people (see 'Back to Bondage'). The Semra landowners lived in the village proper while the bonded labourers lived in scattered groups on surrounding hillocks. On one such hillock we celebrated May Day by forming a Bandhua Samiti. At that time we had seen how bonded labourers who had been liberated by the landlords had not benefited at all. The reason was the social structure of Palamau, which, simply put, is medieval. The upper-caste landowners cannot and will not touch a plough although they own the land. Society is sharply divided between landowners and bonded labourers.

Located on the western border of Bihar, Palamau lies in the north-western part of the Chhotanagpur plateau. At one time the district boasted of great jungles. Today, the jungles are largely destroyed and the district can be described as dry upland. The district is predominantly rural and 88.6 per cent of the working population depends on agriculture. Like other districts where the incidence of bonded labour is high, the district has a very high concentration of scheduled caste (SC) and scheduled tribe (ST) population (44.53 per cent as against a total of 22.86 per cent in Bihar). There is practically no industry worth the name and the main commerce is around jungle products like lac. 'Palamau is the most backward district in a very backward state' (T Vijayendra, Maitreya Ghatak and Vijay Rukmini Rao, 'Rehabilitation of Bonded Labour in India: Study of Two Cases,' in *Human Futures*, Delhi, Winter, 1981).

But this most backward district of a very backward state had, in 1857, risen in revolt against the joint forces of the *jagirdars* and the British. The poor and the downtrodden had risen in an armed revolt which had reached formidable dimensions. In Palamau it was a civil uprising, not military. But those are tales of the past. The heroes of the uprising, Nilambar and Pitambar, do not have institutions named after them. In Palamau, today's ministers have colleges named after them. Even the Chief Minister of the state has a school named after him. Their names are mightier than the heroes who fought the British. Characteristically, the ruined fortress-palace of the Palamau kings stands neglected, without even a plaque. The revolt was crushed, the fighters were hanged, the 'loyalists' were granted big *jagirs*. The hereditary zamindars of Palamau, the brahmins and the Rajputs, are mostly descendants of the loyalists of yesterday. After 1857, the zamindars and the moneylenders usurped all the land. The *kamiauti-seokia* or the *bandhua* system or debt-bondage system was born. How callously the district administration 'identifies' the number of *bandhuas* will be clear from the following: 'In the 1920–21 settlement, a survey of such *kamias* was taken and their number was estimated at over 60,000 . . .' ('Rehabilitation of Bonded Labour in India'). It is only natural that the number has increased over the last 6 decades. It is no use to have only a thousand identified and rehabilitated. What about the unidentified thousands who are getting into fresh bondage?

The *samiti* did not sit idle after 1 May 1981. The more courageous among the *bandhuas* themselves came forward and contacted fellow *bandhuas*. It is well known that the liberated *bandhuas* face a lot of hardships—the landowners refuse to employ them—yet they are happy to be out of bondage. It is these people who made the *choupal* (meeting) a success.

The *choupal* began at 10 in the morning of 1 May at the local town hall named after Mahatma Gandhi. It was, perhaps, the first time that harijans, Muslims and tribals entered the hall. The *bandhuas* themselves were on the stage. They conducted the first session, addressing the gathering. For people living in subhuman conditions, they showed great courage and clarity of thought. As they talked, the full horror of the misery of bondage became increasingly clear. Tetri Bhuyin, a woman from Pathalgarhwa, recounted how she had once borrowed Rs 12 from Chamru Sahu and how she had been working for him for the last 10 years for a meal a day and some foodgrain only. Sahu had refused to release her, she said. Under the *bandhua* system, all over India, a man borrows some money—it might be for food, a death in the family, hunger, sickness, a daughter's marriage, anything. The borrower then puts his thumb-impression on a piece of paper and thus becomes debt-bonded. From then on he will work for the moneylender for an extremely low wage till the debt is repaid with interest. In reality, however, the debt is never repaid, for the interest goes on mounting. The process of debt-repayment thus continues for generations.

Tetri Bhuyin was cruelly beaten by her owner (she is nothing but a slave) for attending the *choupal,* yet she had come. Mangru Bhuiya spoke for the 22 participants of Karso village. 'My *malik* threatened to kill us if we came to the *choupal.* But brother Mogol Bhuiya of Semra put courage into us, so we came. The *sarpanchs* and the *mukhias* usurp everything meant for us. See that they don't,' he warned. Chetan Munda, a non-*bandhua,* Birju Bhuiya, a *bandhua* liberated by Rameshwaram the editor, Mogol—all had helped the *bandhuas.* Then stood up Mohammed Kasim, an old man, to narrate his story. He is one of the 32 *bandhuas* owned by Taramoni Singh of village Solay, under Patan police station. 'My father had once borrowed Rs 10 or Rs 15 from Jagga Singh, Taramoni's father. He died after 45 years of bondage. I, too, have been a *bandhua* for the last 32 years. Between father and son we have given 77 years of our lives, yet the debt remains unpaid. Why tell me that the law against bonded labour has been passed? My *malik* does not know—who will tell him?'

There were others, too. Panchu Bhuiya's father had borrowed Rs 35 from Taramoni. Between father and son they had been *bandhuas* for 60 years. Suleman and Sujait have been *bandhuas* for 40 years for debts of Rs 20 and Rs 40 respectively. Tabrumal borrowed Rs 15, worked for 20 years, went blind and the legacy of bondage was inherited by his son who has been a *bandhua* for the past 16 years. Gora Mian's father borrowed 18 kg of rice and worked for 21 years to repay it. Then Gora took over from him. He has been a *bandhua* for the last 27 years. Taramoni owns the above-mentioned *bandhuas.* He is believed to be a scholar and a learned man. He has 'bequeathed' the *bandhuas* to his son Pitambar Lallu.

The *bandhuas* of Palamau are given names like *kamia, seokia, harwaha, charwaha,* etc. Among them the *dharumaru* is in a special category. The *malik* grabs any person and forces him or her to become a *bandhua.* Sachita Panre of Bhandar (under police station Bisrampur) has kept Tetri Bhuyin and her family as *dharumarus* for 2 generations. In the same village Amresh Panre has forced Bideshi Bhuiya to become his *dharumaru.* Amresh has also had Bideshi's meagre homestead surveyed and usurped. The Panres of Bhandar are especially powerful because Badri Panre is the *sarpanch* through whom government schemes for the *bandhuas* will be implemented if ever they are released. The Rs 4000 package scheme for each *bandhua* family comes through the *sarpanch*, no one else.

Badri Panre, the *sarpanch* of Bisrampur, according to most of the labourers, is a very cruel *malik*. He is one of the many *maliks* who demand absurd sums for releasing the *bandhuas*. Nanku Bhuiya said: 'My ancestors borrowed Rs 130 from Badri Panre's ancestors. First my grandfather, then my father . . . who can count how many years? . . . I have been working for him for 30 years. Today, the *sarpanch* demands Rs 400 for my release.' Badri Panre refuses to release Joshini Devi, who borrowed Rs 200 from the *sarpanch* to fight off starvation 5 or 6 years ago. Since then, she has been working for him with her husband and father-in-law.

The list before me is long. I have noted down the names of a few and I find, even from this random sample-list, 74 people who have been bonded in the last 5 years. It is several years since the bonded labour system abolition ordinance was passed.

In faraway Kachan it was almost a different story. Some *bandhua* families live there in abject poverty. Why do they become bonded? And why do the non-bonded poor envy those in bondage? Because the *bandhuas* get meals from the *maliks*, even if it be of inferior quality, while the non-bonded just starve. The *bandhuas* of Mahuadanr do not even have a well for drinking water. There are schools, ration shops, and health centres but there is nothing for them. Even the land on which their homes stand is owned by the *maliks*.

Anyone who thinks that the zamindari system has been abolished should visit Palamau. There is no such word as land-ceiling. The poor say they live on the zamindar's land, yet Bihar passed the land reform bill in the 50s. An 8-year-old child became a bonded labourer in Kachan. The administration is not interested, neither are the political parties.

The miracle had been achieved. The *bandhuas* of Palamau had united to make the *choupal* a success. And Tetri was not afraid any more. From now on the *bandhuas* themselves would be able to assert their rights, with a little guidance and some assistance. And there were people who would willingly help.

From *Sunday*, 3-9 July 1983.

Palamau in Bondage: Forever?

Palamau continues to remain in bondage and there doesn't seem to be any hope of liberation for the lakhs of poor, tribal, harijan and Muslim people. Yet, there is a sense of awakening. Palamau *bandhuas* have formed a *mukti morcha* which is affiliated to the Bandhua Liberation Front. The district organization was formed in 1981, on May Day, at Semra village.

A *samiti* was born. Towards the end of this year the district-level *samiti* became affiliated to a Delhi-based organization chaired by Swami Agnivesh, who has, through his organization, fought hard for the brick-kiln and stone-quarry workers of Haryana, Punjab and Faridabad. In 1983 more than a thousand *bandhuas* participated in the *choupal* organized by the district *morcha*. The grassroots-level *morcha* took the initiative. The *bandhuas* proved their capabilities. They sat on the dais, conducted the discussions, sang and danced. They marched, for the very first time, in a mighty *juloos*, to meet the almighty Deputy Commissioner. It was a lesson to the friends of the *morcha*. The *bandhuas* may be the most downtrodden of the poor of India. But they are capable, intelligent, able to shoulder responsibilities, and, above all, desperate for a life of dignity.

The 1983 *choupal* did not get very wide media coverage except in an English language daily and weekly of Calcutta. Yet, from the reaction of the district administration, it was clear to me that the stir of consciousness among the *bandhuas* had attracted attention. The Deputy Commissioner was kind enough to discuss with us in detail about future measures for their proper liberation and rehabilitation. He listened to us very sympathetically. With his help (he arranged for conveyance), I was able to cover long distances and visit remote villages under Ranka and Chainpur blocks. I learnt from him that the state government's scheme was to allot Rs 4000 worth of seeds, bullocks, agricultural tools etc. apart from land, for each of the liberated *bandhuas*. In West Bengal, I had already seen how Amalendu Roy of the District Science Centre of Purulia had worked out practical and helpful schemes for the cruelly neglected Kheria–Savaras, a minor community amongst the tribals, in the district of Purulia. Both Amalendu and I believe that only by maximum utilization of available resources, and the involvement of grassroots-level organizations in the implementation of development programmes, enabling the direct beneficiary to receive maximum help, can the poor and the starving be helped effectively.

I requested the Deputy Commissioner to allot land in one stretch, to encourage community farming. If carefully planned and spaced out, even a Rs 4000 package scheme could really help the liberated *bandhuas*. Give them jackfruit, guava, papaya and other fruit–timber–foliage-yielding trees to plant near their dwellings. Give goats for each family. I asked him to invite Amalendu Roy to help in developing the schemes. And, as the Bonded Labour Abolition Act has provisions for seeking the help of non-government organizations sympathetic to the bonded labourer, I requested him to recognize the unique role the district *morcha* was playing by initiating the *bandhuas* to conduct identification work.

The Deputy Commissioner agreed that the district administration had failed to take up the *bandhua* problem seriously. He also told us that the official figure of 1074 for the year 1982–83 might well be far from correct. I tried to convince him that identification work undertaken by the official machinery could never achieve the desired result. The DC would ask the SDO [Sub Divisional Officer], who would ask the BDO [Block Development Officer]. The BDO would shift the responsibility to the *tehsildar*. From there it would go down to the *sarpanch* and *mukhia*, most of whom were owners of bonded labourers themselves. Relief measures meted out through these village agencies would never reach the *bandhua*. The DC agreed with me. I'supplied him with lists and data. And Palamau being the happy hunting ground of various maneaters, some worthy somewhere was angry with the DC and he was transferred soon after. Why and how is another story.

So we were back to square one. But the *morcha* had actually touched the *bandhua* and non-*bandhua* poor. They were eager to work through this very small organization. For each village a *bandhua mukhia* or representative was selected with consent from the *bandhuas*. These *mukhias* (in many cases they were women) came to the town office to submit reports. And the district *morcha* went on tirelessly making lists of *bandhuas* following á set guideline:

(1) Name of the *bandhua* with the name of his/her father.

(2) Name of the owner, *malik*, or *grihastha* as the *bandhuas* call them.

(3) Amount of debt and the cause for taking it.

(4) Years of bondage.

(5) Generations of bondage.

(6) Amount demanded by the *malik* for granting liberation.

The last point is very interesting. I am convinced that the Government of India never really meant to liberate the *bandhuas*. In our India, acts are for enactment and not for implementation. I have been visiting Palamau for so many years. Palamau has at last been declared a bonded labour district. But nowhere will you find posters or a hoarding on the subject of *bandhuas*. Bonded labourers exist everywhere in India, in the agricultural and other sectors. Crores of rupees are being spent on *ek do bachcha* [the family planning slogan] for each couple. As you go from Ranchi to Jamshedpur, the vacuous faces of an idiotically happy child and mother will greet you on the roadside. But nowhere has there been a single attempt to inform the bonded that they are really free, that they need never slave to repay the debt taken from the *malik*, that they can go to the nearest police station and seek help towards liberation. No, the bonded labourers are kept in darkness so that they can slave for the feudal landowners, who can flourish and prove themselves pillars of strength for the ruling powers. Yet, the *maliks* themselves know about the Act. So now they demand a substantial amount for granting release. Bhadoi Bhuiya had borrowed Rs 100 from Chamru Sahu. His family has been in bondage for 2 generations; he himself has served the master for 20 years. Chamru Sahu was ready to release him from bondage provided he paid Sahu Rs 300. Bhadoi belonged to village Putsarunder of Ranka block. I have several lists comprising many *bandhuas*. In this list I find 73 names. In 23 cases the *maliks* have demanded release money. In 31 cases the *maliks* have flatly refused to release the *bandhua*.

Increasingly, the district *morcha* was attracting the notice of sympathetic friends and social workers. The *bandhua* problem was receiving attention. No, the district *morcha* had not been able to move the district administration, or the state government. It was not to be expected. Had the Government of India been serious about ending the bonded labour system, liberating the *jeethas* of Andhra, *gothis* of Orissa, *seokias*, *kamias* and *dharumarus* of Palamau, action measures would have been implemented through the joint measures of the SC and ST Commissioner's Office and the Ministry of Labour. It was never meant to be. India could and would keep the poor as slaves and sermonize to the outside world. The Palamau *morcha* is too small an organization to make the authorities listen. Yet, the *bandhuas* were astir. The people living well below the poverty line joined the *bandhuas* in the hope of deliverance.

Perhaps this made the organizers convene the national seminar on bonded labour at Panheribandh village near Daltonganj this year: a 3-day seminar and a big *juloos* of thousands of *bandhuas* and non-*bandhua* poor. Even a film unit was present and media people came from many places. A cultural activist group from Andhra came to sing. This time the *bandhuas* did not have a leading role. They listened to speeches, sat patiently through the sessions and marched in the *juloos*. If there was a communication gap between the *bandhuas* and the speakers, it was bridged when 13 children from Chhichhouri village were brought to the *choupal* to narrate their experiences as bonded child labour in the carpet factories of Mirzapur, Uttar Pradesh. The very presence of these children made clear to the outsiders the curse of being born in Palamau in a poor man's house.

These children, aged between 6 and 13, were lured away to Mirzapur by a barber with the surname Thakur. In some cases the parents might have known, in others they did not. They were promised a wage of Rs 10 a day and plenty of good food. According to Damodar Mahato of Chhichhouri, the *thekedar* managed to convince the parents that all would be well with their boys and they would soon be back with their wages. After 20 days one boy, Nathni Thakur, had to be sent back home as he was too ill to work. Now the truth came out. One Pannalal, the owner of the carpet factory, made the children work 20 hours a day on a starvation diet, beat them mercilessly and kept them locked in a room. There was a furore in Chhichhouri. Some parents actually went to Mirzapur but were denied access to their children and asked to bring Rs 500 as release money for each child. After much debate, the police station was approached. The Palamau police broke all Indian records by actually going to Mirzapur and bringing 27 of the 30 children back home. Nathni had already returned. Two were missing from Mirzapur.

I write as the children spoke. Why did they listen to Thakur, the *thekedar*? Suresh, a child of 7 or thereabouts said candidly, 'We were starving at home.' Chhichhouri is not the only place children had been taken from. One informant said that 6 boys from Murtangi village, Ranka block, had been taken to Benaras district, Uttar Pradesh. Needless to say, neither Pannalal nor the *thekedar* Thakur have been brought to justice. The Palamau police version might be that the parents of the Chhichhouri boys had consented to the arrangement. It might correctly be argued that even with the parents' consent, forcing the children to render virtually free and forced labour was a cognizable offence. But the point is that in Palamau no one really has a choice. The *bandhuas* are cursed. The non-*bandhua* poor, no less so.

What is Palamau? There is no industry, no alternative job opportunities. The lac-yielding *palas* trees have succumbed to the avarice of the timber contractor and the corrupt forest directorate. The forest line is fast receding. Ranchi and Singbhum might be in another pole altogether. In Palamau there had been no *kisan, khetmajdoor, khadan majdoor*, forest-centred movement or general movement for the tribals' cause. Only socio-political movements can provide the impetus to fight for better lives and assure better wages. It is because there is little option that the poor have to go into bondage for meagre *lukma* or thin gruel for tiffin and a small quantity of coarse, inferior foodgrain for daily wages. I discerned, from the lists I collected and the applications the poor gave me, that there is an alarming rise in the number of *bandhuas*. Thousands are entering into bondage every day, because only as a slave can they eat even a quarter belly full. The non-*bandhuas* might even think that if they become *bandhuas,* some day they too would be liberated and get help from the government, which is inaccessible to them as a non-*bandhua.* The situation is abysmally dismal. So it is inevitable that the *thekedar* will lure away Palamau's starving children to faraway places and that the parents of the children will enter into bondage.

One might well ask, what then is the achievement of the district *morcha* and what is the purpose in continuing it? Many of the speakers called for a movement, even concerted class war. The speakers were well-intentioned, but perhaps over-enthusiasm made them over-optimistic. The district organization comprises *bandhuas* and a few dedicated, strictly voluntary workers who are not funded by anyone for the work they are doing. It is incapable of launching a dynamic and radical movement strictly on its own. The sole achievement of the district *morcha* lies in the fact that the *bandhuas* have increasingly become conscious and fearless. The *maliks* are dead against any *bandhua* joining the *morcha.* In 1983, the bonded labourers of village Bhandar, under police station Bisrampur, came to the *choupal* braving great obstacles. The owners threatened them with dire consequences if they even mentioned the *morcha* to others. A speaker from Beha village said that almost all the scheduled caste and scheduled tribe people of his area were in bondage. The *maliks* were very vengeful towards the *bandhuas* connected with the *morcha.* They would not release them from bondage, would bar them from working, thus denying them the *lukma* and their wages. If they went to the jungles, the forest guards and the police would harass them. Now the *maliks* were snatching the land and *mowa* collected from the forests. Bano Bhuiya, a *morcha* activist from village Kurun, said that only the *morcha* had supplied them with the courage to fight the wily Mahato bond-masters. The *maliks* harassed the *bandhuas* all right, but when they had beaten Ganesh Bhuiya and injured his legs to stop him from coming to the *morcha* office, Bano and other villagers first *gheraoed* the Mahatos and then carried Ganesh to the police station. The officer-in-charge listened to them and let Ganesh go free after chastising the Mahatos.

The representative from Andhra, belonging to Raithu Coolie Sangam, said correctly that the bonded labourers in their area were getting better deals, and were working as agricultural labourers for minimum wages. This had been made possible not through government measures, but through the relentless struggle of the agricultural labourers and the *bandhuas*. That, perhaps, is the only solution in Palamau, too. But the district *morcha* is not the organization for it. Identification, liberation and rehabilitation—these issues need to be taken up in a time-bound programme. If there could be a movement to liberate the *bandhuas* and force the maliks to employ the *bandhua* and non-*bandhua* poor at the declared minimum wage, a solution might be reached. But there is no movement in Palamau for the rights of the poor. To date I have not seen any political group or party take up the cause of the *bandhuas*.

That the district *morcha* has succeeded in touching a chord is apparent from the number of *bandhua* and non-*bandhua* participants. Ramabatar was bonded to Mukha Singh of village Naria, Chainpur police station, for innumerable years. The original debt might have been incurred by his father; he did not know how much was taken, and by whom. Ramabatar died while working for the *malik*, leaving behind a widow Lakhmania Sahu and 5 children. Two years ago, Lakhmania joined the *morcha*. For the last 2 years, Mukha Singh, according to Lakhmania, has been pressing his demand for a payment of Rs 2000. Lakhmania belongs to village Gurdhi. Etoas Bhuiya, the *morcha mukhia* for Gurdhi, raised a question. 'Twenty-four harijans have been granted land by the *sarkar.*' Were they liberated? Etoas does not know. He has been vocal, fighting, pressing the authorities so much that the *sarkar* might well have liberated them. Liberated or not, they had been granted land and once they got possession of the land, they were not going to serve the *maliks* any more. But they did not know where the land lay. No demarcation, no *patta*. Now the block *karamchari* was demanding Rs 200 from each person to get them possession of the land.

At village Gurdhi, the Jadav *maliks* are all-powerful. They are extremely annoyed over the Gurdhi *bandhuas* joining the *morcha*. According to Bitthal Bothia, the Jadavs have started terrorizing the poor of the village. Three non-*bandhuas* possess meagre patches of land. The Jadavs are saying, 'You may possess *parchas* (ownership papers), for the land but we are going to occupy it.' Bithal said, 'Zamindari *zulum* is going on. It began after we started coming to the *morcha* office.' I looked at the list submitted

by the *morcha mukhias* and found that 56 harijans of villages
Dulahi and Chakrodpur under Patan police station have become
bonded after the Act. From Bhandar village, Bisrampur *thana*, 7
have become bonded after the Act. Twelve others have been
serving masters for decades. According to *morcha mukhia* Balkesh
Bhuiya, 22 harijans became bonded to the moneylending Sahus
and Rajputs of village Purnipatan under Patan *thana* that very
day. At village Solley under Patan *thana*, Taramoni, a powerful
zamindar, reigns supreme. Mohammad Kasim's father borrowed
Rs 10 to Rs 15 from him and served the master (most probably
Taramoni's father) for 44 years. Kasim has been slaving for 32
years. For their father's debts, Raghwar Mahate has been serving
him for 44 years, Sujait Mian for 40 years, Tabrul Mian for 36
years, and Hosaini Bhuiya for 65 years. The original debt was
between Rs 10 to Rs 40 only. It might perplex the readers as to
how a person could work for 65 years. Hosaini's father was in
bondage for 30 years and he himself has been slaving for 35
years. The Solley list has 15 names. All slaves of Taramoni. There
might be more.

Some of the speakers spoke relevantly, keeping the reality of
Palamau's backwardness in mind. A keen social worker stressed
the need for village-centred committees of the *morcha*. He said
that the problems of non-*bandhua* agricultural labourers and
those of the *bandhuas* should be treated together. Rural bank
loans should be arranged for the poor of Palamau. He was
working in Garwa subdivision and had been making lists for the
villages. Munsiram, a tribal from Maneka *thana*, said that the
district *morcha* should make lists of grievances suffered by the
non-*bandhua* poor. He had purchased a patch of land from the
Rajput owners in 1968, but the original owner was trying to usurp
it. He repeatedly said that the *bandhua mukti morcha* should look
after poor people like him. There was no other organization for
the poor.

Laru Jonko, a tribal woman leader from Singbhum, said that
the district *morcha* should press demands for land and forest
rights. The rights to forest products should be given to the poor
of Palamau. Oilseed press machines could help the women.
Balram Tiwari, an advocate from Palamau, and one closely
associated with the district *morcha*, stressed that the Act of 1976
had made provision for special magistrates and special courts to

try *bandhua* cases. Palamau had none. The 3 subdivisions Daltonganj, Patehar and Garwa should have 3 special magistrates. Balram fights for the *bandhuas* in the civil court. Cases come up after much delay and even if he wins in the lower court, the *maliks* appeal to the High Court and go scot-free. He also admitted that the Palamau *morcha* had hundreds of lists, but they had to be verified before pressing for action. Rameshwaram admitted candidly that the *morcha*'s achievement so far was the gradual removal of fear from the hearts of the *bandhuas* and non-*bandhuas*.

Swami Agnivesh referred to the Supreme Court judgement by Justice P. N. Bhagwati and made it clear that the contractors' labourers were as bonded as those in the agricultural sector.

If this conference has succeeded in drawing attention to the system of slavery, it is a measure of success. I think that the district *morcha*, with the help of the Delhi-based Liberation Front, should concentrate on a rehabilitation-cum-liberation programme. The non-bonded poor are with the Palamau *morcha*. Local writers, journalists and activists are alive to the problem. But who can make the rusted and corrupt district machinery move into action? According to media reports, the Bihar Chief Minister claims more than 80 per cent achievement in the implementation of the 20-point economic programme in the state. What does he have to say on Palamau? The Kutku Dam and other such mega projects will submerge villages and make thousands destitute. What does the central government have to say? For Palamau, is it to be eternal bondage? The *bandhuas* and non-*bandhuas* demand answers and some action.

From *Economic and Political Weekly*, 21 April 1984.

Report From Palamau

This is a report from a group of active social workers who have
been working in Palamau among bonded labourers for some
time. I cannot divulge their names as they have requested
anonymity. But their experience and analysis should interest all
those who care about the tragic fate of the Palamau *bandhuas*. I
value the opinion of this group, as they are working dedicatedly
and their words are based on actual experience. The town-based
morcha is fortunate in having this dedicated group working for it.

While at Paneribandh, during the *choupal*, the officer-in-
charge of the Chainpur police station came to enquire about the
number of *bandhuas* under his *thana*. Why, he was asked. He
answered that since the system was illegal, it was his duty to know
and try to help. The group I am referring to is working in a
subdivision. They had gone to the SDO, who listened to them
sympathetically and promised to do his utmost towards the
liberation-cum-rehabilitation of the *bandhuas*, if supplied with a
list. The *bandhuas* were supposed to go to him in a procession on
May Day last and submit a list.

My informants divide the issues between those directly
related, and those more indirect. The direct issues are to win
liberation for the *bandhuas* and see that they are properly
rehabilitated. They do not believe in approaching the Supreme
Court first. They believe that the district administration should
first be offered the chance to do justice. Village committees
should be formed from among the *morcha* workers to make the

villagers conscious, and also to assure them that in times of need they will not be left to fend for themselves. Since the *maliks* have started a crusade against the *bandhuas* joining the *morcha*, the district authorities must be asked by the *morcha* to give protection to the *bandhuas*. Both the identification and the rehabilitation committees must have *morcha* members, or else the government people would go directly to the *malik* to ascertain the number of *bandhuas*, who would be too terrified to come forward and declare themselves. Identification was the primary task, and it had to be conducted fairly. There were instances when a non-bonded labourer was declared bonded and rehabilitated in Palamau. The group thinks that financial facilities should be properly utilized and not just distributed at random.

The government's scheme for the liberated *bandhua* is a 4000 rupee package meant for livestock, seeds, agricultural implements and a patch of land. Making provisions for irrigation and drinking water should be added to the scheme. What use is land if there is no water? Palamau villages are mostly dry. Even this time round, the bonded and the non-bonded begged us to see that they do not die from thirst.

The indirectly related issues are more vital and actually closely woven with the problem of bondage. What are the causes that make the poor enter bondage? How can a system like *dharumaru* exist anywhere? It was reported to me in 1983 that in a *bandhua* village under Garhwa *thana*, one Kashi Singh Punjabi had forced 40 Parhayiya tribal families to become his *dharumarus*. A Kharwar tribal had reported the incident. I have also heard from a very responsible government official of Palamau that the Parhayiyas of Palamau are considered and treated as criminal tribes, like the Lodha and Kheria tribes of West Bengal (who are now denotified tribes, though denotification did not change their situation till they united and formed their *samitis*). Now there is less unnecessary persecution and harassment than before, though they still live much below the poverty line.

The group identifies the following causes for the poverty of the people: low development of agriculture and lack of intensive cultivation; lack of irrigation facilities; the village moneylending system and the total failure of a corrupt government banking system to help the poor; lack of employment opportunities other than in agriculture; the low wage rate for the daily wage-earner (there is hardly any gap between the daily wages of a bonded and a non-bonded worker); lack of marketing facilities for forest produce and the low rate for *tendu*-leaf collection; the forest policy of planting trees for industrial use only, such as eucalyptus.

These and other problems plague the lives of the poor. It is very necessary to create, through mass organizations, mass consciousness; unity; the courage to shake off the shackles of fear; an awareness of the necessity of saving, which they can hardly do; an understanding of the necessity of spending less on social occasions like marriages, funerals etc.

The group thinks that the district government should take the following measures in right earnest:

(1) The government should extend all possible help to the poor farmers in developing their agricultural pattern.

(2) Irrigation facilities should be created by digging wells and small tanks.

(3) The minimum wage rate should be strictly enforced with a due fine and punishment in cases of violation of the rule.

(4) The laws regarding the village moneylending system should be strictly enforced and offenders duly punished. The rural banking system should be made more effective and freed of corruption.

(5) Employment for the rural poor must be ensured. An Employment Guarantee Scheme, as in Maharashtra, should be introduced in Palamau. Employment under the Forest Directorate must be given priority.

(6) A fair rate should be fixed for forest produce such as *mowa* and *sal* seeds. The wage rate for *tendu*-leaf collection must be increased and enforced.

(7) Mixed forest plantation must be given preference over plantation for industrial use only. In the mixed forest plantation only such trees must be grown as can help the village economy.

The group has rightly said that unless a concerted effort is made to raise the poor above abject poverty levels, even vigorous implementation of the Bonded Labour Abolition Act will fail to be effective. The poor of Palamau have no choice. Between death by slow starvation and bondage, they will choose the latter.

About children being taken to Mirzapur, the group made their own investigation. They came to know that 36 children had been taken to Mirzapur from 6 or 7 villages. They registered complaints with the relevant authorities. They also met the parents. What they found out is very important: 26 children had gone with their parents' consent; 10 went because their friends did. No one was physically forced. They met some children who had already returned from Mirzapur. When the parents were asked why they had sent their children so far away, they spoke candidly. The children had nothing to do in the village. There was no guarantee that they would get jobs even if they studied upto class 5 or 10. Some villages did not have a primary school in the vicinity. What could the children do except graze goats and cows for others? There was hardly any work in agriculture. There was no facility for the children of the poor to obtain technical education. One person was brutally outspoken, 'We cannot feed our children. What is the use of keeping them and seeing them die? Let them earn a living, let them eat.'

The children said that they did not like school education. According to them, most of the time schools in the remote areas remained closed as the teacher was absent. So what was the use of going to school ?

It is clear that merely releasing a group of children from forced labour will not solve the problem. The problem must be treated in totality. Raise the parents above the poverty line, and ensure a better life for the children. In West Bengal, too, little children are hired out as cattlegrazers or farmhands. There are thousands of primary schools in West Bengal. But a large number of children, due to poverty, are forced to remain illiterate.

The group thinks that the government should see that children who cannot continue their studies are employed after the primary or upper-primary level. The number of primary schools should be increased and schools should be freed from corrupt practices. The villagers say that the school inspectors take a cut from the teacher's salary and the SC and ST students also have to give a percentage of their stipends to people in office. Introduction of technical education for the children of the poor is a must, along with job assurance.

That there is a need for a mass movement of the *bandhuas* is clear to the group. They think that it is possible to move the authorities to action through a *bandhua* movement, but that it would take time. They met the villagers after the national seminar. The villagers did not think that the *morcha* was ineffective. In fact, they thought that the *juloos* had had effect. According to the group, the villagers of a certain village under Dhurki block found such courage from the *choupal* that they joined together and and collected *mowa* from the trees which had been under the Sahus for 10 years. This is the first time that they have found the courage to do this.

Considering the reality of Palamau, I think that it is a really good beginning. A few baskets full of *mowa* might fetch very little. But the poor of Palamau have taken the initiative and have done something for the first time. There is the group (a part of the *morcha*) to help them. But the poor, too, are waking up to the fact that they must work unitedly to change their own lives. It is an achievement for Palamau's poor. The credit is all theirs.

From *Economic and Political Weekly*, 5 May 1984.

Contract
Labour

Contract Labour or Bonded Labour?

On 16 May, *The New Republic* of Ranchi published an account of some bonded labourers rescued from Sasaram after they had served their master for 22 years under subhuman conditions. They had been lured away to Sasaram with promises of 'good jobs', kept in captivity and made to break stones and blast rocks.

The bonded labour system was formally abolished in November 1975. Following that, a new system of recruiting bonded labourers was very quickly introduced in the bonded labour areas. Since their ex-masters would not give them work and since little was done by the state governments towards their rehabilitation, the landless ex-bonded labourers were in acute distress. Now came the agents of various masters to lure them away to faraway places with promises of good jobs. Once they reached these places, they found themselves in a worse form of bondage.

The young ones are waiting for the inevitable *dalal* to come one day and take them away. Many are going. They hear of their good fortune in the weekly *hat*. The masters are good, give 2 square meals a day. Even the young ones are not against becoming a *kamia* or a *seokia*. 'What to do? There is nothing else for the likes of us.' The land given to the freed bonded labourers is uncultivable. The good land is held by the master, though the ownership-paper is in the freed labourer's name. There is no water for drinking or irrigation; no chance of being employed by government agencies for road-repairing, timber-felling, etc.

Though Palamau is a labour-surplus and poverty-stricken district, outside labour is brought in for such work. Forsaken by the government and society, these people, in order to stay alive, enter debt-bondage. They do not have any alternative.

I stared at the face of the young boy. What would he become? A *seokia*, a *kamia*, a *jonwar*? A *harwaha*, a *charwaha*? Would he receive some *tanr*, dry *palhatu* land? *Palhatu* land is not given away to the cattlegrazer or *charwaha*, who just cultivates it as long as he is in service. I have spelt out the background in some detail in order to stress the conditions in which poor adivasis, Muslims and scheduled caste people are recruited by the labour-contractors.

Some of my friends in the villages and forests are very unusual, but Purnendu Mazoomdar is in a class by himself. I am sure that there are very few like him anywhere. His is a household name in the poor villages of Tamar, Bundu, Torpa, Khunti, Chakradharpur, Monoharpur, Gua—over a wide region covering the 2 districts of Ranchi and Singbhum. He is with the poor tribals and non-tribals in their struggle to gain their forest rights, in their fight with the factory and mine owners against prolonged lockouts, in their battle to cling to the land others snatch away from them. Short, animated and simple, this middle-aged man speaks many tribal languages and is considered to be the tribal's true friend. He starves with the tribals, stays with them, and walks hundreds of miles to visit his people when they are in distress. He is also the general secretary of the Mineral Workers' Union, Chakradharpur.

A few months ago he came to me with Laru Jonko, a remarkable Ho woman. She was the president of the Mahila Samiti of Chiriburu and had just succeeded in tracing several adivasi girls who were missing from the interior villages of Singbhum. These girls were working in brick kilns around Calcutta. The story was revealing.

The brick-kiln owners of West Bengal are mostly from north Bihar. This practice of recruitment of adivasi labour must be quite old. Adivasi women, ex-concubines of the kiln owners, are sent to remote villages. The link railway stations are Chaibasa, Sonwa, Pendrasali and Chakradharpur. These recruiting women are called *sardars*. They go to the village *hats* and lure young girls with tales of good jobs near the magic city of Calcutta.

Chiriburu is the place where the Orissa Cement Company has a quartzite mine. This mine has been under illegal lockout by the owners since 8 March 1979 and 2000 adivasi *rejas* have been starving as a result. Gua leaped into the limelight in 1980. This is the region where militant and indomitable tribals and non-tribals are fighting for their rights to the forest and the land. Relentless police and military repression goes on here. After the Gua firing, ploughs have been broken, cattle and poultry seized, foodgrains destroyed; women have lost *izzat* and huts have been razed to the ground. Women can survive on jungle roots and fruits but they need money to buy clothes. So it has been easy for the *sardars* to collect a willing batch of girls, bribe the police, railway police and the political parties, and bring the girls to Calcutta.

Each kiln employs 200 to 400 *rejas*, and each *sardar* receives Rs 30–40 commission for each *reja*, so it is easy to understand that the lure of ready money is too much for the *sardar*. Why does the *sardar* do it, being a tribal herself? I have said that the *sardars* are one-time concubines of the kiln owners, and close association with the owners corrupts these women. They are usually despised by their own folk. They become virtual outcasts.

I find, from the written account of Purnendu Mazoomdar, that the women *sardars*, Sona Jonko and Nandi Jamuda, have supplied 34 *rejas* to the kilns of Magra in West Bengal from the villages of Komay, Ichakuti and Banka, all under Chakradharpur police station. Two male *sardars*, Dibru Lohar and Madru Angari, have supplied, to the same kiln, 5 girls from the villages of Sagipi, Shengao and Otuoti under the same police station.

The kiln owners or *bhatta-maliks* begin by buying paddy land from poor peasants to build the kiln. Since the adjoining paddy fields are ruined by constant use by the *rejas* as passage to the *bhatta*, the owners ultimately sell them to the *bhatta-malik*. The *rejas* receive 1 token or *tikli* for carrying 10 unbaked bricks over 300 to 400 yards. The same payment is received for carrying 10 baked or *pucca* bricks. For unbaked bricks, 20 tokens mean Re 1. One rupee for carrying 200 *kutcha* bricks. For *pucca* bricks, 44 tokens mean Re 1. One rupee for carrying 440 *pucca* bricks. The *rejas* cannot earn more than Rs 4–5 per day. Children aged 10–12 constitute 25 per cent of the total labour strength. Where an adult *reja* earns Rs 25–30 a week, a child earns Rs 10–15. However, an adult actually receives only Rs 15 per week and a child Rs 10. An adult can buy 4 kilos of rice per week and a child 3 kilos. Rice with salt is their only food. Do they get the rest of their wages when they go home? No, never. Paupers they come and paupers they go. Yet they come again the next year. Why?

Sardars who have become too recognized do not approach the prospective *rejas* directly, but send sub-agents. They explore fresh areas. The *rejas* who have had a bad experience are easily misled when a new agent approaches them and promises better working conditions. The last and ultimate decider of their fate, of course, is the state government's total apathy towards them. 1980 was a drought year, so there was remission of land tax. This year, tax arrears are being collected with much *zulum*. Cause enough to drive these people to desperate measures. We are talking of a region where Rs 30 a month is considered a handsome income for an adult and an income of Rs 20 per month is nearer reality. The villagers have land, but it is unproductive and dry. Villagers living in the neighbourhood of a town can sell firewood in the town market. Those living in the remote interior cannot. So they go to the *sardars*. The *sardars* prefer young unmarried girls. They are better workers and good for sale.

They force these young girls to sleep with the owners, the supervising staff, the truck drivers, *khalasis* and local *mastans*. Anyone who refuses to cooperate is first locked up in a room, beaten and then seared with a hot iron. It is usual to make a girl drink heavily and then send her for the master's pleasure. A young Ho girl, aged 16, has been compelled to become the *aurat* of an aged kiln owner at Gajipara in 24 Parganas, West Bengal. She is from the village Dharamsai under Chakradharpur police station.

In politically conscious West Bengal these *rejas* are denied a minimum wage, medical facilities, maternity leave or any kind of leave, and, of course, the right to form a union. There is no attendance or pay register, identity card or employment card. The set-up is very cruel and very cunning. It is impossible for an outsider to break into the fortress of the *bhattas*. The *rejas* cannot leave the *bhatta* or talk to anyone without the prior permission of the owner. The *sardar* never lets them out of her sight. A close guard is kept on them.

These unfortunate beings live in *jhopris* worse than pig-holes. There are no sanitary arrangements, nor any drinking water

where they work through the summer days. The kiln is closed
with the onset of the monsoons and the *rejas* are sent home.

Male recruiting *sardar* Ponka Gagrai of village Dhipasai,
Chakradharpur police station, avoids entering village Bari for
fear of a possible encounter with Budhu Oihar and Kanklo Gop.
He had taken away Budhu's daughter Pechi and Kanklo's
daughter Jema 6 years ago to Patna and the 2 girls have not come
back ever since. From Kharswan and Sagipi villages he supplied
100 labourers to Bakhtiarpur for a farm owner. In November
1980 he took to Benaras 7 girls from Sagipi. From Kharswan he
supplied Shilai Bodra and 34 more girls to a kiln owner of
Ayodhya. Kachi Daroga, P.O. Jatla, Patna, received 30 to 35 girls.
All these girls are young and many of them physically attractive.
Not all of them will come back after the brick-making season is
over. A mother sings to the baby on her lap:

My Bali could live on forest fruits,
My Bali could live on jungle roots;
But trees, alas, do not saris grow,
So to the *bhatta* my Bali had to go.
My Bali had to go.

Where are the Jagtas and Balis and Charibas? If you ask the
parents, they say simply that life was too hard, survival was
threatened, the *bhattas* called out to them and they left.

I have spoken of West Bengal. What happens in Bihar? Bihar,
to me, is the true mirror of India. Bihar has everything in plenty.
Even bonded and contract labourers.

The Oraon, Ho and Munda tribals meet the needs of
hundreds of kilns on the Ganges, at Muzaffarpur, Samastipur,
Bhojpur, Begusarai, Monghyr, Purnea, Gaya, Patna and Chhapra.
The coolie *jhopris* are within the towns and cities, yet the tribals
stay imprisoned there, closely guarded by the musclemen of the
owners. Theirs is a medieval existence far beyond the reach of
statutory labour law benefits and democratic rights.

The recruiting end is in the hands of the *sardars*. They take
the *munshis* of the owner to their villages and keep them carefully
concealed. August and September, the monsoon months, are the
worst for the tribals. This is the time when they are starving,
totally helpless. The *munshi* and the *sardar* arrange grand feasts
and invite the local youth. Through them they get to know of the
whereabouts of girls. Then they make the rounds with ready cash

in hand. The *munshi* pays *dadan* or advance money to the parents of the girls. Once the parents accept Rs 100–150 from the *munshi*, the girls become contract-bound. They cannot refuse to go and work. In the *bhatta*, life undergoes a change: 12–14 hours of work a day, loading and unloading bricks, compulsory sex with the owner or his men in the early hours of the night, sleep in the *jhopri* in the late hours. No medical or sanitary arrangements.

A *reja* may have earned Rs 30–35 in a week, but receives only Rs 15 as *khoraki*. The rest she never gets. When the kiln closes down, the *reja* is given a sari and a railway ticket. The rest, she is told, has been adjusted against her *khoraki* and the *dadan* her parents received.

None of these facts can be verified easily as there is no wage or attendance register, no employment card. Women in the late stages of pregnancy work, because there is no maternity leave. Their lot is worse than that of those in the unorganized sector. A beggar can go abegging where he chooses. A contract-labourer cannot. He does not have any freedom.

What drives them to the brick kilns? Poverty does. Poverty and the deeprooted apathy of the state government towards adopting any remedial measures to remove the root causes of chronic poverty. Singbhum and Ranchi. The cradles of the Kol, Tamar, Birsa, Jharkhand and other movements. By the Bihar Government's own admission, Chhotanagpur has only 2 per cent land area under irrigation and 5 per cent under electrification. Only the industries and the towns receive electricity. There is no arrangement for irrigation through electricity. Lift irrigation is for show and publicity, not for the cultivator. The Chaibasa project is supposed to be under operation, but thousands of villages do not have even a well for drinking water. Under Gua police station, the tribals drink water from the Koina river which is polluted by the Khiriburu washery plant. The Munda-dominated Khunti subdivision has had no project for irrigation.

The Bihar Government collects, on each rupee paid towards land rent, 40 paise as cess for health, 40 paise as cess for education and 20 paise as cess for roads. Sounds very nice and reads better on paper. But how is this money spent in the region from where the contract-bound labourers come? Banka, under Chaibasa police station, has no school building, though there is a teacher. Guigaon under Chakradharpur police station has a school building. Dalbhanga is a predominantly Munda region and is now under Kuchai police station within Seraikela subdivision. It belonged to Tamar police station till 1954. Then came the Boundary Commission and, in order to have Oriya-majority Seraikela within Singbhum, Bihar, 30 *moujas* from the predominantly Mundari language area under Tamar police station were added to Seraikela. Seraikela became a part of Singbhum. But the Mundas of this region are not at all happy over the surgical operation on the regional map. They have to keep close connections with the Mundari area for social purposes and they feel cut off. In 1968 the government took over a high school at Dalbhanga and a hostel for the tribal students. Both were built with mud. The Bihar Government has not found time to convert these into *pucca* buildings in 13 years, nor funds to repair them. These are only a few of the innumerable instances of governmental apathy towards the tribal regions. There are lakhs and lakhs of tribals in Singbhum and Ranchi. A majority of them pay land rent. What does the almighty *sarkar* do with the 40 paise cess per rupee of land rent they pay for education?

For the poor tribal, money is blood. Land is *tanr, banjhara.* Each rupee is earned by selling so many bundles of firewood, so many baskets of *chiranji,* by breaking so many stones, by working so many hours in the mines. Even after the sanction of a primary school for every 100 homesteads, the people remain illiterate. In many schools the teachers don't attend work. They have their own business or trade or shop to look after. The *pradhan* of Sagipi Primary School carries on a brisk business buying *mowa,* goats, silkworm, etc., from the villagers and selling them to traders. This worthy was once *gheraoed.* Complaints against him were submitted to the proper authority, but to no avail. Teachers from north Bihar posted in the tribal region have been caught lending money, buying land or taking *bandobasti* land. Stipends for scheduled caste and tribal boys in primary schools are a great blessing to the teachers who take a nice 'cut' from the money which is sent in lump sums. A Mundari song runs like this:

Rando, Rando, come to school!
Mata, Mata, where are you?
Rando and Mata and the other boys
Graze the cow, tend the goat.
The *Masterji* sits in his shop.

The tribals pay 40 paise for health and medical care and what do they get in return? Lotapahar has a primary health unit but no doctor. So the unit is useless. Dulmi has a doctor but the health unit building is only half-built. Kukru has a dispensary attended by a compounder but no medicine and no doctor. Chhotonagra under Gua police station has no doctor but there is a dispensary. Situated in the deep interior, Chhotonagra did not have any Sahus till 1962. Now there are 4 Sahus who act as moneylenders, land-usurpers and police agents. The poor of the area are malaria-ridden. Women die at childbirth. Infant and child mortality is high.

The lack of doctors and medicine causes death. And when death, disease or epidemic frequents the lonely villages, the villagers launch a witch-hunt, identify someone as a witch and kill her. In Sagipi village in 1978 child mortality was high. The villagers were sure that a witch was causing these deaths. An old Christian tribal woman was identified as the witch. She was a person of some means, had a husband, grown-up sons, grandchildren. The villagers invited her for a *diang* (rice liquor) drinking session and killed her. In January 1981, at Dhangaon under Chakradharpur police station, a Ho woman aged 54 was killed in broad daylight. After a week her widowed daughter was also killed at night, while she was sleeping with her children in their hut. Reason? Some 4 or 5 people were suffering from the same sort of sore on their right legs. The witch must have caused those sores.

Chiriburu Mahila Samaj, under the leadership of the courageous Ho woman, Laru Jonko, has launched a mass signature campaign against witch-hunting. Their cry is, 'Medical facilities are needed. This witch-hunting is barbarous and wrong. Doctors and medicine will bring succour to the people. We achieve nothing by killing innocent women.'

Till now almost Rs 3000 crores have been spent on 'tribal development' in Chhotanagpur. The Sixth Plan has allotted Rs 800 crore. But even after 5 Plans nothing has reached the area. The people have been left in primeval darkness. Officially, the leasing of forests to contractors has been abolished. The declaration has been given much publicity. The announcement came after the Gua firing. But contractors are felling trees in the Jaraikela forest under Sarenda division, all right. The forests in the Ranka *mouja* under Chandil police station are serving their death sentence. Mango, *jamun, pial, kendu, bael,* all fruit-bearing trees, are exempt from felling under the Forest Acts. But the contractor's axe is felling them, too. The tribals and poor villagers are, naturally, desperate. After the Gua firing, the government declared that there would be no collection from the weekly *hats.* The *hat masul* was abolished. Yet *hat masul* is definitely exacted in one of the biggest *hats* of Singbhum district, the Kukru hat under Ichagarh police station. Previously, the *masul* was shared equally by the tribal buyer and the north Bihari seller. Now the purchaser of a cow or vegetables or paddy or clothes has to pay the full amount. In the dry months *hat masul* from Kukru is Rs 2000 per week. In winter it is Rs 4000. The Raja of Ichagarh is the recipient of this *masul* which is said to be collected for the development of Ichagarh High School. It is hard to understand why this school has not been taken over by the government. It is certain that the money does nothing for the school. Students pay their fees. The school goes on. The landless Jhora people have been running the ferry boats on the Koel, Koina and Subarnarekha for ages. Now the Bihar Government has leased out the ferries to contractors. The Jhoras are unemployed. At places the village panchayat has been handling the contracts.

What happens to the *kendu* or *bidi* leaves? Previously the poor villagers grew *kendu* trees on their land and sold the leaves to the traders. January to March is the plucking season. A family could earn Rs 400–500 per season. The Bihar Government leased out the plucking right to contractors; now the villagers are the contractors' labourers. For 100 *kendu* leaves (about a kg) he receives Rs 1.75 when he plucks in a government forest. And in the open market the rate is Rs 10 per kg. The contractors' rate is Re 1 for 100 *keris* or bundles. One *keri* contains 25 leaves. To pluck 2500 leaves a man or a woman works from 4 in the morning till 4 in the afternoon in the depths of the forest, and receives Re 1. The contractor will sell that quantity for Rs 250. I cite these figures to show the pattern of exploitation.

The Mahalis, like the Jhoras, have been reduced to destitution. They are traditionally basket-weavers. Previously they collected bamboo from the forests. Then came forest laws. They had to obtain permission from the Forest Department and pay *masul* for bamboo, the raw material for baskets and winnows. The ruthless deforestation by the contractors has caused them great suffering.

Tales of woe and exploitation on the one hand; the pulse of resistance mounting on the other. The Jharkhand demand is set against such a background. When these people take to violence, they do it out of sheer desperation.

I started with contract-labourers and shall conclude my account with them. Not only women, men, too, are helpless. I cite 2 cases.

(1) Amar Ekka, a Christian Munda and the son of Albis Ekka, was 19 years old in 1976. The family had 8 members, 10 to 12 acres of land with a yield of 30 maunds. Amar was educated upto class 8. Fagu Sahu recruited him in 1976. Amar says, 'I went to Hurda Basar and this agent said that he would take us to Punjab and get us good jobs. I went to Bano, from there to Tati, from Tati to Batia, from Batia to Gomoh. At Gomoh I got into the Amritsar Mail. We got down at Tanda Hurmur station. Then we went along with Mahendra Singh who was the coolie agent for Punjab. Fagu Sahu sold us to Mahendra. We were 5 or 6 boys. We stayed for 8 days at Pathankot. The farmer Makhan Singh promised to pay Rs 60 per month as wages plus food, clothes, etc. From 4 a. m. I looked after cattle till 8 a. m. From 8 a. m. I watered the wheat fields. I was ill-treated, beaten and harassed by Makhan Singh and his family members. My wage was raised to Rs 80. After 6 months I wanted to leave. Makhan did not give me 2 months' wages. He said he had paid me and was adjusting the money. I ran away from his place one day at 3 a. m. By train I reached Tanda Hurmur. There Darshan Singh, a teacher, employed me at Rs 100 per month. He had 2000 cows and buffaloes and milking was operated electrically. I worked till 1979 and my wage was Rs 175 per month. Then I left.'

(2) Sura Pai, a Raotia boy from Buruichanda was brought to Ferozepur by Shivshankar Sahu and sold to Diwan Singh of Sandwala for Rs 250. 'Diwan Singh told me, "I have purchased you, so I won't give you anything for 2 months. After 2 months, I will pay you Rs 100 a month with food." I worked there for 4 months and was inhumanly treated. The local agricultural labourers asked me, "Why do you work for so little? We work for Rs 10/12 a day." I ran away after 4 months when my owner

refused to pay me anything. I sold some wheat for Rs 8 and went by train to Ludhiana. There I met Barna Karkota of Harta village who was sold to Surjeet Singh, Diwan Singh's brother and a *sarpanch*. Barna was running away from his owner, a very cruel man. At Ludhiana we worked at Jagdamba Wool Mill at Rs 170 per month and 4 hours' overtime benefit. After 2 months I got Rs 180 per month. I spent Rs 100 on food and lodging. After I saved some money I returned home.'

We know some of these details from Purnendu Mazoomdar's untiring efforts to uncover the pattern of exploitation in Singbhum and Ranchi. The Bihar Government realizes Rs 30 crore from the forests of Chhotanagpur and Rs 10 crore from the Excise Department. The royalty received from the mines and industries must be fabulous. If forest revenue received by the government is Rs 30 crore, what must the contractors be earning? Their palaces in Ranchi and north Bihar give some idea. As long as Chhotanagpur is kept for exploitation alone, agents and *sardars* will go on haunting the destitute villages. Men and women will migrate to faraway places. Some will come back, some will not. Punjab and Haryana will have slaves. West Bengal and the rest of Bihar, *bhatta-coolies*. Kiln owners, *mastans* and truck drivers will have their pot of flesh and all will be happy except the tribals and the non-tribal poor. But they are expendable.

From *Economic and Political Weekly*, 6 June 1981.

An Eastside Story: Construction Labourers in West Bengal

Narayangarh and Sabong are adjacent blocks in the district of Medinipur. Both are very dry and the subsoil water level is poor. Last year's drought has hit the 2 blocks most severely. Since last September the poor people, unable to wait any longer for the panchayat to come to their relief, have started migrating to other districts in search of work. Narma, Maligerya, Fulgerya, Gama—I know these places well. Not from direct acquaintance but from my close association with the poor of the area, especially the hapless Lodha and Munda tribals. They come and stay with me and from their letters and verbal accounts, I have come to know of their suffering.

Gunadhar Singh, a poor peasant of Gama village, is a Munda, and a keen contributor to my journal *Bortika*. He is highly intelligent. He came to me with Thaleswar, another Munda from Gama, towards the end of March. Thaleswar's son had come to work on the Eastern Metropolitan Bypass (EMB), a gigantic Calcutta Metropolitan Development Authority (CMDA) project. Hounded by continued starvation at home, his teenage son had refused to sit for the Higher Secondary examination and had come to Calcutta to dig earth for the project.

Gunadhar had showed them the way to my house. Now groups of them come to me in desperation. The working hours are too long, the work too hard. They long to go home, but the babu refuses to pay their wages.

On 6 April I had to rush to the work site. The babu and his toughs were dragging the sick labourers from their hutments, beating them and forcing them to work. I went with a young journalist friend of mine. I asked my friend to accompany me as the area we were going to was notorious, the toughs trigger and bomb happy. The babu was all apology and politeness. How wrong of the labourers to drag me all the way. Why, he was treating them like his own. Wages? He would certainly pay them down to the last paise. But it would not do to leave the job and go back. If the labourers did not work for a full month, the contractor would not pay and the *khatadar* knew it only too well. The toughs were not that patient. They threatened to beat up the labourers, and the hapless villagers thronged around us, crying bitterly. They wanted to go home. The toughs were too rough, they feared for their lives.

They had reason to. The place was a vast desolation. Not a single tree in sight. The hutments of the labourers were too low and the heat inside was intolerable. We promised to talk to the authorities and left the site. The *khatadar,* a young boy, insisted that there was no agreement of a month's minimum working time. The babu differed with him but one point was clear. There was nothing in writing. In a CMDA project, the labourers had nothing to depend upon but the mercy of the babu.

The *khatadar* and his friend stayed at my place that night. The babu had left as soon as we turned our backs, leaving the labourers to the toughs. The toughs threatened to murder the *khatadar.* On 8 April, 25 labourers came to me with their meagre belongings. On the previous day the toughs and a relative of the babu had tried their best to incite the labourers against the *khatadar.* The labourers stood united. They knew the *khatadar,* a poor boy from their village and they would not harm him. The toughs, on the morning of the 8th, threw them out, dismantled the hutments and left the place. The labourers did not have a single rupee between them and did not know the city at all. They stayed with me and I sent them home in the evening. This is the Eastside Story in a nutshell, but now the details must be told.

And before I do so, I must pay my homage to the savant Ramakrishna who had once said, in contempt of money, 'Earth is money, money earth.' For the simpleminded, the usual interpretation is that dust and gold were the same to him. I think, being a seer, he must have known that in future, earth—dug, shifted, transported—would mint money for the almighty contractors of independent India. India is truly mortgaged to the contractors. The only commodity the contractors have failed to lay their hands on, as yet, is the air we breathe.

The Eastern Metropolitan Bypass project employs thousands of labourers to dig earth, to uplevel lowland and level the fields. It is a CMDA project. I came to know of a contractor. There may be more, I would not know. The practice is that the contractors appoint agents or *dafadars*. One *dafadar* recruits and handles 70–100 labourers. The labourers are recruited through sub-agents or *khatadars*. One *khatadar* recruits and handles 25 or more labourers. The labourers have no direct connection with either the *dafadar* or the contractor.

The babu of my story is said to be one Saktipada Sau of village Bamunara, Medinipur. In December 1982, he managed to recruit, through a *khatadar*, 32 labourers from the villages of Gama, Narma, Sagria, Sabong and Mangalpur, for digging and levelling work at the Kolaghat Thermal Power Project. According to rules, these labourers were to be paid according to the measure of the ground excavated, and not daily wages. Paid correctly, a labourer would earn something like Rs 12 a day after 8 hours' work. This *dafadar* promised the labourers Rs 3.50 a day plus food. This is how the contractors mint money from earth-work. The labourers are shamelessly cheated. The *khatadar* works for a salary. The *dafadar* manages his cut. The contractor makes the largest profit and the labourers work on slave pay even in much publicized government projects.

The *dafadar* did not pay the labourers after his term at the Kolaghat Thermal Power Project was over. Some left. Some stayed on. The *dafadar* appointed a new *khatadar*, a young boy from Gama, hitherto working as a labourer. He promised to pay the *khatadar* Rs 350 a month and food, and told him that he must recruit labourers for work on the Eastern Metropolitan Bypass. The labourers would get Rs 4 per head per day, the working day would be strictly 8 hours only, and the food good and plentiful. (It must be admitted, in all fairness, that the labourers who worked at the site always said that they had no complaint about food.) Sudhir Parya, the new *khatadar*, was further told that the labourers would get arrears paid at the new work site. So 51 villagers came to work on the project. Some worked from the end of February and the rest joined in the first week of March.

After joining, the labourers found that living conditions were wretched, and that working hours were from 5 in the morning till 7 in the evening with a 15-minute tiffin break at 8 in the morning and an hour or an hour-and-a-half lunch break. The *dafadar* refused to pay any sum against their wages; what were the women and children at home to live on? Many left and only 25 stayed till 8 April. The *dafadar* paid the *khatadar* only the train fare for the labourers. There was great resentment against the *khatadar* at first, but soon they realized that the young and naive Sudhir Parya was no match for the wily Sau. Relations between the *dafadar* and the *khatadar* grew worse as the latter insisted that the labourers be paid. I have reported what happened next.

Till 8 April the *dafadar* owed Sudhir Parya Rs 3,849.25—Rs 841.75 for work at Kolaghat; Rs 1,782.50 for work at EMBP; and Rs 1,225 for the *khatadar*. The *khatadar* insists that he wants nothing, but the labourers must be paid their arrears. This at the *dafadar's* rate. Who expects contractors' labourers to be paid at the government rate? An appeal has already been submitted to the State Labour Directorate with signatures and thumb-impressions of the labourers. Some of them are mere boys, not even 13 years old, and some are old men.

Why do I write this Eastside Story? I have always suspected that the bonded labour system is very much present in the agricultural and unorganized sectors of West Bengal in the form of contract labour under different names. And, today, it is not enough to liberate the bonded labourers in the agricultural sector alone. A new bonded labour system has come up all over India. Careful scrutiny will prove that the contractors' labourers are nothing but bonded labourers, in reality. You will find them working on building projects, dams, roads, brick kilns. When labourers come from Ranchi to work in West Bengal brick kilns, they come under the migrant labour act or something, not that it helps them any. But when labourers move from one district to another of the same state? This EMBP project is worth how many crores of rupees? If the almighty contractors with powerful connections are a necessity, then where is the machinery to enforce labour protection laws? In a project where a small boy like Ajit Adgiri does not get a single paisa for 44 days' work, what profit is made by the contractor, his *dafadar,* and the inevitable local toughs?

On the threshold of Calcutta, the mighty city, thousands of hapless labourers are slaving. Why have they come? Because of the drought. And who is there to see to them? Twelve hours of backbreaking work under the scorching sun—for food alone. After nightfall the vast stretch of land comes alive with *mastans* selling and consuming liquor. If the local panchayats were helpful, they would not have come. If the working conditions were tolerable, they would not give up and leave. Who will check and find out how many have left and why? And what are the guardians of liberty doing? Let the contractors make their packets. But why deprive the poor of meagre amounts?

From *Economic and Political Weekly,* 16–23 April 1983.

No Escape

Witch Sabbath At Singbhum

On 8 September 1980, the Bihar Military Police (BMP), confronted by tribals assembled under the flag of the Jharkhand Mukti Morcha in the small and picturesque town of Gua, chased some tribals who had to run to the hospital carrying a comrade injured in police firing. Eleven were shot dead within the hospital. The BMP had, according to a tribal, fired 60 to 70 rounds and people of the surrounding area remain convinced that many more than the officially admitted number of 11 died that day. As I write this, I have a list of 8 names; 3 names are still missing to complete the list.

Singbhum is an unfathomable mass of untold miseries. It needs a lot of time, tenacity and toughness to unearth even the names of the officially dead here. It needs stamina to cover long distances on foot. Number 5 on the list was a landless labourer and the others were small peasants, all very poor. Chandra has left behind a 14-year-old daughter, Ramo 3 small children, Rengo a child, Bagi a girl-wife, Joto 2 children, Mangala 4 children and Mata a daughter. What happens to the mothers, fathers, wives and children the killed persons leave behind? One simply does not know. Singbhum is like the white-haired old woman collecting firewood in the jungles, who never answers a stranger, never looks at anyone. Keeping the intruders into her grief at a distance, beyond the barrier of her silence, she continues collecting firewood. According to a tribal, a militant youth organization with a number of 'iron pillars to tie their elephants to' (in other words, important connections) attributed the Gua firing to the missionaries and opposed the demand for a judicial inquiry.

Why, after more than a year, do I refer to Gua? Because, from what others are telling me, it seems that Singbhum has been chosen for a witch sabbath; after the Gua firing the process has been accelerated. The district gazetteers will tell you of the Larka Ho people who dared the British army and successfully withstood the onslaughts of intruders into Kolhan for a long time. Even today, one finds some remnants of the characteristics of this tribe, even after the minerals and forests of Singbhum have been leased to outsiders. The Ho people have a relatively lower rate of conversion to Christianity; they have also retained their hold over land to a greater extent than the other tribes. It is also true that the Ho people's migration to other states has been minimal. But all this is changing fast.

Now Ho men and women are being taken to work in the brickfields of West Bengal, North Bihar and elsewhere as contract labour, on terms which are more like those for bonded labour. They are taken to Punjab to be sold, literally, to rich farmers and brickfield owners by crafty agents. If they went in hundreds before, now they are going in thousands. Why? Because on 8 September 1980 at Gua, the tribals retaliated with arrows and killed some BMP personnel. A tribal says that from that day an undeclared war of revenge has been raging unabated. The villagers are forced to accept absurd work terms for survival. The avengers are on the rampage. At Gua, the arrows hit their targets and the tribals are being taught a lesson. An old tribal says angrily, 'Yes, yes, 11 in the hospital. But so many rounds of firing, can it really be that no one was killed? It was a big crowd. Why did the trucks come? What did they take away? Why was the place kept cordoned off?' A young academic tells me smilingly, 'Please don't believe him. They exaggerate so.'

The mad one tells me—the true Gua story must be written the Kolhan way. The Kolhan way is to walk miles to godforsaken places across the jungles and over the hills. You utter the name 'Gua' ('Guey' as the Ho people say) and they withdraw into a shell, their faces become expressionless. After a long pause an old woman suddenly speaks of the twin iron *nagaras* of Chhotonagra. Once upon a time the *nagaras* would be beaten when the enemy tried to enter Kolhan. But the Ho people forgot this sacred ritual when the hordes of sahibs and *dikus* entered the scene. What does it matter if one *nagara* is taken to Manoharpur and the other left behind? What is done, cannot be undone. Kolhan, from that day, has seen her sun steadily setting. A middle-aged tribal says angrily, 'Why refer to Gua? Read the Bihar Police Manual and you will see that murder was done that day. Our sons die and nobody cares. Our people are taken out of Kolhan to be made slaves elsewhere and not one word of protest from anyone.' He spits on the grass.

Thus Gua remains a mystery. And however strange it may seem, this beautiful small town, cool even in summer, lies at the root of the present witch sabbath in Singbhum. Hidden forces have surfaced to break the solidarity of the tribal people and to demoralize them.

What I write here is assembled from reports from various sources; my correspondents prefer to remain anonymous. According to one, the communal forces have joined hands for a takeover of Singbhum. His account is revealing. In 1964, for the first time, a major communal riot broke out in Ranchi and Singbhum. The particularly affected areas were the towns of Ranchi, Jamshedpur, Chakradharpur and Chaibasa. Communal frenzy engulfed the political, social and moral sanity of the people. One communal riot prepared the stage. Now entered the militant Hindu-ists like one Sarangi and others. They succeeded in influencing some of the tribals, too, which explains the participation of some misled tribal youth in the communal riots of Chakradharpur in the 70s. This Sarangi is a notorious criminal. He has the singular honour of having been entered as a 'Bad Livelihood' case in Bihar Police records. In order to be convicted as a BL case, the police has to have 110 witnesses on its side.

The takeover by professionals soon paid handsome dividends. According to my source, the Jamshedpur riots of 1979 started from the Daigutu tribal *bustee*. For some time now the tribal youths have been participating in the Ramnavami processions. Chaibasa and other towns grow frenzied with the militant display of lethal arms and weapons in the hands of the processionists. The same faces can be seen in the Jan Sangh and Bharatiya Janata Party (BJP) circles. That the militant Hindu-ists are really determined to win over the tribals will be clear from the account given by my source.

In Chaibasa, dominated by traders from Rajasthan, *dharmasabhas* are held with great regularity and various gurus often visit their different disciples. From the bookstall set up at such a *sabha*, my friend bought a booklet for 25 paise. The book bore the title *Adibasiyon Bhi Hindu Hai* (Tribals are also Hindus). The author had taken great pains to prove that the tribals were Hindus and cited freely from the epics to prove his point. After 1978, the Rashtriya Swayamsevak Sangh (RSS) has been active in the region and has opened units in far interior villages. Since the RSS gives martial training to its cadres, it has a better chance than the missionaries, since *lathi* and sword exercises tend to attract the tribals. The candidates selected on BJP tickets have joined the Congress (I), but BJP influence and RSS activity continue hand-in-hand.

There was a new impetus in the tribal movement with the Jharkhand Mukti Morcha (JMM) gaining ground; and places like Sonua, Goilkera, Gua, Serengda, Putida etc. became strongholds of the movement.

After the Gua firing, money poured into the region from different sources. Money came in under the Subarnarekha plan financed by the World Bank, and large amounts of it were mis-spent for want of specific plans. Tenders were accepted for 6-inch-deep concrete roads, and cement roads are being built, providing daily work to the tribal *rejas* and *majdoors*. Banks were asked to provide finance for silkworm cultivation, animal husbandry and agriculture. Ministers and their secretaries came to grace the inauguration ceremony. How the loans are being given and what benefit the tribals are receiving from such loans would need another long article.

Then the Deendayal Institute, named after the Jan Sangh leader Deendayal Upadhyay, made its entry. Nanaji Deshmukh, according to my correspondent, came to Chaibasa to hold meetings. Addressing the meetings, he spoke of the necessity of developing tribal villages and of the Deendayal Institute's achievements in such work elsewhere. He declared that the tribals were being converted to Christianity, that this had to be stopped, that there would be no dearth of *sevaks* or money for this: *sevaks* would be coming from Delhi and Kanpur. He met the managers of the different banks. What passed between the banks and Deshmukh? I have a copy of a memorandum from a certain bank. It is most revealing. The Deendayal Institute is interested in developing areas connected with the Jharkhand movement: the Kuira area of Goilkera block, Chakradharpur block, Potka block, Chandil block and Bhargaon block are to be developed. The programme would be 'intensive' and the Institute 'planned to post a good number of field staff at each centre'.

After the Jan Sangh-dominated Deendayal Institute came the RSS. A man from another part of Bihar, who prefers to remain anonymous, writes that the RSS organized workers' meetings, and helped convene a *sahityasabha* where the works of Golwalkar were sold. The 1981 Ramnavami festival brought the role of the RSS to the surface. At Chaibasa, the BMP and the police were already on patrol. The organizers built an image of the divine Mahavir surreptitiously behind the cover of 3 buses which blocked the road, seemingly parked for repair. In the depths of the night the image was carried to a piece of *khas jamin* meant for the building of an Urdu library in the Muslim-dominated Barabazar area, and placed there on a pedestal. A priest came and, after uttering mantras, did *pran pratistha* of the hitherto lifeless idol, rendering it 'divine'. Hundreds of worshippers came to worship the god. Tension enveloped the town. Mahavir continued to stand there even after Ramnavami was over. Communal feelings ran high. The DC had the idol removed. This created havoc. Women continued to worship it and men courted arrest over the issue. The tribal and non-tribal slums displayed hundreds of BJP flags, the lotus on a field of saffron.

One fears that a communal riot is being manufactured at Chaibasa. The JMM movement is going through a lull. The tribals are being preyed upon by militant communalists. A local CPI leader is said to have declared, 'I am first a Hindu, then a Communist.' Converting Singbhum into fertile ground for communalism, the activists are aiming to break tribal solidarity. The ultimate aim is not a Hindu–Muslim riot but a riot between the Christian and non-Christian tribals. When that is achieved, the witches will have fulfilled their mission. According to my source, some of the missionaries, too, are working towards the same goal. How real the witches are, will be clear from the following account.

In 1980, some enthusiasts at Chaibasa decided to observe Birsa Munda Jayanti Utsava, the birth anniversary of the tribal rebel leader Birsa Munda. The editor of a local left-wing journal came forward to help. The tribals and most of the non-tribals remained aloof and did not participate. Just an hour before the scheduled beginning, the local missionaries sent a large painting of Birsa as a gift. And a young European, accompanied by a Bengali youth, arrived. He said that he was a member of the West German Communist Party and had come to make some surveys. My correspondent was very surprised. Incidentally, this 'West German Communist' stayed there for 2 days, collected information about the JMM movement and the tribals, and then disappeared from the scene. The Jayanti was thinly attended by the tribals. Afterwards a tribal student told my correspondent, 'Why should we participate? Was not Birsa a man of the missionary camp? Why else were you helped by the missionaries? That left-wing journal is financed by a Belgian Mission. Money comes from Bangalore. We know.'

Well, my friend did not know. But isn't a clear picture emerging? If the missionaries help Birsa Jayanti, then Birsa's name is sullied in the non-Christian tribal mind. When missionaries or their people give support to a name, or a cause, the very name or the cause becomes suspect. Once this happens, a purpose has been achieved. Rob a tribal of the sanctity of a name or cause which can forge unity, and he will be suspicious of everything for a long time to come. The tribals have always been wary of non-tribals. Now they will start suspecting tribals too. It is not just a coincidence that a local influential big-noise, a close associate and friend of Sarangi, held a meeting soon after the Birsa Jayanti and spoke vehemently against the missionary-influenced Birsa Jayanti. Or that the Gua firing was attributed to the machinations of the missionaries, by a powerful block.

The anti-missionary stand is given publicity to gain the confidence of the tribals. A truck carrying contract-labour from Chaibasa overturns. The priest and the students of a local convent rescue the injured tribals and offer them first-aid. The big-noise enters the scene and insults the priest. It was all right to administer first-aid, but who gave him the right to offer water to the tribals and make them lose caste by becoming *jati bhrasht?* The locals say that the big-noise received money from the contractors of the labour tráde to raise a furore. Who knows? And how do the contractors and middlemen take thousands of contract-bound labourers from Singbhum? Whom do they bribe in order to run the operation smoothly? These questions need to be probed. Today, the tribal existence in Singbhum is symbolized in this simple song about a cowherd lost in the jungle:

In the east, the tiger prowls
In the south, the black bear growls
In the west, the wild wolf howls
In the north, the serpent's jowls
So the little boy he waits and waits
To be eaten by the tiger
To be crushed to death by the bear
To be torn to shreds by the wolves
To be swallowed by the snake.

What are the tribals to do? Old Mother Kolhan never answers. Her children did not beat the *nagara* when the outsiders entered Kolhan. How can she tell them what to do? What is done, cannot be undone.

Why this assemblage of reactionary forces in Singbhum? The answer is, Singbhum is rich in forests; Singbhum is a labour-recruitment centre; Singbhum is very necessary for India's *pancharangi* programme of wealth for the wealthy and poverty for the poor. That is why the communalists, missionaries and the so-called friends of the tribals have joined forces there. Tribals and tribal interests are sacrificial beasts. Nothing else. No one can help Singbhum simply because no one can afford to annoy the big industrial houses which own the rich minerals of Singbhum. The immunity these big industrialists enjoy makes them totally blind to human misery. They are capitalists and their outlook and dealings are as feudal as can be expected. Two instances of the callous brutality of the big-ones have come to my notice through the endeavours of a tenacious person.

The Birla mughals own the Roro Asbestos-Cement mines of Chaibasa, Singbhum, and Hyderabad A-C Products operate it. Asbestos is a 'naturally occurring silky material' but unlike other fibres it is nonflammable and, therefore, invaluable in the manufacture of fireproof cloth, rope, paper, millboard, sheets, paint, etc., and in the making of fire-proof safes, insulators, lubricants, felts, etc., according to *Minerals of India* by Meher D.

N. Wadia. The Singbhum asbestos is of the actionolite variety, which is not as soft and flexible as the chrysotile variety. In 1966 asbestos was valued at Rs 24 lakhs for 10,000 tonnes. This should give us some idea about how valuable it is. Asbestos, mined at Roro, is taken to Hyderabad to manufacture roof-sheets, A-C pipes, etc.

Roro is in the heart of Kolhan, surrounded by hills and jungles. The mine is an underground one and is situated at the top of a hill at an altitude of 2000 ft. About 1500 tribals workers come to work there from villages both near and far. They cut the fibre while crawling in the pits, as the ceilings are low. While cutting or taking out chunks, they freely inhale asbestos fibre and dust. HACP Ltd. gives the miners nothing but a daily wage of Rs 7–10. No DA, no cost of living index, work-uniform, living quarters, hospitals or creches. No transport to take them from base-camp to pit-head. Birla builds temples, prints and distributes the *Bhagavad Gita.* The liquor sellers rob the miners of their wages on pay day.

But all this is the usual situation for tribal and non-tribal miners anywhere in India. The greater danger is exposure to asbestos, which causes asbestosis, a scarring of the lungs, leading to death. Asbestosis today is incurable. Asbestos plants have been closed down in America. Sweden has imposed a ban on the mining and manufacture of asbestos. It is compulsory for asbestos mining and manufacturing authorities to put a skull-and-crossbone sign near asbestos stocks, etc. It is also necessary to provide the miners with a set of work-uniforms, since asbestos dust and fibre spell death. The Roro miners work in the mines in their daily-wear clothes. According to one who knows, they go home and spread the dust. The visit to the weekly market at Chaibasa spreads the chances of death by asbestosis to other visitors. The crusher-plant exhausts release asbestos-dust into the air which the villagers of the surrounding area breathe. The miners and the other employees of HACP are daily and hourly being exposed to asbestos dust and fibre. Birla could not care less.

Between January and August of 1981, 30 people, including miners and villagers, died of asbestosis. Once, in 1978, due to the efforts of the United Mineral Workers' Union, this issue was raised in the Rajya Sabha by an MP and the Labour Minister asked the Director General of Mines Safety, at Dhanbad, to undertake a health survey. Robert John Hamilton of the ILO visited Roro on 28 November 1978. No one knows what his suggestions were about controlling dust from the crusher-plant. Anyway, nothing has been done. Asbestos mining remains profitable. Birla prints and distributes the *Gita*, the miners and the tribal villagers die, reactionary organizations take care of tribal solidarity; Kolhan, the old woman, waits somewhere and watches the *tamasha* at her children's cost.

Asbestosis for the Roro miners and silicosis for the Jhikpani cement miners and those working for the factories of limestone and clay. Silicosis is a form of pneumoconiosis characterized by the formation of small discrete nodules. In advanced cases, a dense fibrosis and emphysema with impairment of respiratory function may develop. Silicosis is a fibriotic reaction occurring in the lungs. It is produced by the inhalation of silica dust by persons employed in tin, zinc and gold mines, and also cutters of marble and stone. The treatment is the removal of the cause; changes already produced in the lungs are usually permanent; chronic bronchitis or pulmonary tuberculosis are common accompaniments of the condition.(Pierce, Miller and Cunningham, *Medical and Nursing Dictionary and Enclyclopaedia*, Faber and Faber).

The Jhikpani cement factory exhausts release cement dust into the air, and the adjoining villages and fields and trees are smothered under a layer of fine cement which, in contact with moisture of the atmosphere, hardens. This cement causes damage to crops, trees and human beings with the same destructive fury. Someone writes that a 35-mile radius around the factory is under threat; that some villages had to be abandoned because the paddy was cursed and trees withered; that village huts, under cement dust, look grey and haunted; that villagers suffer from acute breathing trouble. The owners could not care less. Why build a dust control tower? The Jhikpani ACC earns huge profits. A non-tribal philosophizes, 'What to do? If they don't die from silicosis, they'll die from something else. They aren't immortal.' He utters these words out of a despair and anger born of frustration.

Roro and Jhikpani are twin mirrors to Singbhum. Inhuman exploitation is to continue and the children of Kolhan are to be kept in eternal bondage. In order to keep the exploitation running, tribal solidarity must be broken into atoms. The witches will see to it. Where is Kolhan, the mythical mother of the Kols? What is happening to her children? Who has the answer?

From *Economic and Political Weekly*, 3 October 1981.

A Countryside Slowly Dying

A visit to Singbhum was long under contemplation, so the invitation to attend a meeting, or *sammelan*, of the tribals of Rajenka and other villages was most welcome. The ACC factory of Jhikpani is causing much distress in the locality because cement dust carried by the wind is ruining crops and vegetation. The *sammelan* was organized by a committee constituted of people belonging to the Jharkhand Mukti Morcha, Kolhan Raksha Sangh, United Mineral Workers Union, Mahila Samaj of Chakradharpur, Roro asbestos miners and nearby villages. The approach to Jhikpani from Chaibasa was marked by a changing landscape. The fields lay barren and grey under layers of accumulated cement dust. The trees looked ghostly, the leaves hanging listless, heavy with cement dust. In the weekly *hat* at Jhikpani the air was hazy with grey dust. Cement dust fell relentlessly upon everyone and everything. Within minutes we, too, were covered with cement dust. The tribals bought and sold, going about their business without concern. The open sheds selling liquor were doing brisk business.

In the afternoon we went and saw the places nearby. Rajenka village is one of the worst sufferers. It lies permanently enveloped in cement dust. There were several of us on the team. What we saw defies description.

Big lakes mirror the sky and it is soothing to the eye to see water after traversing a scorched countryside. These are not natural lakes, though they look like nature's gift to a dry and savaged landscape. They are abandoned mines. According to the Metalliferous Mines Regulations, they are illegal. 'Shaft and open cast workings temporarily or permanently out of use and any place in or about an excavation which is dangerous shall be completely filled up or kept securely fenced' (5A of chapter XI), says the rule. And, in the same chapter, 'Before a mine is abandoned or the working thereof discontinued, the owner, agent or manager shall cause the top or entrance of every shaft, incline or other opening into the mine to be fenced by a structure of permanent character sufficient to effectively prevent persons falling into or entering the same' (5B of chapter XI).

The huge water tanks around Jhikpani are abandoned mines which have not been filled up. Even a fence or a permanent structure around them will not help solve the peculiar problem caused by the huge pits. The surrounding area consists of agricultural fields. It is also a non-irrigated area. Rainwater is the only source of relief for the peasantry. The water which is so soothing to the eye is actually stolen water. During the rains the rainwater flows into the pits, leaving the fields dry, where enough irrigation can help vegetation-growth. This was amply proved by the greenery around the rural health centre. The menace is very real and the peasants are justifiably aggrieved about it. The steep drop to water level was almost vertical. It looked as if only Jim Corbett's *ghoorals* could tackle the descent. Yet we found vegetable patches covering the same vertical landline. We crossed the fields and tanks and reached the main road towards the plant. Open drains on both sides carry cement dust to another pit. The day is not distant when this pit, too, will be filled up with cement waste. In Singbhum district a 50-km belt of limestone extends from Chaibasa to Jagannathpur.

ACC has about 19 cement factories in India and Jhikpani might be the oldest. It employs about 2000 workers in the factory and the quarry, consisting of about 800 permanent and 1200 casual labourers. Are the casual labourers recruited by contractors? I don't know. And while all the unskilled labourers are tribals, only about 20 per cent of the skilled labourers are from the tribes. Not a happy picture at all. The Jhikpani plants produce something like 7,20,000 tons per year. Production has gone up in the last 30 years, but the number of labourers remains static. The factory runs in 3 shifts, round the clock.

The twin giant chimneys emanate cement exhaust. My informant told me that every day about 700 tons of cement dust are released from the chimneys. The term he used was 'cement gas'. I don't know his method of calculation. The difference between crude limestone and cement, both measured by weight? Whatever it is, the dust menace is a real threat. A 10-mile radius area around the factory looks like a vast nightmare. Cement dust, accumulated and hardened by night moisture, kills vegetation slowly. Trees wither, paddy, lentil and *jowar* plants give up and die, unable to survive in soil hardened by cement dust. The peasants and. casual *majdoors* inhale cement dust and die of tuberculosis. It has never been properly investigated whether the tuberculosis found in the area is caused by silicosis or not. A fair and impartial survey of tubercular deaths could be revealing. The workers in the factory and the people living around suffer. The cattle suffer, too. When the health of humans is treated with callousness, who thinks of animals? Cattle inhale cement dust, contract tuberculosis and die. The Singbhum lifescape is one of savage indifference.

The Metalliferous Mines Regulations 1961, amended upto 1980, has 8 clauses on dust control in chapter XII (precautions against danger from fire, dust, gas and water). All the rules are ignored with supreme contempt. A proper exhaust system will control the dust menace, but why install it at so much cost when 2000 workers can produce 2000 tons of cement per day and when every day casual labour queues up at the factory gate, begging to be taken on for the day?

The *sammelan* was held in the open before a beautiful pavilion of split bamboo covered with leafy branches. Peasants and workers of the area had united in hundreds. Most of them were tribals, largely of the Ho tribe. The Ho people of Singbhum are a mighty race—both the young and the old had come. A significant section of the gathering was non-tribal. Rasiklal Honaga, the *mukhia* of Dokatta panchayat in Tonto block, said with quiet despair that fields previously yielding 15 *maunds* of paddy per acre were now yielding 5. Cement dust affected his panchayat, crop failure was an everyday experience and cattle died of eating dust-laden leaves and grass.

Moreover, the ACC plant was expanding and usurping the villagers' lands in a most arbitrary manner. The villagers never

know how much land the company will take, or whose. The ACC
does not bother to take the permission of the owner of the land.
It just says that money against the land has been deposited with
the treasury. In the past, it used to consult the *mukhias, mundas,
mankis, sarpanchs.* Now it does not.

Landgrabbing by the ACC goes on, seemingly in an illegal
manner. Kandwa, Rajenka and Dokatta are already in the
acquired area. Nimidh, Kudahati, Jorapokar, Barajhikpani and
Dodonga are under threat. Since the area under the factory falls
under the limestone belt, the villagers have to give up their land
so that ACC can increase cement production. According to the
rules, leases have to be renewed every 30 years and the
landowners properly compensated. Acquiring tribal land is illegal
but it can be done under the cover of law when a factory needs
expansion. Land is being taken forcibly and the cultivator
harassed by the police if he tills his own land. Surprisingly, he is
told that he is cultivating ACC land.

In this acquirement of land lies hidden the promise of a job in
the factory. It became clear when a casual labourer showed an
appeal by several casual labourers, venting their grievances. Their
land was taken over, but no compensation was paid. Promise of
work was given but they were kept on as casual labourers at the
factory for years with 8–10 days of work a month. They did not
enjoy earned leave or sick leave benefits, nor did they receive *gur*,
soda, hats or boots. They were not being made permanent.

Gumia Shundi of Baihatu village was a discharged labourer of
the Roro mines. He was very vocal and spoke most impressively.
After 2 deaths in the Roro mines there was a 48-hour *gherao.* The
authorities gave assurances about adopting preventive measures
against accidents and undertaking asbestos dust control. After
that, 7 workers were discharged, including Gumia. His livelihood
now depended upon gathering and selling firewood. But life in
the villages was hazardous. The police were seizing paddy, too. So
the villagers had to keep paddy hidden in the jungles. Because of
the JMM movement the police had set fire to the village of
Sangajatha. Gumia squarely condemned the *mankis* and *mundas*
for their inaction against the asbestos dust hazard. (These *mundas*
are not necessarily Munda tribals. The village heads are known as
mundas, too.)

The figures I have mentioned have been collected from the

people working in the factory. It baffles me why there has never been a militant movement against forcible land usurpation by the ACC, the cement dust hazard and negligence over filling up the abandoned mines. The factory has unions. The Jhikpani plant of the ACC is the other example of the dubious role of the established trade unions. The abandoned pits converted into water reservoirs can be solidly walled around so as to stop rainwater from pouring or seeping in. The water can be used for irrigation purposes, too. But the cement dust hazard? Sunil Sengupta, another member of our team, said from his European experience that cement factories were common but such health and cultivation hazards caused by cement dust were uniquely Indian. I thought of the limestone quarries I had seen between Bilaspur and Rajnandgaon in Madhya Pradesh. Many more factories and a slow death of the countryside. It is easier, in Singbhum, to kill and terrorize the ordinary people with the law on your side. The ACC is too powerful to abide by the law.

On the morning of 30 January we had gone to Serengsi Ghati where the Ho people had fought the British in the 19th century. We left the jeep at Serengsi village and covered the distance on foot. The jungles were beautiful, with wild plums ripe under the sun and early *palas* flowers heralding the spring. A favourite haunt of the elephants, the area was in the interior. The tiny rivulet, Charna, accompanied us. Three old villagers led the way. They still remembered the story of the battle handed down by their ancestors. The tribal king's war-cry could be heard from a place which was named Rajenka to commemorate the event. A flat stone under a *mowa* tree marked the line of advance by the tribals. The atmosphere was charged with the past of a people who still record everything in the mind, not on paper. Nor do they believe in commemorating things our way. I asked them to keep a stone plaque at Serengsi village with the notification of the battle. A quick dip in the Charna brought the past even nearer. Once the rocky and steep banks of the Charna had witnessed a fierce battle where the mighty British had fought and lost. Those were the days the brave Kolhans dreamt of. The forests were primeval. No 'social forestry' as one sees in West Bengal. No eucalyptus plantations with the forest floor bare of undergrowth, as one sees in Jhargram. Here the *sal, arjun, sidha, kusum* and *palas* crowded the skyline. The undergrowth was undisturbed. I saw *basakas, anantamul* and other medicinal plants. The sight of Ho women pumping water from newly sunk tubewells was a pleasant surprise. The Gua firing and the accompanying stir had moved the administration a little and the tubewells were sunk after that. That's what they told me.

From Serengsi we had come to Jhikpani. The grey countryside is still a nightmarish memory. Who can save the countryside from a slow and inevitable death? What is going to happen to the hapless villagers so wrongly and cruelly deprived of their land? Only the people of Singbhum can work out a solution with a continuous and consistent movement, not a merely sporadic and thunderous one. Under whose leadership ? I do not know.

From *Economic and Political Weekly*, 5 March 1983.

Eucalyptus : Why ?

'Eucalyptus is a myrtaceous genus of trees, mostly Australian. Most of them secrete resinous gums, whence they are called gum trees' (Webster's Dictionary). Stebbing's *The Forests of India* (1926) has only a few words for eucalyptus. The genus is also referred to as an experiment in new plantation.

In the 1961 district gazetteers of Palamau and Singbhum, in the chapters on forests, there is not a single reference to eucalyptus. Nor in a handbook prepared and published by the Government of West Bengal does one come across the name now deified by union and state governments. The destruction of natural forests and the plantation of eucalyptus is quite a recent affair. The eucalyptus policy and the insane and ruthless new forest bill are closely linked.

Forests consist of trees, plants, creepers, shrubs, bushes and undergrowth of grass and lesser plants. A lot has been written about *sal* forests but almost all Indian trees have a social and economic relevance to the immediate society. In the *Bouddha Jatakas* we come across a story—Jeevaka, Gautam Buddha's physician, was once sent to a forest by his teacher to collect plants which have no use for mankind. Jeevaka came back after a long search and said that he had failed to find any such plant. In the book *Common Trees* published by the National Book Trust, H. Santappu has discussed 36 trees and plants. *Kadam*, 'in Bombay forests, is considered after teak, one of the five most valuable timber trees.' It has medicinal properties as well. The Flame of the Forest or the *palas* serves mankind with lac, gum, seed, leaf and firewood, and due to its adaptability to dry, sandy and hilly areas is a good species for the regeneration of poor soil. The *mahua* has so many economic uses that in the proposed Jharkhand area of West Bengal it is justifiably known as Kalpataru or the divine tree. Lodha brides are first married to the *mahua* tree, then to the groom, who has to get married first to a mango tree. *Toon, bhendi,* tamarind, *kusum,* jackfruit, ironwood, gliricide, *amaltas,* purple *bauhinis,* silk cotton, *kendu,* mussaenda, the tree of heaven, all have economic uses and a mixed forest sustains the immediate populace. Not all of them are tribals. In the forest areas, tribals and non-tribals, all the poor people, somehow make a living from the forest. We, in India, know very little about the economic uses of our trees. We know about the traditional uses only. Any advanced country (other than India) in 36 years, would have undertaken extensive research on the subject and, with a sensible forest policy, would have made maximum use of the knowledge.

Take the case of Jhargram and Purulia of West Bengal. A carefully grown forest of *sal, palas, kendu, piasal,* wild *jamun,* jackfruit, *amla,* plum and other species would have provided the region with food, fuel and various means of livelihood. Such a forest would help life to flourish and, importantly, the soil-moisture would be retained. Only such a forest justifies the term 'social forestry' because it sustains the neighbouring rural society.

And, from the not-so-old district gazetteers of Bihar, we find that the government's forest policy was not always aimed at the total destruction of natural species. The 1961 gazetteer on Singbhum states that sal was the principal forest product of that district. Only a small quantity of *semul* and other softwood species were supplied to WIMCO. The Palamau gazetteer stated that *sal* sometimes constituted 50 per cent of the crop and stressed the importance of bamboo cultivation, as it was in great demand at the paper mills. There is not a single reference to eucalyptus in the gazetteers of the 2 districts mainly dependent upon forest revenue. Today, with finance from Sweden, Singbhum is felling natural forests and planting eucalyptus. WIMCO needs eucalyptus for the matchbox industry. I was shocked to see Palamau robbed of the magnificent bamboos, *palas, kusum, sidha, shisham* and *sal,* and newly clothed in eucalyptus. But it is still possible to come across real forests in Palamau and Singbhum here and there. In the Bankura, Purulia and Medinipur districts of West Bengal, it is all eucalyptus. Our villagers have been robbed of food, fuel and means of survival because of the state's social forestry policy. One cannot eat the leaf, bark or fruit of eucalyptus. Eucalyptus does not offer shelter from sun and rain. But protest against eucalyptus, in West Bengal, is interpreted as the influence of Jharkhandi propaganda.

Why this sudden forest-departmental frenzy for eucalyptus ? Well, eucalyptus means matchboxes, rayon, furniture, medicine. Which class benefits from factories, workshops, plants and markets connected with various eucalyptus products ? Definitely not the poor and the downtrodden. The forest is meant for society and society is sustained by the forest. I have not heard of a Ho from Singbhum, or a Parhayiya from Palamau or a Lodha or Santhal from West Bengal who has gone in for big capital investment in eucalyptus products. Social forestry for which society? Not for the poor and the downtrodden. For the rich, then? It must be so. But at what national cost?

Eucalyptus was introduced to India in the 1840s from Australia. It used to be seen in the big gardens of the well-to-do as a decorative tree. No country in the world really went in for eucalyptus plantation as it was not a safe tree to play with. As a full-grown eucalyptus consumes 80 gallons of water a day, it is not good for dry soil but beneficial for marshy land, and for the desert, where the sandy layer has already been exposed. A sturdy species, eucalyptus will grow in any type of soil. The chief of Terai forests, Nainital division, admitted in 1975 that wherever eucalyptus plantations came up, the tubewells went dry and water-levels of the wells fell. He had also noted that the forest floor in an eucalyptus plantation was devoid of undergrowth. According to experts, eucalyptus trees were to be uprooted if the river or stream nearby went dry.

According to ecologists of Bombay, the eucalyptus hazard was affecting the ecological balance of the Terai, where natural forests had been felled to make way for the eucalyptus. During the summer, the hot winds blowing from the plains got no resistance from the eucalyptus, and hit the snowlines. Previously they would absorb the moisture of the Terais. As a result the Pindari glacier is already receding. Nainital and Mussourie are not so cold anymore. In 1982, a world-renowned specialist on the subject had visited the Dehradun Forest Research Institute and expressed his dismay at seeing eucalyptus plantations between Dehradun and Rishikesh. He said that it was senseless to fell fruit and fuel-yielding trees to plant eucalyptus. Eucalyptus would suck the soil dry. If any tree in India needed uprooting, it was eucalyptus.

When I was touring the faraway regions of Purulia, a soil conservationist confided that the extensive eucalyptus plantations were consuming whatever little water the Purulia soil had. That no undergrowth covers an eucalyptus plantation-floor is very apparent. Nature's process of creation also gets hampered, as the strong smell of eucalyptus repels flying insects like bees, butterflies, etc., causing pollination stoppage. A eucalyptus forest does not encourage or harbour wildlife of small animals and birds. I am concerned with the India I know. My India is of the poor, starving and helpless people. Most of them are landless and the few who have land are happy to be able to make the most of given resources. To cover Purulia, Bankura, Medinipur, Singbhum and Palamau with eucalyptus will rob my India of drinking and irrigation water. These are the areas where there is a chronic water scarcity.

The water consumption of a eucalyptus tree is equal to that of 10 *sal* trees. Its slim trunk and narrow leaves are incapable of resisting wind. Nor can it offer shade. So the upper level of soil, which conserves water and nitrogen salt, gets eroded due to direct exposure to the sun and wind. The sandy sub-level gets exposed. During the monsoons this sand gets carried down to the river beds. Thus the rivers and streams of the dry areas are getting filled with sand, and denudation of vegetation on the banks is causing the widening of the river bed. Such rivers flood easily, causing havoc to the countryside.

It is downright hypocrisy to destroy the natural habitat of wildlife, to plant eucalyptus, and yet to publicize India's great concern for the protection of wildlife.

An impartial and objective survey by a team of experts will prove that (a) eucalyptus plantation is a threat to India's store of subsoil water-reserve which is already diminishing; (b) it is a threat to the country's ecological and atmospheric balance; (c) eucalyptus plantation on the Himalayan foothills should be cut down and uprooted to protect the snowlines from the hot winds blowing from the plains; (d) rivers, streams, wells, tanks and tubewells in the eucalyptus area are drying up; and (e) it is monstrous to plant eucalyptus in the drought-prone regions of West Bengal, Bihar and elsewhere in India.

Such a team should also bring out who the beneficiaries from eucalyptus are and who the losers. Will eucalyptus sustain India's starving millions? How? Most of the bonded labourers of Palamau do not have rights over homestead land, though Bihar passed the land reform bill in 1952. The Kheria–Savaras of West Bengal are constantly being hounded by the forest guards and the police and regularly evicted from homesteads. The Lodhas of Medinipur lead a threatened existence. The Santhals of West Bengal are constantly on the move in search of work. The Birhors and Parhayiyas live like paupers in West Bengal and Bihar. In my India, children of 7 years are hired out as child-labourers just for a meal. Will eucalyptus help them? Are these people going to operate rayon, plastic or matchbox industries? Will they own and operate paper mills, or open furniture shops ? We know the answer. Then for whom are we sacrificing our Himalayas, our monsoons, our agricultural fields, our people ?

An anti-eucalyptus movement on a national scale seems to be the only answer. Since the eucalyptus-oriented forest policy and the abominable forest bill are closely linked together, such a movement should thwart and ultimately defeat both.

From *Economic and Political Weekly*, 6 August 1983.

Land and Employment

Land Alienation among Tribals in West Bengal

Both in terms of laws and their implementation, West Bengal has a relatively better record in land reforms than most other states of the country. The main comprehensive land reforms act of the state was enacted in 1955 and has been amended several times since. In the main set of acts and their subsequent amendments, several provisions have been incorporated to prevent alienation of tribal land, particularly from tribals to non-tribals. But despite all these laws, the process of land alienation has reached serious proportions in the state.

It is true that there are several reasons for this, including the poor level of development among the tribals, lack of literacy and education among them, and their deeprooted mistrust and fear of the legal system. But the real cause is their class position. India, that is, Bharat, doesn't consider them to be an integral part of society. How else can one explain the role played by the dominant sections of society, the administration and the political parties, doing everything within their means to ensure that the tribals do not enjoy any right to which they are entitled?

Under the laws of the state, a tribal can sell his land only to a tribal and any sale or even gift to a non-tribal is illegal. Sale or transfer of land to a non-tribal can be done only with the written permission of specially designated revenue officials. In case of a tribal seeking to transfer his land, the district and subdivision level SC and ST Welfare Officers have been empowered to act as

Revenue Officers and the formalities have to be carried out through them. Any violation of these provisions would make the transaction illegal.

A tribal can, however, transfer his land, without selling it, in a few specific cases:

—He can transfer the land to another tribal for a period not exceeding 7 years under usufructuary mortgage (called *khai khalasi* in rural areas) against money borrowed. The idea is that the person who had lent the money would recover the loan with interest from the crops within the mortgage period. If, however, the loanee is in a position to repay the remaining amount before the stipulated period, the Revenue Officer would ensure that he regained his land on payment of the remaining amount.

—He can sell or gift the land to the government for a charitable purpose.

—He can mortgage the land to the government or to a registered cooperative society.

—No interest in land or transfer of the land itself by a tribal would be legal unless registered according to the provisions of the law.

—If any tribal had transferred any land to a non-tribal in contravention of the laws within a period of 30 years prior to the amendment of 1976, the transferred land would have to be restored to him.

The very idea behind specially empowering the SC and ST Welfare Officers to act as Revenue Officers (or *kanungos*) relating to transfer of tribal land was that they would have an advantage in protecting tribal interests by virtue of their official position. I learnt from the Land and Land Revenue Minister of West Bengal (no less!) that the necessary notification empowering these officials had been sent to them at the district and subdivision level after the amendments were made. It was sent once again after my enquiry. However, whenever a tribal approaches the SC and ST Officer at the district or subdivision level, he finds that either the concerned officials are not aware of the notification or they are evasive about it. The net result is that the tribals do not get the support of the Act. This is the general experience of a large number of tribals in Bankura, Medinipur, Darjeeling, Purulia, Hooghly and South 24 Parganas district. Due to their poverty, lack of education and the callousness and even collusion of officials with land sharks, land is constantly being transferred to non-tribals. I shall discuss 2 cases here. Both the cases have taken place in north Bengal, hardly a few kilometres away from Naxalbari.

In the first case, some businessmen from outside the state are taking over the land of the local tribals at Ethelbari in Alipurduar subdivision of Jalpaiguri district. They are running a flourishing brickmaking business. The *pradhan* (head of the village panchayat) is turning a blind eye to it. According to the villagers, he himself has an interest in the brick kilns. The *upapradhan* or the next person in the village panchayat, protested against this. The brick-kiln owners went to the police. The police promptly acted to protect the interests of the brick-kiln owners. On 20 August 1987, the Subdivisional Police Officer came to the village with 60 policemen and beat up a large number of tribal men, women and even children. The *upapradhan,* himself a tribal, was not spared, because he had taken the side of the villagers against the brick-kiln owners.

The residents of Ethelbari háve been trying to draw the attention of the authorities for thé last few years, protesting against the brick kilns on their land. They had sent letters to the District Magistrate of Jalpaiguri, Subdivisional Land Reforms Officer, SC and ST Welfare Department, the Chief Minister, the Minister of Agriculture, the Superintendent of Police of the district and the Prime Minister of the country. No one cared to reply. Finally, an organization of tribals wrote a letter to the Supreme Court of the country. The Deputy Registrar of the Supreme Court wrote to the State Social Welfare Department, the Chairman of the Legal Aid Advisory Committee and to the Deputy Secretary of the Law Department of the state. There has been no response from any of them.

But how did the brick-kiln owners get access to the land they are occupying? In 4 out of a total of 5 cases, some money has been paid to the owners and then the land has been transferred to fictitious tribal people. It should be noted that this is the most widely prevalent method for registering sale of tribal land. Land is purchased in the name of people who do not exist, or do not have anything to do with the transaction other than lending their name. The person who actually buys the land is not a tribal but has money and political clout. It is not difficult for him to influence the local political parties, panchayat, police and officials—in other words, the very people who should protect the interests of the tribals. On how many fronts can the tribal carry on his battles?

In the fifth case, a non-tribal has declared himself to be a tribal and got the transaction registered.

These cases, if anything, expose the blatant violation of laws that goes on all the time. It is not enough to enact laws without making sure that they are also implemented. All these people continue to violate the laws with impunity.

A major problem is that the tribals do not even know that the SC and ST Welfare Officers are competent to provide them redress. The officials themselves seem to have no concern for a matter that is of such vital importance to the tribals. Restoration of illegally transferred land is possible only through the legal process, which is often protracted and always expensive. But the system that exists for providing legal aid to the poor people in this state is a farce. What generally happens is that whenever an aggrieved tribal goes to the police to make a complaint or seek protection, the police gets the tribal implicated in false lawsuits. The lawyers of the government end up fighting against the tribal, instead of protecting him. Those who take over land from the tribals in total violation of laws can do so because they have the necessary clout and are helped not only by the police and the administration, but—and this is more serious—by the political parties of all colours and shades. These political parties have destroyed the unity among the tribals and they usually operate through a small section of privileged tribals who do not protect the interests of the community and often create discord amongst fellow-tribals at the grassroots level.

After the 1982 elections, when the Left Front came to power for the second time, there was general jubilation among the landless and poor peasants and sharecroppers. There was widespread apprehension among the *jotedars* and rich peasants that their surplus land would be taken over by the government. So far, many of them had been supporters of the Congress Party and most used to exploit the agricultural labourers, sharecroppers and marginal farmers. They sensed the winds of change and started switching sides. They mostly became supporters of the major partner in the Left Front, the CPI(M).

With these sections joining the ruling parties, those within the Left Front, particularly within the 2 Communist parties, who had been fighting for the poor peasants and sharecroppers, started feeling cornered inside their own parties. The very people against whom they had so far been fighting for land and for sharecroppers' rights, even achieving major success, were now within the ranks of their own parties. But their class interest remained unchanged. Now, as members of the major partner in the ruling Left Front, they had all the backing of the administration and there was little to prevent them from evicting sharecroppers even if they belonged to their own parties, or taking over the land of the small peasants. In several areas of West Bengal, tribal peasants and sharecroppers of the major ruling party had to fight against *jotedars* who belonged to their own party, and community.

The other side of the picture is that if an ordinary peasant does not belong to the ruling parties, he does not have any protection. Take the case of Pasupati Murmu, a tribal peasant of Medinipur district. Pasupati belonged to the CPI, which was not a partner in the ruling Left Front in 1982. He had an acre of land, for a family of 9. As this was not sufficient for survival, the members of his family used to work as agricultural labourers. But as he was outside the ruling parties, his land was forcibly taken over by the local panchayat and distributed among landless tribals. When he objected and tried to harvest paddy from his own land, he was mercilessly beaten up and killed and his family forced to leave the village. I had repeatedly informed the district administration of Medinipur and the Land and Land Reforms Department of the state about the incident, seeking restoration of the land to his family. Nothing happened.

The reason why I am mentioning this incident is that party politics has sown seeds of bitter conflict and violence at the grassroots level among the tribals. All the political parties are doing this, directly or indirectly, and causing division among the tribals, all for narrow party interests. This has further complicated the issue of land alienation among tribals and those eyeing their land take advantage of this.

These crafty people are fully aware that even the educated among the tribals do not know of the laws which could help them get back land already transferred, or that officers at the district and subdivision level have been empowered to help them. They know that the tribals are unaware of the benefits of the 1986 amendments to the laws relating to restoration of transferred land. This ignorance is fairly widespread. I have received a large number of applications and documents from tribals who have lost their land in the districts of South 24 Parganas, Bankura and Purulia, which proves how pervasive this ignorance is.

Those who take advantage of this also know that the tribal would get no help from the local officials and the police, as no one would listen to him. Any tribal without clout would ultimately have to abandon his rights and hand over the land to the land sharks because they have money and influence. Those showing the audacity to seek legal redress would get lost in the labyrinth of unending civil suits.

They also know that if the tribal goes to the panchayat or political parties, he would not get any justice, as these are controlled by the mainstream people. The simple tribal, not used to lying or the complex ways of the legal system, loses his case even before he starts it. As a result:

—Land is often bought in the name of a non-existent tribal or a tribal who acts as a front for a non-tribal buyer. The concerned departments oblige by registering the sale-deed, once a few palms are greased. No inconvenient queries are made, of course.

—In more blatant cases, a non-tribal manages to procure (read ·buy) a certificate identifying himself as a tribal, and through further fraudulent means gets the land transferred in his own name without the knowledge of the actual tribal owner.

Other means are simpler but no less effective. The Ethelbari case gives some idea of this—through political clout and with help from obliging panchayats, the police and goons, if necessary, the lawful tribal owners are physically evicted from their own land. When goons terrorize people, they are supposed to go to the police. But if the police are hand-in-glove with them, what chance do the people have? It is not the tribals alone who are at the receiving end of this process. But this is certainly happening more in the case of tribals.

One aggravating factor in the case of a tribal is that he often does not keep papers and documents properly. If he is told that all the papers should be carefully preserved, he is nonplussed and wonders why, since everyone knows that he owns a particular piece of land, he needs papers to prove it. It may sound amazing, but I have met such people. They just do not understand many of our ways, the ways of mainstream society.

Those among them who understand the importance of papers and documents face numerous problems in trying to get these documents or their copies from concerned offices. In this matter, the worst culprits are the Land Revenue Department personnel.

While papers are necessary, they may not be enough, as Agnu Panna learnt the hard way. Agnu is an Oraon. His forefathers, along with thousands of other indentured tribal labourers, were brought from Bihar and Madhya Pradesh to the tea-garden area in north Bengal over a hundred years ago. The tribals were also brought to several other areas of West Bengal to clear forests and reclaim land for agriculture.

Agnu's forefathers were brought to the Matigara police station area in the Siliguri subdivision. If it doesn't ring a bell, the place is within walking distance of a place called Naxalbari, a name that has become a symbol of protest and the struggle of peasants and oppressed people all over the country. But that was of little help to Agnu Panna.

Agnu's father was a regular tenant of 32.99 acres of land since pre-independence days and he used to pay annual rent and had all the papers and documents in order. When zamindari was abolished after the passing of the Estate Acquisition Bill in 1954, it was suddenly discovered that Agnu's father's name was no longer in the records and the land was shown to be in the name of Shiva, the family deity of the landlords under whom Agnu's father was a tenant. This was nothing unusual, as records of debates in the West Bengal Legislative Assembly would show—crafty landlords even recorded their lands in the names of animals. Transfer of land in the name of a family deity was very much within the purview of the law. Only, in this specific case, he who got the land transferred in his family deity's name did not have a right to the land. But such small problems are easily surmountable for people with money and influence.

This blatant manipulation of records could only have been possible in connivance with the land revenue officials. When Agnu's father went to his own land, he was severely beaten up by the landlord's goons.

Agnu's father complained to the Land Revenue Department office at Siliguri and an order was issued in his favour, nullifying the earlier change. Agnu was a minor at that time. Then the landlord submitted a forged document and got the land recorded in the name of his own brother-in-law. Then the same land was transferred by the brother-in-law to the son of the landlord. Thus, the same piece of land was transferred twice, all on the basis of forged documents, in total violation of section 5(A) of the relevant law. This, too, could only have been possible with the cooperation of the Land Revenue Department officials.

Then a part of the land thus acquired was sold off by the landlords and the deal was duly registered. After several years, the landlord Kaliprasad died. By that time, Agnu had joined the Border Security Force (BSF) and was serving in its 93rd Regiment in Nagaland and Tripura. The son of the landlord brought an eviction suit against Agnu's father and his family, from their own land. This was also a blatantly false case and ultimately the judgement went in favour of Agnu's family.

The son of the landlord started a new lawsuit against Agnu's family, claiming their land. The case was started in 1979 and dragged on for years. All this time Agnu, who was posted away from Siliguri, had to make arrangements for following up the cases. While the case was dragging on, the landlord's son sold off the land to some local criminal elements, generally described in West Bengal as 'antisocials'. By the time the case ran its full course and the order went in favour of Agnu and his family, the antisocials had already forcibly evicted them from their land and built a house there. Agnu had to take leave several times to follow up the case. He needed more leave now. But the BSF sacked him without showing any reason, after many years of service.

Throughout this period, when these blatant violations of law were taking place, Agnu and his father complained to the police station. Records show that between 1976 and 1987, 24 formal complaints were made at the Siliguri and Matigara police stations. Of them 6 were made in 1976, 3 in 1977, 2 in 1978, 3 in 1979, 2 in 1980, 1 in 1982, 2 in 1986 and 5 in 1987. But this tribal family didn't have a chance against the machinations of the landlord, antisocials and the police working together.

During this period, Agnu's family sent applications to a

large number of people, praying for intervention and justice. The list includes the District Judge; Deputy Commissioner; Superintendent of Police; SC and ST Welfare Department of Darjeeling district; Subdivisional Officer; Subdivisional Police Officer and Scheduled Tribe Welfare Officer of Siliguri subdivision; the local head of the panchayat; Settlement Officer, Cooch Bihar; the Chief Minister and Land Reforms Minister of West Bengal; the Law Minister; the Home Minister and the Prime Minister of India and many others. To no avail, of course.

Though the State Land Revenue Minister has repeatedly declared that tribal land cannot be acquired and converted into tea gardens, this is happening nevertheless. One example of this is the Nagpur tea garden which is being developed over 450 acres near Belakoba, adjacent to Siliguri in north Bengal. The land has been mainly acquired from the tribals.

Fatinga and Paglidhuri villages are under Sikarpur *mouja*. The Nagpur tea-garden owners have acquired most of the land of these 2 villages. As a result, 61 tribal families of Fatinga and 101 from Paglidhuri have been rendered landless. Except for 1 family, the rest are tribals. The Nagpur tea-garden owners have acquired about 477 acres of land from them. The acquirement process was started in June 1989 by middlemen. The land was surveyed in December 1989. It is learnt that each family was paid at the rate of Rs 1000 per acre. Ninety per cent of the acquired land of Paglidhuri is *patta* land. The Fatinga tribals, too, had *patta* land.

In acquiring tribal land, Nagpur tea-garden owners allegedly resorted to foolproof methods. It appears that 162 tribal families of the 2 villages are applying to the tea-garden owners and giving them land voluntarily. This appeal is written on a twenty-rupee stamp paper. It reads like this: 'On 23.12.89, we have given to you land owned by us, till date cultivated by us, sustaining our livelihood. You, too, have helped us by giving one thousand rupees per acre. You will give the land-giving families one job per acre . . .' It ends like this: 'We will enjoy the same facilities and benefits followed by other tea gardens, such as schools, permanent jobs as labourers, rations, bonus, hut, fuels, hospitals, clubs, work-tools, umbrellas, blankets etc. Whatever we have written here is just a repetition of your promises.'

The Divisional Commissioner, Jalpaiguri, said that

administrative letters were issued to all new tea-garden owners to postpone work. It is clear that this letter did not deter the Nagpur tea-garden owners from proceeding with plantation work.

The cases discussed here are merely examples of what goes on in the state, under all regimes. Numerous other similar incidents are taking place all the time. I receive complaints from tribals over loss of land almost every week. And this happens despite the existence of laws for the protection of the tribals with specific responsibility given to the administration and the police. Unfortunately, those contributing most to the process of land alienation among tribals are the officials and the police themselves. It is through their direct support that the process goes on. Political parties who could have ensured the proper implementation of the laws in favour of the tribals remain silent spectators, or even worse. In none of the districts of West Bengal have they taken up this issue. It is also a harsh reality that people belonging to the various political parties are themselves involved in depriving the tribals of their land.

With a mainstream society long used to exploiting them, a bureaucracy that is, at best, indifferent to their problems, and political parties mainly interested in mobilizing their votes, the largely illiterate and numerically few tribals can do little. In recent years, after every election, many tribals have been branded as 'non-supporters' of the ruling front and thus turned into vulnerable prey for land sharks. The influx of immigrants first from East Pakistan and then from Bangladesh, further complicated matters. In the neighbouring state of Tripura, it has entirely changed the demographic composition, reducing the tribals to a minority in a few years. In the northern parts of West Bengal, also, the periodic influxes accentuated the process of land transfer from the tribals.

And now, with the recent changes in economic policy and the obsession with big projects, the process is likely to be accentuated. Already, in the erstwhile West Dinajpur district of north Bengal, largescale conversion of agricultural land into tea estates has started. Another factor that has contributed to the eviction of tribals from the Terai region of north Bengal is the repressive action of the police in the name of containing the Gorkhaland movement. A large number of tribals have already been evicted from this area. With the prospect of the movement taking a new course, that of demanding a separate state, this process may be further accentuated.

In West Bengal, the Santhals are numerically and otherwise stronger than the other tribal groups. But even they are often forced to part with their land in the face of the combined assault of political parties–bureaucracy–rural rich–brick-kiln owners–antisocials–panchayats–development projects. The panchayats have become the den of vested interests in rural areas.

The least that the government can do is to inform the tribals about the laws which exist for protecting their rights to land. The legal provisions should be explained in simple language and widely circulated among the tribals. They should be displayed in panchayat offices at all levels. Repeated announcements should be made over the radio and TV. Why are they not being published in the Bengali and Santhali publications of the state government, titled *West Bengal*, and the very largely circulated daily newspaper of the CPI(M)?

The government needs to send circulars to the district and subdivision-level SC and ST Welfare Officers on a regular basis, informing them of their legal obligations. Special courts should be formed in areas with a high tribal concentration.

Another important step that needs to be taken is the formation of legal aid cells for the tribals, which won't exploit the tribals, and will take up their cases as public interest litigations. While a lot of initiative has to be taken by the tribals themselves, they alone cannot go far without support from the more aware and responsible sections of the mainstream. A beginning has to be made, and made now. Or else, by the time the country reaches the 21st century, most of the tribals who have land today will be landless. If that happens, the smaller tribal groups would be completely wiped off the map of the country.

From *Bortika*, October–December 1989; and incorporating segments from 'Tribal Land Alienation', *Frontier*, 3 August 1991.
Translated from the original Bengali by Maitreya Ghatak.

The Call Never Comes

Bimala Hari (24) was a poor harijan woman of Kanchrapara in Nadia district of West Bengal. A resident of Dengapara sweepers' colony, she had registered her name at the Kalyani Employment Exchange in 1979. Now she need not wait for a call from the exchange any longer, because she has solved her problems by committing suicide. I saw her in early 1982 when I visited the colony after Rajendra Bansfor, a spirited youth, was killed. Rajendra had dared to oppose the underworld *mastans* who had made the harijan colonies of Kanchrapara centres of the *chullu* (illegally distilled liquor) trade. The Harijan Kalyan Samiti has many grievances and this *chullu* business is only one of them. The school in Dengapara is in a dilapidated state, the roads are in ruins, the open drains are a threat to health, abject poverty and neglect stares you in the face. Yet the harijans of Kanchrapara are thousands in number and their dwellings are either on railway or municipal land. They want to change their life-pattern. But others want them to continue in squalor and neglect. Bimala Hari wanted a change. She had waited for 4 years. The call never came. It never does.

The list before me contains names of 45 harijans with names registered at the Kalyani, Barrackpur and Naihati exchanges, all near Calcutta. Whatever industries West Bengal has are largely concentrated in these areas of the state. Some have been waiting since 1978 for a call.

Compared to these places, Purulia is a backward district. It would be more apt to call it the most neglected district of West Bengal. Bandwan and Manbazar-II blocks are amongst the more backward blocks within the district. Those are the places where you will find the shy Kherias, silent Birhors and persecuted Paharia tribals. Bandwan and Manbazar-II still do not have a *pucca* connecting road to the headquarters. In Manbazar-II you must be ready to walk miles if you want to go anywhere. Purulia suffers from gross neglect even after 35 years of independence and the places I have mentioned are mainly tribal zones. The Santhals are more advanced and the rate of literacy among them is also higher. They are socially and politically conscious. In Churku village lives the freedom fighter, Kanuram Savara. He receives a political pension, the only one among the Lodhas and Kherias to enjoy this honour, but his sons have failed to secure a job through the Purulia Employment Exchange/Bandwan Block Branch.

In a list I find 55 names, mostly of tribals, registered at the above exchange. A few of them are graduates. Jiban Chandra Murmu registered his name in 1970. I find names registered since 1975. A Santhal registers his name, he is a graduate, but even then employment agencies pass him by. These boys and girls come from villages where primary schools have been opened and teachers taken on. The educated tribal remains unemployed for years and ultimately loses interest in education.

In comparison to other districts of West Bengal, Medinipur is politically more alive. South-west Medinipur has a large tribal population. You will find Santhals, Mundas, Bhumijas, Lodhas, Doms, Mahalis, Hos and others here. Poverty compels the poor to hire out their children as cattlegrazers, chiefly for food and clothing. The present state government has literally carried primary education to the remote villages, yet the percentage of primary school students remains low. When a son or daughter from a poor family completes some years at school, it is often done at great sacrifice to the household economy. When a Gandhi Mallik from Dalkati village or a Krishnaprasad Bhakta from village Chakua (both Lodha boys) studies upto class 8 or 9, and registers his name at Jhargram exchange, they are grown-up enough for regular jobs. They and others situated as they are feel that they have avoided family responsibilities long enough by going to school and should get a job somehow. Gandhi's name

lies registered from 1976 and Krishna's from 1978. I have a list of
177 names of educated unemployed Kurmi, Santhal, Munda,
Lodha and Mahali boys. Most of the names are registered at
Jhargram and Belda exchanges of Medinipur, some at Medinipur
town and Kharagpur exchanges. Kharagpur is a major railway
town of the region and boasts one of the premier institutes for
engineering and technological education. Mahali is a small tribe.
Six unfortunate Mahalis have been waiting since 1975 for a call
from the exchange. At least 100 names have been registered since
1975.

Parameshwar Marandi, a Santhal of Murshidabad, is a keen
and intelligent boy. He is employed in the agricultural income-
tax office at Berhampur, the headquarters of Murshidabad, a
thoroughly neglected district which doesn't have any industry to
speak of. Yet it houses the Farakka barrage and a super-thermal
power station. Being the seat of power in the region before the
British takeover, and the capital of the nawabs of the period, it
has a lot of potential for tourism. But even that is neglected. The
people of the district are still waiting for the proper takeover and
management of the justly famed Hazarduari Palace.
Parameshwar's desire to learn about the first migration of
Santhals to Murshidabad brought him to me. Murshidabad is
located near the Dumka region of Bihar. A sizeable Santhal
population has embraced Christianity in the district. The
percentage of literacy is fairly high among them. The Santhals are
the largest tribe in West Bengal. It is amusing how even highly
educated people think and talk of all tribes as Santhals—
someone even praised my novel on Birsa Munda as the story of a
'Santhal' rebellion.

In my list of educated unemployed Santhals I find that Suren
Murmu of village Dhobaguria registered his name in 1974; other
registrations date from 1975. The list contains names of girls too.
My list has 109 names.

Purulia, Medinipur, Kanchrapara, Murshidabad, these lists are
only a small sample of the current situation. There must be many,
many more, who have been waiting for years.

Since the names belong to human beings, and since I know
many of them personally, the problem of SC and ST
unemployment is very real to me and not merely a matter of
statistics. I admit that the problem of unemployment is acute in

West Bengal, even among non-SC and non-ST people. Also, there is great resentment against SC and ST quota reservation.

The declared policy of reservation does not, in reality, benefit the ST unemployed. Rarely does a tribal enter the science stream and even more rarely, higher studies in science. So jobs requiring graduation or postgraduation in specialized studies may have reservation quotas for tribals, but which tribal becomes a marine biologist or a nuclear physicist or haematologist? Neither do they generally enter the commerce stream. A tribal with an honours or postgraduate degree in economics, accountancy or business management is almost unheard of. Usually a tribal will leave school after primary education, class 4 level, or middle primary, class 6, or at best after class 8. The Lodhas and the Mahalis will rarely complete the School Final course. A Santhal, an Oraon or a Munda/Bhumij will try to complete the School Final (SF) or Higher Secondary (HS) course. When they cannot, it is usually due to poverty. Even among the Santhals who complete the BA or MA course, it is usually in the arts subjects. So when the employing agency wants an ST doctor, engineer, technician etc., in 99 cases out of 100, the vacancy is finally filled up by a non-tribal due to non-availability of a tribal candidate. An impartial survey will prove that in good, competitive jobs, tribal candidates are really not available and non-tribals fill the posts.

Then there are the jobs for which the SC and the ST candidates can apply. Clerkship in bank and government offices, for example. My finding is that when the job is duly advertised, there is little time for one living in a village to avail of the opportunity. Sure, there are reservations for ST candidates. But they live in the villages. Seldom are the district exchanges duly informed. I was surprised to know that the Tribal Welfare Directorate has an ST employment cell. This cell should keep track of the various genuine tribal organizations so that the tribal candidates can be reached in time. I was greatly surprised to know from someone working in the recruitment section of the banks that they have been given such a list and that they inform some organizations. When I asked if a tribal candidate was ever recruited that way, he shook his head. Do those organizations exist? How many tribals have been given jobs against the scheduled quota in the banks in the last 10 years ?

Last of all, the various employment exchanges should be

asked how many tribals have received jobs through their efforts between 1973 and 1983. How is it that the unfortunate tribals never receive a call? What is happening to the ST reserved jobs? Who is getting them? Is it true that many non-SC and ST candidates are managing caste/tribe certificates and availing themselves of the quota-jobs? Most tribals are fit for class IV jobs in the state and central government agencies. Is there any truth in the often-heard charge that these days one has to bribe the political *dada*, the local exchange clerks and officers, in order to get a call? If one is fortunate enough to get a job, one must be prepared to bribe the all-powerful union *dada* to be able to retain it.

Purulia and Medinipur are often swayed by the Jharkhand *hawa*. It is very, very bad to be a Jharkhandi in this state. But if educated tribals are kept deprived of employment chances for a decade, for 13 years (as in the case of Bangshi of Purulia), is it surprising that they will be resentful and suffer from a sense of gross injustice? If the state government's policy is to do justice to the minority tribes, then how is it that Lodhas are not found fit enough to be considered for the posts of even forest guards? Last of all, what about the thousands of posts of primary teachers in the tribal zones in recent years? How many primary teachers have been appointed from among the local educated tribals, with names duly registered? The common practice of filling an ST vacancy with a non-ST candidate and offering the glib explanation—suitable tribal candidate not found—is often a cover-up. The tribals themselves and many fair-minded non-tribals say so.

The educated tribals of the state are not to be envied at all. Outsiders believe that they are the specially favoured children of the government. Just a visit to the remote tribal areas will disprove such an assertion. The countless unemployed non-tribals are often angry because the tribals are supposed to be getting job benefits. In reality, not only are they not getting any special benefit as tribals, they are being deliberately deprived of the quota-reserved jobs in many cases. The position of the Lodha and the Mahali tribals provides no incentive to their communities to take up further education. Santhal girls from Burdwan and Purulia, after completing secondary school, find themselves in a dilemma. Neither is there an employment-incentive, nor are they agreeable to working as common labourers on daily wages: School education is thus a hindrance to a tribal, not a benefit.

Gomastaprasad Soren, a sensitive and quiet Santhal, has written, 'Please go through the list and try to help them. Most of them live in remote hilly and forest areas, far from the town of Purulia. There is little communication facility there and they do not have radios, nor do they subscribe to newspapers. Postal communication being in jeopardy, they do not get letters in time. Nowadays the employment exchanges are full of corruption. Both the exchanges and the political parties are indifferent to them. So they do not receive calls even after renewal of the registration cards. What are they to do?'

I do not have any answer to Gomasta's question. I only know that the problem of educated unemployed tribals and SC candidates is a monumental one. The district employment exchanges are of no help to them. The situation is not healthy for the promotion of education among tribals. And it is dangerous for any government to give them education and then keep them unemployed for years. It leads first to frustration, then to anger, and widens the gulf between them and us further. Gross negligence of their interests for 4 decades has already convinced them that no one will look to their interests, ever.

From *Economic and Political Weekly*, 9 July 1983.

Palamau, a Vast Crematorium

Once it was exciting to go to McCluskiegunge, Palamau, by various routes. On one occasion, I remember buying pomfret from a tribal at Bhurkunda station, a pleasant surprise for the 'gunge' people. One always went to McCluskiegunge, which was a home far away from home, to plan further explorations. But this time I was going not to McCluskiegunge, but to Daltonganj via Ranchi.

Sitting straight-backed on my reserved seat, I dozed through the night. The sight of Gautamdhara, a hill station, in the morning and adivasi girls selling *kendu* fruit and purple *karbinda* berries in *palas* leaf containers, woke me up. They sold them for 10 paise per container. *Kendu* leaf is *bidi* leaf and *kendu*-growing belts are generally taken on lease by traders and merchants. Revenue from any forest produce is always taken away by outsiders. In order to get the wild fruits, berries, tender shoots and leaves which sustain them through the lean months, the local people are forced either to steal or to bribe forest guards. The forest dwellers of India do not have a single right to the forest today.

Ranchi has a scarcity of electricity and water. Mosquitoes abound and prices of essential commodities soar every day. Ranchi is a fast-growing monster battening on the wealth of industrialists, middlemen, touts and forest contractors. Much money flows through the government department channels of

Ranchi in the name of tribal development. Dr Biseswar Prasad Kesri reported that in a development project, over Rs 50 lakhs had been spent for the 'upliftment and development' of a certain area but the money had been pocketed by a few individuals. Bharat Coking Coal issued 20 to 25 contracts in the name of tribals and harijans for supplying *bichi*, a rock with iron ingredients used in coal washeries. All the contracts are held by non-tribals and non-harijans. The tribals and harijans bring the rocks. The usurpers take the payment in cash from the State Bank of India. My friends once challenged the bank official about making a payment of Rs 10,000 to a usurper. 'You know very well that you are not paying the right man. He is not Dukha Singh from a remote village.' I do not know what the official's answer was. People like my friends are thoroughly disliked by those who benefit, for they pull the alarm chain to stop a smooth-running sleek operation.

An acquaintance complained that the tribals of Ranchi were becoming too wealthy and cut off from the grassroots. Another protested, 'Why, walk up and down the busiest streets of Ranchi, you will not find a single tribal going in for high-priced goods.' I have found that such notions are quite prevalent among West Bengal intellectuals. As far as they are concerned, tribals can have their sympathy as long as they remain half-clad, starving and illiterate. Such intellectuals are admirers of adivasi culture and they expect the starving adivasis to forget their misery in *mahua*, music and group dances. Their knowledge of tribals is derived from books and magazines. After a few decades of exposure to the general educational stream, many tribals of Ranchi and elsewhere are officials, educationists, doctors and engineers. Their lifestyle has expectedly undergone changes. But they, according to the people I am referring to, are no longer true tribals. This attitude infuriates me.

An experience at Grosner College in Ranchi was very illuminating. After a short talk and some discussions, the time for leave-taking was near. The students, tribals all, both boys and girls, Christian and non-Christian, bade us farewell with songs and dances. Education has not taught them to discard their culture. A young Bengali boy asked me an unnerving question after the evening meet at the Union Library Hall, Ranchi. He said, 'There are thousands of us here in Ranchi for generations.

Our ancestors entered the region following the footsteps of the British but we have a hunch that we are still *dikus* to our tribal friends. What should our approach be to win their trust? We want to make atonement for the wrongs we have caused them to suffer.'

It is surprising how the Hindi translations of my book have brought the Hindi-reading people closer to me. Birsa Munda's name always comes up in their conversations with me. In Birsa's time, Ranchi was the symbol of British power and Birsa breathed his last in Ranchi Jail. I found an awareness of Birsa and his *ulgulan* in Ranchi, which was very satisfying. So I was surprised to find no voice of protest against the statue of Birsa standing on Birsa Chowk. Today, Birsa Munda is loved and respected by all. Our patriotic poets were not aware that the tribal movements were very much part of India's national struggle for independence. They drew their inspiration from Shivaji, Rana Pratap and other kingly heroes, not from Baba Tilka Majhi, Sidhu or Kanhu or Birsa. But the statue was shocking. It showed a captive Birsa standing with his hands tied, copied from a photo of a captive Birsa in Dr K. S. Singh's book *Dust-storm and Hanging Mist*. Here Birsa is a mute spectator of the new industrial township of Dhurwa. The statue is a symbol of the tribal existence in India today. Why did the artist have to be so faithful to the photograph? If one raised a statue of Bhagat Singh or Khudiram today, would one put chains on them? The British put Birsa in chains. Do we have to do the same? Or is it to emphasize the fact that tribal existence is better preserved in chains and that to protest against bondage is futile? The outer plaster is peeling off. The writing underneath is almost wiped off. It is not a tribute, but an insult to a great leader of the people.

We started for Daltonganj in the morning. We paid a very high price for the tickets on the state bus, which was in worse condition than any condemned state bus of Calcutta, and that's saying a lot. As we crossed Kuru, leaving Ranchi behind and entering Palamau, blasts of hot wind greeted us. 'Mark well the *banjhara* soil,' my companion said. According to the local people, the scorching wind is an indicator that Palamau is, in reality, a vast cremation ground.

I was fortunate in having Dr Bireswar Prasad Kesri with me. Closely associated with the Kshetriya Adim Jati Bhasa

Sanatokotara Bibhaga of Ranchi University, he recently published
the first comprehensive history of Chhotanagpur in Hindi. Owing
to the 'untiring efforts of people like him, tribal languages are
getting introduced at the postgraduate level at Ranchi University.
I found the Oraon and Mundari school primers very useful. Kesri
is a quiet and soft-spoken person. He knows Palamau at the
grassroots level. Compassion and concern for the poor drew him
to the Jharkhand movement. This close contact with the
grassroots level is a special feature of the Jharkhand leaders I
have met, such as Monoranjan Mahato and Bishnu Soren of West
Bengal. 'Didi, just have a look,' he said and I saw the stretch of
scorched barren land right from the wayside to the distant hills.
Not a tree, not even a blade of grass. I was visiting Palamau after 7
years and my eyes were not prepared for such a sight. Palamau is
hot, very hot, during the summer months. The soil is dry and
yields per acre very low. The forest compensated for this
imbalance of nature. The forest gave the poor of the district food
and fuel.

After independence, Vanodyog or forest development work
came into existence. And that sealed the fate of Palamau. Land-
hungry outsiders usurped all the cultivable land, evicting the
original tenants. They are the people whom bonded labourers
serve. Palamau has the distinction of being a bonded labour
district, a merit earned by having more than 40,000 bonded
labourers. The Palamau *seokia, kamia, jonwar* and other bonded
labourers are rich material for theoretical research works on the
subject. The 'maneater' of Palamau, the Mauar of Manatu,
received some publicity some time ago. But his story was not
followed up. The Mauar was discharged because when the
bonded labourer was asked by the defending lawyer, 'Did you
borrow money from this man?' pointing to the Mauar, the answer
was, 'No.'

'Then who did?'
'My grandfather did.'
'What? From this man?'
'No.'

The case was dismissed. The bonded labourer never got a
chance to explain that his grandfather had borrowed money
from the Mauar's father or grandfather. We do not know what
happened to the man who gave evidence against the Mauar. The

Mauar is only one of the countless maneaters of Palamau who
thrive on forced labour by people in debt bondage.

The Mauar story goes to prove that Palamau is in the dark
ages as far as landownership is concerned. The supremacy of the
upper castes is totally accepted in Palamau. And along with this
feudalism, the forest-hungry outsiders came to Palamau after
independence. In a forest-rich district, the governmental Forest
Directorate plays an exploiter's role. Deforestation is necessary,
but not without simultaneous afforestation. It is absolutely
imperative to leave young trees while felling timber. But forests
were leased out to forest contractors. Savage and merciless
denudation of forests began. The poor villagers used to worship
the *palas* tree because they used to cultivate lac on the *palas*.
Palamau used to supply almost 50 per cent of India's total lac.
The forest contractors are the new tycoons in Ranchi and
Daltonganj. Because of their avarice, miles of earth lie bare. Even
the *palas* trees stand severed. The truncated trunks look like
hell's sentinels. Palamau is a vast crematorium, indeed. Trees
were felled, wood was burned for charcoal, and who did it? One
always hears of tribals ruining the forest. The forests survived as
long as the poor people and the villagers used it. A tribal or a
poor person has neither the money nor the organization to cause
devastation to the forest. Hundreds of trucks roar along the roads
of Palamau carrying timber and charcoal and bauxite mineral
rocks. The land and the forests and the timber of Palamau go to
make the outsiders rich. Birla companies take bauxite from
Palamau for their aluminium factory at Renukot, U.P. where they
are provided with cheap electricity. They make skyhigh profits.
The forest contractors build luxury palaces in Ranchi and
Daltonganj. The poor of the district enter into debt bondage.

I pointed to occasional breaks of trees here and there. A
fellow passenger said, 'Mataji, those are young and slender trees.
Not yet ready for the axe. Wait a bit, you'll see. How can the
rakshasa eat a person when he is all skin and bones? Previously
the young trees were spared when felling timber. Now they do
not leave a single tree behind. This is against forest law.'

But the very word 'law' is meaningless because the contractors
and Forest Directorate people have joined hands in the carnage.
Only the poor villagers and tribals are harassed, fined, beaten up,
fired at and jailed if they fail to bribe the forest guards while

collecting firewood or edible fruits. I found fields sown with a thorny plant called *morabba* in the local dialect and *sialkanta* in Bengali. The flower is yellow and the seeds of the fruit are like black mustard seeds. In desperation the villagers have sown these plants. The next day, while walking to a bonded-labour village, I saw women carrying these fruits to the faraway market. Why? Why not? These seeds are ground for extracting oil. The oil has medicinal property. The middlemen purchase them. From the distant villages of Palamau, these *morabba* seeds come to us mingled with mustard seeds. Food adulteration even in the raw-produce stage is a big industry today. The village women get 15 to 20 paise per basket. The fruits have almost no weight.

My friends pointed at the dried-up little river and said, 'Ruthless felling of trees caused this.' Palamau rivers never ran so totally dry so soon. I remember some hand-outs given to me by the State Forest Directorate long ago. Trees store water in their roots and keep the soil moist. Then came the question of the much publicized river dam projects. According to the concerned, the Ranchi-Koel-Karo and the Subarnarekha project, when completed, will be connected with Paradip and Haldia. Built with World Bank money, the waterways will carry and export uranium from the largest uranium deposit in the world. Palamau will not receive the irrigation and electricity benefits derived from these, either. Other districts will receive all the benefits at the cost of Palamau. After a lot of protests, 3 smaller projects have been taken up for Palamau. The Kutku, the Oraya and the Malaya projects. But all these 5 river dam projects will drown hundreds of villages and, in the project plans, the sites for the dams have been shown as barren, *banjhara*, uninhabited land. So the villagers are not going to get any compensation. Kesri's prediction is that within 25 years these dams will be sand-silted.

It will not be out of place to mention what I learned of the Birlas and their vast wealth in Palamau. On my way back from Daltonganj I met Lal Ajoy Nath Sahadeo, descendant of a local chief. He belongs to the Yuva Congress but was very outspoken. In the 20s his family failed to pay the revenue and the Birlas got hold of their lands. Birla agents have *kachharis* in all the villages. They have, according to Sahadeo, thousands of acres of land, all under cultivation. They have 3 or 4 bauxite mines too, on a 100-year lease. Bauxite for the Renukot factory is carried to U.P. by train and by truck. They would not consider building an aluminium factory at Palamau. So the local labour is employed as unskilled labour alone.

From *Business Standard*, 20 May 1981.
Previously part of a longer piece entitled 'The Chains of Untouchability'.

*Political and
Cultural
Dimensions of
Discrimination*

The Jharkhand Movement and Separatism

In the opinion of the state and central governments, the Jharkhand movement is a separatist one. It has even been argued that the real objective behind the demand for a separate Jharkhand state is to secede. It is, however, not clear to us— secede from what?

Those participating in the movement want a Jharkhand state or autonomous region covering the tribal areas of Bihar, West Bengal, Orissa and Madhya Pradesh. Does the very demand for a separate state amount to the intention to secede? Hasn't one separate state after another been formed in India after independence? If they haven't seceded, why should Jharkhand secede?

And how can it be assumed, on the face of it, that the Jharkhand state is being demanded only for the tribals ? In all the major meetings of the movement, it has been repeatedly asserted that the movement is in the interest of all the oppressed people, both tribals and non-tribals. Are the exploited and poor non-caste Hindus living in the Jharkhand-movement areas feeling threatened and scared? Not at all. On enquiry, it may even be found that they are sympathetic to the movement, and, probably, support it.

I have heard from many people in Jharkhand that the campaign 'Bengalis leave Jharkhand' has never been considered by them to be a Jharkhandi campaign. I have also heard from a *gramsevak* in a Medinipur village how thousands of leaflets crying

'Bengalis leave Jharkhand' have been brought into the area in a clandestine manner, with utmost efficiency. None of those involved was a tribal and all belonged to the anti-Jharkhand movement camp. Though their machinations did not succeed, it created some temporary confusion.

The fact is, if the Jharkhand movement was not branded as separatist, the administration would be in an embarrassing situation, because the movement hasn't grown out of, nor does it stand upon, thin air. Periodic eviction from their own land and villages, atrocious exploitation by moneylenders, landlords, contractors, traders and officials, perpetuation of slavery under the bonded labour system, luring of tribal women who are coerced into the flesh trade, constant assault on their traditional culture and social structure—all these age-old practices have in the past led to both localized and widespread agrarian uprisings by the tribals in many parts of the country: the rebellion of Tilka Majhi, the Kol rebellion, the *hul* of Sidhu-Kanhu or the *ulgulan* of Birsa Munda were protests which grew out of desperate attempts to retain their traditional rights over forests and land. Are not the causes which led to these uprisings still present? The root cause of the Jharkhand movement is the wanton appropriation of tribal land, flouting all legislations. If we who are not tribals forget this, we would be blind to a glaring fact. The movement originates in the long history of deprivation and exploitation of the tribals. And, compared to all the movements of the past in scope and objectives, it is much more widespread, political and dynamic.

But let us come back to the issue of whether or not the Jharkhand movement is separatist. A movement does not become separatist merely because it demands a separate state, because, even though the circumstances may have been different, several such states have been formed since independence, and in their case, the bogey of secession has not been raised. Also, it has been pointed out by some that Nehru himself had promised a separate state for Jharkhand to Jaipal Singh. If Jharkhand becomes a state, a vast opportunity for rapacious exploitation would slip out of the clutches of the caste Hindu forest officials, forest contractors, moneylenders, traders and landlords. Is that the real reason behind the bogey?

These are not biased and irresponsible statements. A scandalous reality looming behind all campaigns against the tribals is the arrogant shadow of an India ruled by caste Hindus.

After a recent massacre committed by the police in Gua in Singbhum, the Bihar Military Police, in a vicious move, even entered the hospital and killed 11 people who had been admitted with injuries incurred in the firing (see 'Witch Sabbath at Singbhum'). Predictably, it is the military police who are getting all the support of the entire administration. If what a local non-tribal activist says is correct, then Gua, Jamda, Guilkera, Manoharpur, Chaibasa, are full of military camps. Hundreds of tribals have been arrested, an orgy of violence continues in village after village, crops have been looted, houses have been burnt, cattle and poultry forcibly removed. Of the 150 tribal officers of the district, 130 have been transferred away to north Bihar. Two tribal ministers and the Chief Secretary of the state were going to Gua for an on-the-spot investigation under the direction of the District Judge. When they reached Jamda, the BMP allowed only the Chief Secretary to proceed and the ministers had to go back to Patna.

The reason why so much is being said about Gua is that in the Singbhum district, where Gua is located, the tribals dependent on the forests participated in the Jharkhand movement as a protest against their misery. Between 1974–77 they launched an intense movement, the Sagoana movement, which became quite strong. In 1978, the Congress, the Revolutionary Socialist Party (RSP), Jharkhand Mukti Morcha, Marxist Coordination Committee, Birsa Sevadal, Muslim League, 2 factions of the CPI(ML) and the Jharkhand Party, all joined the Jharkhand United Front. Behind this United Front was the pressure of the grassroots-level people.

The Jharkhand Party and the Jharkhand Mukti Morcha formed electoral alliances with separate parties. But it is also true that despite this, these 2 parties could, and actually did, work together. This is something which is beyond our comprehension. It is not possible for us non-tribals to appreciate the deeprooted sense of insecurity, embedded in the race memory of the tribals, from which this feeling of solidarity grows. Another implication of the Jharkhand movement is that high-level leaders are not the last word for the grassroots-level people. The local leaders have a strong influence over them.

In order to understand the real nature of the Jharkhand

movement, we have to face many unpleasant facts. It has to be remembered that the creation of a separate state will not end exploitation in tribal life. The Jharkhand leaders are aware of that. The various interviews and statements of leaders like N. E. Horo, A. K. Roy and Shibu Soren have claimed that their struggle is against socio-economic exploitation. In the joint statement of Roy and Soren, it has been stated clearly that the movement is not against any party, people or individuals. They have based the movement on certain objective realities. For an understanding, one has to go deeper, to the root of the movement. And here one needs to try to understand the movement in its totality.

It is a fact that at the leadership level, the Mukti Morcha of Shibu Soren and the Congress(I) have come to an electoral understanding. It is also true that the Congress(I), in the past, had opposed the Mukti Morcha-led movements in support of agricultural minimum wages or Santhal sharecroppers. But no easy equation is possible in the case of this movement, because the Mukti Morcha is participating in the movement on the basis of its own experience and assessment of the ground situation.

Somewhere in the very depths of tribal consciousness lie some experiences which still hurt. No tribal, educated or illiterate, can forget them. For instance, from this resource-rich region of Ranchi–Singbhum–Palamau, minerals and money are being systematically taken out but the tribals of the region are being pushed to the bottom of the so-called poverty line. Tribals are being evicted from land which is passing into the hands of non-tribals. Forest contractors and officials are using and exploiting tribals and they are losing all their traditional rights in the forests. The moneylenders are lending them money at high rates of interest and consequently they are losing land and getting trapped into debt-bondage. In the tribal experience, forest contractors, officials, moneylenders and landlords are the people who get support from the police, courts and the administration.

Those who oppose the Jharkhand movement would do well to remember that even though there are laws to protect the interests of the tribals, in reality they are of little use. These exploitations and injustices are a hard reality for all tribals, whether educated or illiterate. They feel that the redressal of these injustices is possible only in a separate state, hence the demand for Jharkhand. Many feel that the movement is being branded as separatist solely with the objective of perpetuating these injustices.

In no statement or charter for Jharkhand so far has it been claimed that the Jharkhand state is meant only for tribals. In this context, the charter of demands of the Keshiari (Medinipur) unit of the West Bengal Jharkhand Party may be discussed. The document contained several demands. No one would disagree with the justice of those demands in the charter which are applicable for the people in general. These demands may be put into 2 categories.

Category 1

a) Protest against partisan behaviour in land distribution.

b) Protest against favouritism in the distribution of mini-kits and other government materials.

c) Demand for investigation into charges of corruption among panchayat members.

d) Demand for distributing 5 acres of land to each landless person.

e) Demand for unemployment allowance for the rural unemployed.

f) Parity in pay for public and private sector employees.

g) Minimum wages for agricultural labourers.

h) Imposition of ceiling on urban property.

i) Submission of statement of assets by all government employees.

j) Credit for cultivators, *bargadars.*

These demands by no means suggest that the Jharkhandis want to remain isolated from the mainstream in rural West Bengal. On the contrary, it would seem that they consider the interests of the common non-tribal people to be the same as their own. If they are met, they would benefit both tribals and non-tribals. Many of these demands have often been included in the electoral promises of political parties. But promises of distribution of land among the landless irrespective of party affiliation, elimination of corruption in the panchayats, giving credit to the *bargadars,* still remain mere electoral promises.

But I must also tell the Jharkhandis that by asking for an account of the assets of the government employees, they have immensely hurt the feelings of the administration under all regimes and political parties. This is a touchy issue, not only in post-independence West Bengal but also in the whole country. Among the government employees, examples of not looting even when they have an opportunity to do so, is quite rare. This larceny and looting has now become a part of the Great Indian Tradition.

Category 2

And what are the other demands?

a) For comprehensive development, the 16 proposed districts and adjacent areas must be formed into a separate Jharkhand state.

b) All calumny against the Jharkhand Party must be stopped at once.

c) Those organizer-teachers who are yet to be appointed on a regular basis must be recruited in permanent posts. The school boards must not be allowed to recruit a teacher for the position of the organizer-teacher in a partisan manner.

d) Children of less developed communities like the scheduled castes and scheduled tribes must be provided government aid on a regular basis.

e) Unemployed youth from each Jharkhandi family must be given government jobs.

f) The Kurmis (Mahato) must be included in the scheduled tribe list.

g) Teaching of the Santhali language through the Alchiki script must be introduced.

h) The Jharkhandi festivals must be included in the public holiday list.

i) Explanation has to be given as to why central government resources meant for tribals are returned unutilized.

j) 75 per cent of the shops in the Keshiari (Medinipur) mini-market must be given to the scheduled castes and scheduled tribes.

Let us examine the demands. The first demand requires little elaboration. It is the main demand and because of this, the Jharkhand movement has been branded secessionist. The second demand is also just. Which party would like to be maligned? The third demand requires some explanation.

Under the present norms, a tribal who is an aspirant to the post of a teacher may become an 'organizer-teacher' after passing the class 8 examination. Then he has to teach in a primary school without any pay for one-and-a-half to two years. Then he may get the post of a permanent teacher. But these norms are not being observed. Hence the demand. It is not that there are thousands of tribal aspirants for these posts and the competition so tough that many tribals cannot be recruited. There is a long story of rampant corruption behind this demand. I am giving a few examples. I refrain from mentioning the names of the concerned villages and the people, all tribals, for obvious reasons. An organizer has been working for 9 years, without being appointed on a permanent basis. A man and a woman started a school years ago. Under the previous regime, the school was placed before the panel for recognition. Under the present regime, the school has been recognized. But the 2 teachers who had started the school were thrown out. Those who have got their jobs are caste Hindu men and women. The area is a tribal one. The original woman teacher is now an agricultural labourer.

Keeping the organizer-teacher under probation for years, recruiting non-tribal favoured persons over the legitimate claims of the tribal organizer-teachers, has been happening on a large scale for years. That is why such a demand has been raised. If this context is objectively assessed, the legitimacy of the demand is clear. If the demands of the educated tribals are bypassed and non-tribal teachers are recruited even in tribal majority areas, it would be foolish to expect no resentment .

The fourth demand is for both tribals and the scheduled castes. The fourth demand is supported by a very large section of the people of this country. The word 'regular' should be specially noticed. There are many who cannot continue with their studies without regular support. In this matter of support, strange are the ways of the administration. Two tribal girl students I know passed the secondary examination and were admitted into Jhargram and Medinipur colleges in the hope that they would get the support to which they were entitled. But then they were told by the officials that they would have to somehow manage for a year before the government support came. The students had to go back to their villages. They came from poor tribal families and simply could not stay in town for a whole year without any support.

In the fifth demand, the term 'Jharkhandi' means a tribal. If an unemployed tribal youth demands a job, he may be branded a secessionist. But not when the demand comes from non-tribals. Is the task of recruiting tribals to posts reserved for tribals completed? Why doesn't the government give an account of how many such posts were reserved and how many tribals have actually been recruited for these posts, or a statement that only tribals are working in posts reserved for them? There are good enough reasons for the government to keep silent over these awkward questions.

Take the sixth demand. It has been discussed in detail by Pasupati Mahato in *Shilalipi* (Tusu Special Number) published from Jamshedpur. One interesting fact cited by the article is that the conservative Hindus played a pioneering role in keeping the Kurmis separated from the tribals. If today the Kurmis want to be united with the other tribals, it is their own affair.

The seventh demand has been, in principle, accepted by the government. And is there anything wrong in the eighth demand? India is supposed to be a secular state—a secular identity now revealed only through various religious holidays. If there can be religious holidays for the Hindus, Muslims, Buddhists, Sikhs and Jains, then why can't the tribals also demand holidays on those festivals which a majority of them observe, like Karam, Sohrai, Sarjom, Baha, or Morenko? If a Hindu's demand for a holiday for, say, Jagatdhattri Puja, does not make him communal, why should a tribal be communal just because he is asking for a holiday on Morenko? Such holidays, on a regional basis, should certainly be declared, even if only to reinforce religious tolerance. If you can have holidays for the Hindu religion, why not for the festivals of the Santhal–Munda–Oraon–Kurmis? Information on major festivals can easily be provided by Tribal Research Institutes in the states where they exist.

The movement cannot be branded as secessionist even in the context of the ninth demand. Why does money meant for tribal development have to be returned unutilized? Is the task of tribal development already over? Tribals live in villages. The Block Office comes to know of the needs of the villages through the panchayat. The *gramsevaks* also report to the Block Office. Are these reports acted upon? What does the Tribal Welfare Officer do? Perhaps all this money would not have been returned unutilized if the Tribal Welfare Officers themselves were tribals. Needless to say, this is a just and pertinent demand. The tribals live under the poverty line, tribal welfare funds are returned unutilized, the state is ruled by a pro-people government, and yet if the tribal demands an explanation then he becomes a secessionist. We refuse to buy this line of argument.

There are many tribal villages where just a small canal or a deep tubewell could have turned the land into fertile fields; if roads existed, local handicrafts could be taken to the market; if health centres existed, maternal mortality would not occur. And these facilities would have helped everyone, not only the tribals.

Those who consider the tenth demand unjust would do well to remember that in the past the tribals had not got the shops earmarked for them. I can cite the example of Jubilee Market in Jhargram. In a newspaper statement, N. E. Horo said that though the shops there were made for tribals, those who actually got them were non-tribals. With such shining examples in the past, the tribals are justified in voicing their demand for the allotment of rooms in the Keshiari mini-market.

Why is the scheme to create doubts and resistance in the minds of the common people about the Jharkhand movement so often successful?

The main reason lies in our not applying our minds to understanding the problem. We accept the Jharkhand demand as secessionist for the very same reason that we end up buying specific brands of products i.e., Rexona soap or Binaca toothpaste—when something is placed before the people, whether a product or a concept, they tend to accept it without applying their minds. Millions are spent on marketing research and advertisement just for this purpose.

Clever marketing of soap–shampoo–toothpaste is not that dangerous, though their steep prices suggest otherwise, But do not the fiercely loyal and often blind cadres of the present state regime believe that the root cause of all the anarchies in this state is the stepmotherly attitude of the central government? In this state, whether it is erratic power supply or garbage accumulation on the streets, everything is blamed on the centre. The people's task is only to continue voting for those in power.

Another reason is lack of familiarity. Behind this lack of familiarity lurks the age-old belief that 'India means India of the caste Hindus.' We do not know the tribals nor do we care to know them. In the past, possibly even today, a large majority of the educated have a stereotyped image of the tribals, promoted largely by films and plays. Tribals on the screen or the stage inevitably wear feathered head-dresses if they are males and flowers if they are women, wear scanty clothing—near-nakedness is compulsory—just to emphasize their innocence. And lastly, the typical dance and music. Not that these are not part of tribal life, but certainly not in the way they are shown. This synthetic image still exists, even in the minds of the educated people.

I remember, some time ago, there was to be a conference of tribals somewhere in Medinipur district. When a suggestion was made to someone quite learned and otherwise enthusiastic to attend the conference, he replied, 'I am not interested in meeting synthetic tribals who wear sophisticated clothes and attend conferences.' Another young person, cultured, very widely read and working in a position of high responsibility, himself a writer, told me about tribals, 'They are urban and sophisticated to the point of being unreal.' For them and their like, I have the same reply. Is it realistic to expect that the tribals would wait patiently for ages, forgoing education, wearing loin-cloths, bows and arrows in hand, in their 'unadulterated' and 'unsophisticated' form, completely alienated from the mainstream of life, in the hope that someday people like these would have the time and inclination to go and meet them?

Even those who are highly educated and otherwise quite well-informed somehow have a notion that tribal means only Santhal. For many such people there is little distinction between a Santhal and a Munda. The following is typical of exchanges I have often gone through:

'Are there Mundas in West Bengal?'
'Yes. Many.'
'In which language do you speak to them?'
'Bengali, of course.'
'Bengali? How surprising!'

This simple fact, that Mundas who live in West Bengal speak Bengali, get their education through the Bengali medium, seems incomprehensible to many. I have seen many thoroughly surprised when they learn that Birsa Munda was not a Santhal. It doesn't mean that they are not well-meaning people. It's only that they know very little about rural areas and village people in general, and even less about the tribals.

It is time to make a serious effort to understand the people who live in the heartland of Jharkhand objectively. One has to analyse the situation and understand why the demand for Jharkhand is raised at all. The fact is that exploitation and abuse of people doesn't only have political, economic and social dimensions. Such exploitation also continues in the cultural field. And this all-out assault cannot continue for ever. We could, of course, continue to behave like the proverbial ostrich. Only, the loss would be ours.

From *Anik*, December 1980.
Translated from the original Bengali by Maitreya Ghatak.

August 1987

Tribal Language and Literature:
The Need for Recognition

When I was in Chakadoba village in Medinipur district on the occasion of Sadhu Ram Chand Murmu Day, the well-known poet of the Santhali language, Saradaprasad Kisku, enlightened me on the dead Santhali litterateur who was being felicitated. Sadhu Ram Chand had a high degree of social awareness and he had tried to enlighten the Santhal people through his poems, lyrics and plays. He spoke of the poor people and of the need for unity amongst the tribals. In those days, there was no printing press for the Santhali language, nor any magazine or paper where writings in the language could be published. Sadhu Ram had died an untimely death. Very few people know today that he had prepared a script for the Santhali language.

Sarada was introduced to Sadhu Ram Chand's writings way back in 1948. His lyrics had inspired Sarada in those days. Sarada had met Sadhu Ram Chand in Bankura in April 1954. He still preserves the letters he received from the poet in those days. Much of his writing is lying scattered and needs to be put together and published. There are people who can do it, if a Santhali press is available. Ideally, the writings should be published in Santhali, with a Bengali version.

We are paying, and will continue to do so, a heavy price today for our age-old tradition of ignorance and negligence of the tribals. Take the history of the freedom struggle as it is read by students of history, as well as by others. In the period between 1757 and 1947, all over India, particularly in eastern India, several anti-imperialist struggles of the tribal peasants occurred. Yet they find no mention in books of history. Non-tribal India has not acknowledged these glorious struggles as part of the freedom movement.

In the 1981 census, India had 5,16,28,638 tribals. It is a large number, yet the history of their struggles is not considered fit for inclusion as part of Indian history. The many millions of India manage to survive without knowing about this 51 million. That is why, when a young Santhal woman asked me why the story of the hanging of Khudiram Bose is found in our textbooks but no mention is made of all the tribals who had laid down their lives for the country, I had no answer. The time is long overdue for us to join the tribals in supporting this demand. The Kheria–Savara tribals of Purulia who participated in the freedom movement in 1942 and were imprisoned, do not get the freedom fighters' pension even today, with the probable exception of Kanuram Savar and Locchu Savar. Even they do not get the full pension of Rs 500 or the railway pass for free first class travel for a year.

We have had enough of the disgusting government-sponsored extravaganzas on the occasion of the 40th anniversary of independence and are probably going to see more of the same on the 50th anniversary. This time, at least, the first task should be to take up a programme of publishing books in all the Indian languages about the tribal peoples' participation in the freedom movement. These books should be written both in the state languages as well as local tribal languages.

Tribals know very little about the various government programmes meant for them. The Integrated Tribal Development Project (ITDP) is a case in point. There are innumerable schemes under this project for the development of the tribals. But the tribals are not aware of these schemes; nor do the benefits trickle down to them. This is true all over the country. My suggestion is that in every state, booklets should be published informing the poor (including the scheduled castes and scheduled tribes) of the various government schemes meant for them. Shouldn't they know what their legitimate dues are? Even a clerk in the ITDP office knows clearly what his or her pay and allowances are. But no tribal in any state knows what is due to him or her under the various government schemes. And this includes the 30,70,672 tribals of West Bengal. Take the case of the Rural Landless Employment Guarantee Programme (RLEGP). The money for these schemes comes from the central government. One of the schemes under the programme is providing houses for homeless tribals. How many homeless tribals have actually benefited under the scheme? Even those who get anything under the schemes have to receive it like alms doled out to a beggar, all the time being reminded of the kindness of the political bosses who have thus favoured them. It is not surprising, under the circumstances, that the tribals are being forced to seek shelter under the umbrella of whichever political party wields power in the area, for their sheer survival.

But the real problem of the tribal is not just that of getting material support for survival. Mainstream society is carrying on a continuous, shrewd and systematic assault on his social system, his culture, his very tribal identity and existence. Think of the type of films which are shown in the local video parlours in tribal areas, or the books which are provided to the rural libraries in tribal areas of West Bengal. There is nothing there that they can relate to.

My contention is that history should be re-written, acknowledging the debt of mainstream India to the struggles of the tribals in the British and even pre-British days. The history of their struggles is not to be found only in written scripts but in their songs, dances, folk tales, passed from one generation to another. So much of it has perished with the people who have died with all this history carefully protected in the very depths of their hearts. But so much still exists. For this, one has to go to the older people. The present generation knows very little because they were never told. And the people who had started the *hul, ulgulan* or the *mulkui* struggles have been forced for the last 200 years to move away from the areas where these struggles started.

In this context, when one reads in the Gazetteer of India, 'The tribals form the bedrock of the people of this country' or that 'they laid the foundation of Indian civilization,' one wonders what sort of deadly game the mainstream, the administration and the whole social system are playing with several crores of people.

The paths of the tribals and the mainstream run at a parallel. The country is paying a heavy price for this, and will continue to do so unless it changes its attitude.

In West Bengal, there are several state-sponsored literary awards, but none in the name of a tribal, nor specifically for a work about any aspect of tribal life. At the state level, a literary award of, say, Rs 10,000.00 every year should be declared. The award should go to a tribal, writing on any aspect of tribal life in Bengali or a tribal language. One has to remember that in West Bengal today, the Santhals, despite many constraints, write and publish in their own language. But the Lodhas and Kherias speak in their version of the Bengali language. In the *abad* areas of the South 24 Parganas district, among the Oraons, Mundas and Bedias, there is a declining use of their own language. In the tea-garden areas of north Bengal, there are people speaking Hindi, Sadri, Mundari, Lohar, Gorait, Chikbaraik and Baraik. However, among many tribal groups other than the Santhals, either the original tribal language doesn't exist because they have been in this state for ages, or it is little used. Considering this, the award should not be confined only to tribal languages. Even English should be accepted, keeping in mind that excellent work by Nityananda Hembram, 'The Austric Civilisation in India'. In *Bortika*, people from several tribal groups, with or without formal education, write and write quite well.

Such an award would encourage a lot of people from the various tribal groups to write. One doesn't need a formal education for this purpose. Sadhu Ram Chand Murmu himself was not a product of any university. Let the award in his name become a forum for all the tribal groups.

The government should also provide publication support to those who write or publish in Santhali or any other tribal language. Government grants and patronage go to so many people and publications. Why should not a part of it come to the tribals? Why should not the District Information and Culture Department give advertisements to magazines published in any tribal language? Similarly, at the national level, the Sahitya Akademi should declare an award for literary work in a tribal language.

And, finally, the question of official recognition to language. The Santhali language is yet to be recognized. The data for the following table is from the 1971 census, because even at the time of writing, the government has not made public the data on the numerical strength of various tribal groups. Even then, this table is good enough to indicate which languages should get recognition:

Language	Number Speaking	Recognized?
1. Bhojpuri	1,43,40,564	Yes
2. Chhatisgarhi	66,93,445	No
3. Magdhi	66,38,495	No
4. Maithili	61,21,912	No
5. Marwari	47,14,094	No
6. Santhali	36,93,558	No
7. Kashmiri	24,21,760	Yes
8. Rajasthani	20,93,557	No
9. Gondi	15,48,070	No
10. Konkanese	15,22,684	No
11. Dogri	12,98,856	No
12. Gurkhali/Nepali	12,86,824	No
13. Pahari	12,69,651	No
14. Bhili	12,50,312	No
15. Kurukh/Oraon	12,40,395	No
16. Kumauni	12,34,939	No
17. Garhwali	12,27,151	No
18. Sindhi	12,04,678	Yes

The table clearly shows that there are several linguistic groups which are relatively larger in size than Sindhi and Kashmiri, yet have not been recognized. The issue of recognizing these languages is closely linked to their overall development and their literature. There is no reason to believe that the question of separate statehood would arise the moment the languages are recognized. Some of these linguistic groups are spread over large areas. For instance, the Bhils are spread over Andhra Pradesh, Bihar, Gujarat, Karnataka, Madhya Pradesh, Maharashtra, Rajasthan and Tripura. Gonds are concentrated in Andhra Pradesh, Bihar, Gujarat, Karnataka, Madhya Pradesh and Maharashtra. Santhals are mostly to be found in West Bengal, Assam, Bihar, Tripura and Orissa. It would be a matter of grave injustice if all the tribal languages with a numerical strength higher than that of the Sindhi-speaking people (12,04,678) are also not recognized. And just recognition is not enough. It should be followed by a literary award in that language. For the country as a whole, there should be another Akademi Award for a literary work by a tribal on the tribals, whether in his own language or in the language of the state where he lives. That is the type of positive step which should be taken.

In West Bengal, there are several state-sponsored literary awards in the name of well-known literary figures. It is time to have a literary award in the name of Sadhu Ram Chand Murmu. It should be open not only to the Santhals but to the other tribal groups of West Bengal as well. The Santhals know that Sadhu Ram Chand Murmu is esteemed by all the tribals and recognition of him would be recognition for all the tribals. The issues raised here exercise the minds of the tribals as well and they should have the final say over any decision taken on them. The point is, a beginning has to be made and made now.

From *Aajkal,* 11 August 1987.
Translated from the original Bengali by Maitreya Ghatak.

Lodhas and
Kherias of
West Bengal

Lodhas of West Bengal

I came to know the Lodhas first through a very competent piece of writing from Prahlad Bhukta, the only graduate among the Lodhas, in my journal *Bortika*, a district literary quarterly entrusted to me in 1979, after my father's death. He used to edit it from our hometown, Berhampur. Everyone thought I had gone mad when I changed it to a journal for the people from the lower levels of society.

My experience of our people had already taught me that illiteracy or low literacy need not necessarily mean a lack of culture, understanding and intelligence. So it became their journal. I am proud to say that we have published many village and block reports, life accounts of agricultural labourers, small peasants, rickshaw pullers, etc., all written by the people concerned. I have never insulted my contributors by editing their language or style. Thus *Bortika* has fulfilled its purpose of removing the intermediary educated writer from between the man of the soil and the printed page.

The Lodha and Kheria tribals are both mentioned in the census as Lodha–Savaras and Kheria–Savaras. The Lodhas are concentrated in Medinipur district of West Bengal, mainly in the forest areas. The Kheria tribals of West Bengal are mostly concentrated in the district of Purulia. Some are to be found in the forest areas of Ranibandh (Bankura) and the Banaspahari area under Binpur in Medinipur, too. Even in these days of dwindling forest belts, the Lodhas and Kherias live near forests. Hunters and forest dwellers, they managed to keep their identity intact as long as the forests were intact. Now, with the rapid and ruthless deforestation of Medinipur, they are exposed to the hungry and savage times and are fighting a lost battle for survival. A minority tribe, they feel insecure even amidst tribal societies.

According to the 1971 census, the Lodha–Kherias are 45,906 in number, the Lodhas making up about 35,000. The number in 1981 will not be very different. Both the tribes, but especially the Lodhas, have been leading a hunted and persecuted existence for decades. That this affects the birth rate is not very surprising. The 1971 census shows that only 4.09 per cent of the Lodha–Kherias are primary-school-educated. The percentage of school final or above is 0.31, and only 18,379 are listed as workers in the census. The Lodhas in general are abjectly poor. A survey of a Lodha village made by a Lodha in December 1982 will prove my point:

Name of village:	Sankharidanga
Lodha families:	88
Total population:	470
Cultivable land	
14 decimals to 1 acre:	59 families
No cultivable land:	29 families
Not even homestead land:	18 families
Schoolgoing children:	33
Wage earners:	164
Earning Rs 15 a month:	16
Earning Rs 30 a month:	130
Earning Rs 45 a month:	16
Earning Rs 60 a month:	2

Sankharidanga is a Lodha village. The Lodhas may live in mixed villages but the Lodha dwellings are generally found in separate *mahallas* or *tolis*. They like to live amidst their own people.

Lodhas trace their lineage to the mythical hunter king Kalketu and his tribal wife Fullara. Mukundaram Chakravarti, a great poet of the 16th century, has narrated the story of Kalketu, but the Lodha version is different. The forest and fertility goddess Chandi had blessed Kalketu and he had become a king. But the wily outsiders deprived him of his kingdom and his tribe became poor. However, the goddess continued to protect the

Savara hunters. Even today the forest deities protecting flora,
fauna and forest dwellers are worshipped by the Lodhas. People
of all castes and tribes depend, in many temples, on Lodha
priests for invoking the blessing of the gods and goddesses. The
Baram-goddess temple on the Bombay road is a famous one.
Every bus, truck or car on the road is under the goddess's
protection. Any driver who does not slow down his vehicle to
throw a coin in homage is bound to suffer an accident, according
to local belief.

The Lodhas are no respecters of brahmins. According to
Lodha belief, the great Jagannatha of Puri was once worshipped
by a Lodha. The wily brahmins sent a young man to befriend the
beautiful daughter of the chief priest. He then left the forest with
her and the idol. A Lodha will not bow to a brahmin.

While the brahmins stole Jagannatha from the Lodhas, an
irate god, Ranrangahari-Bishoichandi, left his Santhal priest and
came to the Lodhas himself. The Lodhas say that this happened
in Jamsol village in Nayagram police station area. When Charka
Santhal failed to please the god, he chose a Savara, a Bhukta, for
his priest. This god, when angry, takes the form of an evil demon,
Gyan, who enters the inside of a Lodha and sucks his life-blood.
So the Lodhas believe. But this Gyan is a social reality today. A
Lodha's life is under constant threat, hidden and open.

The British had once branded this tribe 'criminal' and though
the Lodhas were denotified in the 50s, the rural population still
thinks of them in the same way. Whenever there is a theft or
dacoity, it is customary for the police to harass the Lodhas. It is
also well known to the police and the administration that the
upper-class village worthies are the brains behind these thefts, the
Lodhas being only their tools. And only a small percentage of the
Lodhas are employed in the thriving crime industry. Crime is
really an industry now and the receivers of the stolen goods are
the real criminals. But they are usually moneyed and influential
people and no one dares touch them. When thefts multiply,
Lodhas are killed.

How deep the stigma is was nakedly exposed when Chuni
Kotal, a Lodha girl, became a graduate. While Chuni was praised
skyhigh, almost all the journals reported that she came from a
criminal tribe, the Lodha. Chuni herself protested against this,
and her letters were published in some newspapers.

How to remove this stigma from the social consciousness? In a children's journal, one reads that a certain place in Jhargram is unsafe since criminal Lodhas haunt it. How to save the Lodhas from the onslaught by the mainstream unless they themselves become alert? A few months back the secretary of the Lodha Savara Samaj Kalyan Samiti wrote to me asking for my advice. A cheap but widely circulated journal has just printed a story about Lodhas raping women belonging to a major tribal group, thus justifying the killing of the Lodhas.

The position of the Lodhas in West Bengal is best understood from the 'why and how' of some Lodha killings. In January 1982, in the village of Gonua (Narayangarh *thana*), 6 Lodhas were killed (some roasted alive), and 4 were maimed for suspected theft. In July 1982, 6 Lodhas were killed in 3 villages near Jhargram. They were supposed to have raped an old woman. It was a manufactured story. The upper-caste brahmins of the nearby village were the real culprits. But no one bothered to probe and expose the truth. Why? Because Lodhas are expendable. Lodha-killing is a regular feature in West Bengal. Listed below are a few killings which have taken place between 1979–1982:

18 Lodhas were killed at Patina in 1979.

6 killed and 4 maimed at Gonua in January 1982.

2 killed at Jhargram–Nunnunigerya in February 1982.

1 killed in Shakpara village in March 1982.

1 killed in Khejurkuti in June 1982.

6 killed in 3 villages of Saro, Baghjhanpa and Chakua in June 1982.

Not in one case have the political parties protested. Nor has there been any inquiry. We, in West Bengal, kill the Lodhas for being Lodhas and criticize the other states for being intolerant. Who are the Lodhas? Criminals. Well, murder and robbery are not uncommon in West Bengal today. There are no Lodhas in the other districts. Why blame the Lodhas alone? And has a life of criminal activities helped the Lodhas any? Why are they the poorest of the poor? It is a complicated story. Even the non-Lodha villagers admit that it is pointless blaming the Lodhas alone while the real culprits, the receivers of stolen goods, enjoy social immunity. Yet they participate in Lodha killings. Neither the district administration nor the higher-ups in Calcutta have tried to analyse the problem objectively and solve it. The Lodhas get killed, a temporary police camp is set up, some relief materials are provided for the aggrieved families. Then everyone forgets about the Lodhas till another killing takes place. I say 'killing'—what about the Lodhas maimed, blinded and crippled by a frenzied mob ?

Has the state government succeeded in making the big landholders cough up land which is above statutory ceilings? No one knows the answer. But in places, the Lodhas and other minority tribes have been given land. The irate *jotedars* have incited the other poor people to attack and kill the Lodhas when the latter tried to cultivate the land. In Nayagram *thana* (the scene of the Paina carnage of 1979) the rich landowners once evicted Santhal *bargadars* (sharecroppers) and gave *barga* rights to the Lodhas over a wide area. This was in the remote past. They knew that the Santhals were numerically strong, united and militant. The Lodhas could be made to work at the lowest possible wage. As a result, there was hostility and enmity between the starving Santhals and the starving Lodhas. In 1982 in Khejurkuti Parijatpur (Keshiari *thana*) the rich landowners instigated the poor Kora tribals to attack the Lodhas when the latter tried to cultivate the newly acquired land received from the government, and one was killed. In July 1982 in the villages of Saro, Baghjhaapa and Chakua (Jhargram *thana*), 6 persons were killed. The main issue was *khas* land belonging to the rich landholders of Chandri village which had been given to the Lodhas; and, of course, the main architect of the killings was a big receiver of stolen goods who kept a few Lodhas on his payroll. He wanted to teach a lesson to a poor woman whom he had once favoured and then discarded. So he had her attacked by his hirelings, let a day slip by, then raised a hue and cry that the Lodhas had raped her, and led a lynch mob to the Lodha villages. The story was given out by one of the hirelings.

Not in a single case of Lodha killings has there been any protest from the political parties, nor has there been a concerted and painstaking effort to explain to the other tribes that the Lodha is not the enemy of the Santhal. The receivers of stolen goods, the operators behind the thefts and robberies, are the real threats. A Santhal has to understand that not just the Santhal but the tribal entity is under threat of extinction; instead of hostility against the minority tribe, the Santhals, Mundas and Oraons should take the lesser tribes under their protection and forge a tribal unity. When a Santhal kills a Lodha or a Lodha robs a Santhal, the outsider benefits. The outsiders thrive upon tribal disunity.

In 1982 a young man from the village Kapasgerya raped a Lodha girl belonging to Lakhiasol village. The Lodhas of the latter village went to the local political leader for justice.The leader fined the young man Rs 825 and let him go since he refused to marry the girl. When the Lodhas protested, the leader became angry. The Lodhas were refused panchayat work and denied kerosene. They united in a meeting and decided that it was cruelty to ostracize the girl alone and told the father of the girl so. This was taken as an open threat against the leader. So the leader came with armed tribals to terrorize the Lodhas and demanded Rs 500 as penalty. The poor Lodhas pacified him with Rs 300, which they collected in great distress. In fact, one Lodha had to pawn his only possession, an old bicycle.

Saro village in Jhargram witnessed a brutal Lodha killing in 1985. On June 30, 1985, there was a theft at nearby Andharisol village. The village worthies came and threatened 2 Lodhas of Saro: if they did not reveal the names of the culprits, their houses would be burnt and possessions looted. The 2 hid in the forest, as they always do. Do they pray to the guardian gods and goddesses of the forest to hide them? I don't know. I hear that they were arrested; their houses, along with other Lodha houses, looted. Now the wives of the 2 Lodhas trudge wearily from Jhargram police station to the Lodha cell office and back home. Quite a distance, from Saro to Jhargram—and to the Lodhas of Jhargram subdivision, Jhargram town administration is as inaccessible as the bureaucrats in New Delhi.

About a month ago, the Lodhas of Jaralata village were returning home after purchasing rice. The local police accosted them and seized their cycles.

The persecution of Radhanath Savara, a retired armyman, will bring the picture into sharper focus. Radhanath, a man of keen social conscience, a resident of village Chandabila, came back home after his retirement. The Lodhas started to come to him whenever disputes arose or quarrels broke out, and they accepted his judgement. If a man from their own community could solve matters, why run to others? On 16 September 1984, Radhanath was asked by the Lodhas of village Kundalia to settle some quarrel or dispute. Radhanath settled the matter. The controllers of Lodha life did not like it. They must have felt threatened. Weren't the Lodhas becoming too independent? Usually a Lodha in a scrape has to run to others either with a bribe or with a vow of allegiance. They probably thought that this was not the time to teach the Lodhas a lesson by unleashing a lynch mob on them. Methods more sophisticated, more wily, were needed; best to punish a Lodha through another Lodha, thus keeping the names of other castes clean.

At Jaralata village a tank was being dug under the Lodha development project. Radhanath was the supervisor. On 23 July 1985, he was going to the Block Office with the muster roll, for only the work-supervisor was responsible for payment to the workers. Near Patharnalla village, Radhanath was approached by some Lodhas who requested him to accompany them to the *thana* to clarify certain points in a land dispute. No sooner had Radhanath entered the police station than he was arrested. The charges against him, all criminal, are many. After much pleading and persuasion, he was released on bail on 28/29 July 1985. But the case remains baffling. Only an impartial investigation can solve the mystery, but who cares about a Lodha, even if he is a former *jawan* of the Indian army? What an encouragement to the Lodhas!

But the story of the 2 villages, Pataghar and Laljaal, is a fit subject for filmmakers and playwrights who portray social injustice. The background: the Kheria–Savaras of Pataghar wrote to me pleading for a well. The panchayats in West Bengal are doing such glorious work for the villages that till November 1983 many Kheria villages of Purulia did not have a single well for drinking water. The semi-dry streams were all they had. A well was sanctioned for Pataghar, a Kheria village. And it was allegedly snatched by an influential resident of Laljaal, a comparatively well-off village dominated by landowning upper-caste people. Well, the Kherias ran here and there and another well was sanctioned for them. This effrontery of the hitherto submissive Kheria people was unforgivable.

Madhu Savara, according to an almost illegible letter from his son, Manik, was poor, and an alcoholic. The unending struggle to eke out a living slowly affected his brain, already weakened by starvation. Father of a son and daughter, both teenagers, one day he beat his wife and drove her out to her parent's house. Then he became a suicidal maniac. Many times he tried to sneak away to the forest and hang himself from a tree. Each time his son or a relative or a villager rescued him. Hekim Savara, his uncle, was a comparatively well-off person, possessing some land and cattle. Hekim tried to help his nephew as much as he could. It was well known in many villages that Madhu was mentally deranged and suicidal.

On 16 June 1985, Madhu took a *lota* of water from his daughter, went to the forest and hanged himself with a rope made from strips torn from the lungi he was wearing. In the villages, fields and forests are the people's latrine. Manik grew panicky when his father failed to return, went to the forest, found his father, called the villagers and they brought the dead Madhu home. Perhaps the panchayat member or *pradhan* was informed. He and others advised Manik to cremate Madhu. The correct procedure would have been to inform the Binpur police station but that would have meant too much harassment for Manik. So Madhu was cremated. And then the trouble started.

On 17 June 1985, police from Binpur police station came and took Hekim Savara and his sons to the police station on the charge of murdering Madhu and then trying to conceal the fact by hanging him and assisting in the cremation. Manik's letter was very pathetic. He told me that neither his grandfather nor his uncles could have had a hand in Madhu's death. It baffles Manik as to why the police do not believe the residents of Pataghar who are in the know of the facts and why they believe the influential 31 other caste people of Laljaal who have allegedly filed the case and who do not know anything. He pleads that the case is a fabricated one and if the Binpur police do not stop harassing his relatives the result will be disastrous for all concerned, for his grandfather has already tried mediation by other people and failing in that, is pawning his possessions and cattle to appease you know who. Another Savara writes in desperation that the Laljaal people are boasting that they want to teach a lesson to the Kherias who have become swollen-headed with all the attention they are receiving from the government.

The Lodhas have often told me that they are grateful to the

present state government because now the police does not hound
them all the time. Now they can sleep in their own huts.
Previously they had to sleep in the forest. It was quite customary
for the police to come and harass the Lodhas. I cannot say that
the picture has changed very much. Whenever something
unpleasant happens in Jhargram subdivision, the Lodhas become
the first suspects. In a regrettable incident, the Tribal Welfare
Minister's car was attacked by some miscreants. The next day the
news said that 13 Lodhas had been arrested for the incident.
That particular road is well known for wayside robberies and
armed dacoities; it is a law and order problem. It was not a crime
organized by the Lodhas, because the Lodhas, who steal for
survival, have never been known for sophisticated, well-planned
and well-organized crimes. By nature the tribe is shy, withdrawn
and wary of the outside world.

The Lodhas are not safe even when they want to work for
their social upliftment. On 21 March 1983, 4 Lodha boys were
going to Prahlad Bhukta to discuss their *samiti*. One of them was
the secretary of the CPI(M) Khetmazdoor Union. It so happened
that there had been a theft in a nearby village. About 50 men
accosted them, took them to the secretary of the Krishak Sabha
(peasant organization) and had their houses searched. This was
very insulting to the Lodhas and their women came out with bows
and arrows, which made the secretary and others flee. Then the
secretaries of the 2 village Krishak Sabhas called a meeting,
accused the Lodhas belonging to their party of unruly behaviour,
made the secretary of the Khetmazdoor Union apologize and
said that whenever there was a theft, Lodha homes would be
searched with no explanation required. The Lodhas might be
allies and supporters of the rulers but the *bhadralok* rulers
generally make it clear that the Lodha is not to forget that he
belongs to a criminal tribe. The term 'criminal' may not have
been tagged on to the tribe in the records, but the treatment
meted out to them is so insulting and dehumanizing that such
official clemency becomes an absurdity. The Gyan has many
faces.

And the receivers of stolen goods, the village worthies, are the
worst Gyans. They are constantly after the Lodhas, encouraging
the vulnerable ones to steal, now posing as their friends, now
threatening them with dire consequences if they do not obey.

Patina, in Nayagram *thana*, is a village of receivers. So are Fulboni and Chamar-bandhi. Once, in 1979, the Lodhas of Singdui and other villages ran to Patina seeking protection from a lynch mob. But the receivers, of course, did not help them.

Why this vindictive attitude towards the Lodhas and the Kherias? Does the state government want it? No. But the neighbouring society, the controllers of village life, mostly belonging to the affluent class, cannot tolerate the hitherto submissive people wanting to live like human beings. The treatment these unfortunates are receiving is basically class-motivated.

In Medinipur the political picture is very muddled and the minority communities have always tried to survive by being loyal to the ruling party. However, the major constituent of the Left Front in this district may profess sympathy for them but does not come to their help when they suffer. It is also a fact that in the village hierarchy, the controllers and operators have changed flags just to hold on to land. The government's policy for Lodha development has roused the ire of people who considered Lodhas expendable.

According to West Bengal Government rules, every Lodha hamlet or village is supposed to come under the Integrated Tribal Development Project (ITDP). The lavishly glorified ITDP is no solution, either, since nothing reaches the Lodha in reality. But the Lodhas, desperate as they are for sheer physical survival, want these schemes. The schemes never reach them, as no one cares to implement them. Now that the Lodhas themselves are surveying their villages, and sending me the reports, I have some idea, taking a village as an example.

The village is Madhabpur, located in block Narayangarh. There are a total of 32 Lodha households (total population, 99). Of the families, 12 are totally landless; and 17 have received a little bit of land from the government. There are 23 schoolgoing children but they do not receive the books, garments, slates or tiffin they are supposed to. The poverty level of the families would be evident from the following:

Number of Families	Income Per Month (Rs)
17	30
12	60
1	20

1	125
1	nil

When a family of 6 has to survive on Rs 60 a month it is natural that a Lodha child, from the age of 7, will be hired out as a cowgrazer or goatherd and will not be sent to school. Even if a Lodha child goes to school, s/he is taunted and cruelly treated by the teacher. How many times has a Lodha mother told me, 'Please send a Santhal or a Lodha teacher for our village school; the upper-caste teachers hate the boys. They ask the children to water or hoe the garden, or tend the vegetable patch.' In fact, I was appalled to know that the Lodha children of Lengamara village do not go to school because after 4 years at the school, they have not been taught the alphabets properly. The unsavoury fact about West Bengal is that the teachers, especially in the tribal belt, have a strong aversion to the tribal poor aspiring to be educated. If they go in for education, who will do the various chores in the fields, houses and farms? It is also an eye-opener that in the tribal belt of West Bengal, most primary schools have non-tribal teachers, though qualified tribal candidates are available in plenty. And in the Bandwan block of backward Purulia, many schools exist in name only. The teachers do not come. Schools do not function.

Sankharidanga and Madhabpur are just 2 typical Lodha villages. The others are no better off. According to government rules, every Lodha family is entitled to benefit from one scheme or another. But a Lodha is not really entitled to anything. Sudhir Nayek and Suren Pramanik, 2 Lodha boys with SF and HS qualifications, may run 2 night schools in Jasmol and Lakhiasol, but when it comes to the sanctioning of 2 posts, teachers from other castes are absorbed.

In the village of Barochati-Jamsol, the Lodhas must give up their rights over a water reservoir because the owner refuses to sell it to them. This reservoir gives them water, fish and the vegetables grown on its banks. The Lodhas want the government to purchase it and give it to the Lodhas for a fishing cooperative. The owner is reluctant.

What about the Lodha hostels? Niranjan Bhukta is the superintendent of the Lodha hostel in village Chaksahapur in Debra *thana*. There are 17 Lodha and 3 Santhal children in the hostel. Niranjan has been pleading for improvements for a long time. The dwelling is in ruins, the roof leaks in the monsoons, snakes crawl on the cracked mud walls. A child was once bitten by a snake at night. The panchayat heads and other officers have inspected the hostel repeatedly but do nothing. Barring a few exceptions, such is the general condition of the tribal hostels.

Yet, a residential hostel at the primary level is the only solution to the problem of schoolgoing Lodha children. It is very difficult for a Lodha child to continue his/her studies. The apathy of succeeding governments has made the Lodha apathetic towards himself. A sense of despair, a shadow of doom, haunts the Lodha existence. A Lodha mother asked me once, 'Can you assure me that my son will grow to be old?' What could I tell her? In the Saro killing, Miru, a bright young man, was killed. His mother-in-law told me, 'Every day he came to take his ailing father-in-law to hospital for his injection. How could they accuse him of rape?' Her point was, a boy with such a sense of social responsibility would not have done something so vile. The Lodha men and women mourned Miru, as he was a good, bright boy. They asked me, 'What is the use of sending our boys to school? It is better to keep them at home, as one never knows when one's son is going to be killed.' One of them said, 'Why should you be sad because our children have given up school? Our boys, even after going to school for years and obtaining certificates, will not get jobs.'

These words of despair reveal a hard reality. It is very surprising that there is no special consideration for the minority tribes with regard to employment. When a Lodha boy, after obtaining his SF or HS certificate, registers his name in the local employment exchange and does not receive even a call for an interview for 6–7 years, he becomes discouraged, and other Lodha children learn from the example. Since Lodhas educated upto the primary and secondary level are very few in number, it should not have been difficult to get them jobs. In the special Lodha number of *Bortika* I printed names of 214 educated unemployed among the Lodhas. It is surprising that the Lodhas are not considered for posts of forest guards and the like. In the primary schools in the Lodha villages, Lodha men and women with 8th standard certificates could easily be employed as teachers.

Some areas are especially neglected, like the Lodha villages in parts of Lalgarh block. In 5 villages the Lodha families have no ration cards. Only Lalu Savara has studied upto class 4 in these 5 villages, the others are illiterate. There is not a single primary school in 3 villages in a row (Rangamati, Tarki and Karamsol). Each village has 2–3 families who own a bullock and a plough. The others are totally dependent upon the forest for survival. Yet there are blocks, panchayats and smaller panchayat-units. These are supposed to be the implementing bodies for development programmes. There is money available for Lodha development.

The Lodhas need special attention and care, for other SC/ST or non-SC/ST people may be poorer, but their total existence is not immersed in such abysmal despair. They must be loved, respected, allowed to feel that they too belong to the society they live in. The Lodha tribe has been cruelly made to feel that it is expendable.

Districts with high tribal concentrations, like Medinipur, Bankura and Purulia, should locate offices for matters relating to tribals in areas where it is possible for the tribals to approach them. Also, in these districts, the heads of various government departments should be people who understand the problems of the tribals. But officers who try to do their duty sincerely and are trusted by the people are always transferred. No one stops to ponder and think whether the government's declared policy is actually benefiting the Lodhas and Kherias or not. That a policy has been declared is enough to launch repressive action.

It is a matter of great shame that on the one hand the state government declares its policy for Savara development and on the other, the people concerned are threatened, thwarted, harassed and pushed back into prison. This prison lies within the Lodhas and Kherias. Fear psychosis keeps them imprisoned.

Since others are always speaking about the Lodhas, I thought it best to let the Lodhas speak for themselves. I befriended them and when I learned that they had once formed a Lodha–Savara social welfare organization and had even got it registered, I pressed them to have it revived. That was when they revived their hitherto non-functioning Lodha Savara Samaj Kalyan Samiti; and *Bortika* published a special Lodha supplement in which Lodhas and a Santhal contributed articles.

The Lodhas came out with many grievances. First, they held a meeting and sent an open letter to the Chief Minister of West

Bengal with mass-signatures and thumb-prints. We published it.

From 1979 to 1982, 35 Lodhas were killed in Patina, Khejurkuti, Shakpara, Gonua, Nunnunigerya, Saro, Baghjhanpa and Chakua. The first demand was for a judicial inquiry into the killings and suitable punishment for the culprits (no steps had been taken). The second demand was for legal punishment for the receivers of stolen goods and others who kept a small section of the Lodhas engaged in criminal activities (no result). The third demand was for employment for the educated Lodha boys and girls (a complete list with employment exchange numbers of the candidates was repeatedly sent to the appropriate authorities by this correspondent). The fourth demand was for compensation to the families of the slaughtered Lodhas, either by way of employment or cultivable land (D. Bandyopadhyay, then Land Reforms Commissioner of West Bengal, initiated an irrigation project for Patina Lodhas). The fifth demand was for residential schools for Lodha children (no result). The sixth demand was for allotment of such land to landless Lodhas as was free of dispute and *jotedar* hostility, since killings took place over land distributed to the Lodhas. The seventh demand was for making the Lodha community self-supporting through cottage industries, fishery, goat-keeping, piggery, poultry, etc., all on a strictly cooperative basis. The eighth demand was to make the educated Lodhas belonging to the *samiti* responsible for handling the money meant for Lodha development. The ninth demand was for letting the Lodhas live like human beings and freeing them from the dungeons to which they had been confined even 35 years after independence. The date was 3 August 1982.

With the revival of their *samiti*, a new face of the Lodha is emerging. The landless, the marginal peasant, the agricultural labourer, the forest casual-worker, have begun to work for their own development and have already opened 5 branches of the *samiti*. They fully understand that not all of them will get regular employment and cultivable land. They themselves suggest, 'Since many among the Lodhas earn their livelihood by rearing goats and selling them in the weekly village markets, why cannot they be given the contracts for supplying goats under block-schemes for the Lodhas?' One writes, 'Many Lodhas cultivate fish and sell them. It is no good giving us barren and dry land. Instead, a tank would help us more.' They know what they can handle, and given a chance they are ready to show what they can do. Hunting, fruit, root, tuber, leaf and seed gathering, are fast receding into oblivion with the cutting down of natural forests and with eucalyptus plantations coming up. The Lodha women curse the eucalyptus trees, describing them as 'nylon-clad city girls, no good for everyday life'. They have no sympathy for a tree which gives neither food nor fuel to the poor. A forest-centred life is a mere dream now. The Lodhas are desperate to find a way to survive within the existing system.

They are running night schools. Taking to a life of crime is a mistake, they try to explain. And what a flair they have for writing! Prahlad Bhukta, Chuni Kotal, Jugal Kotal, Prashanta Ari, Sankar Kotal, all of them are prolific and competent writers. The Lodha girl Chuni's life-story makes memorable reading. It is revealing to know what the Lodhas think about the Lodha problem. 'We refuse to be killed, maimed and hounded,' they write. 'We refuse to be treated as criminals.' The general view in West Bengal is that the Lodhas are criminals and incapable of organized thinking. And yet, the Lodhas are sensitive, lovable and capable of great love and warmth.

The Lodhas revived their *samiti* out of desperation, for sheer physical survival. The awakening of the Lodhas surprised the state government. The sluggish serpent, bearing the Lodha label, eternally in winter-hibernation, seemed to stir a little. Six Lodhas, including Chuni Kotal, were appointed as Lodha cell social workers. And 3 boys were appointed as village welfare supervisors in Chakua, Chandabila and Pranabpalli, on a temporary basis, at Rs 10 a day. All were employed in September 1983.

This encouraged the Lodhas. Chuni went in for college studies. Boys who had left school in the higher classes were persuaded to complete school. There was need for at least 100 social workers in different areas of the district. It was physically impossible for 6 workers to cover more than 300 villages. Since the village welfare supervisors were working in a smaller area, their usefulness was soon established. Through their devotion and dedication, Lodha and some non-Lodha children started to come to the community centre to study. These workers could persuade the Lodhas to give up drinking, to save their wages, to live hygienically. They felt that the state government was coming forward with schemes for development and the Lodhas should be prepared to reap the full benefit of such schemes.

A tribe, hitherto disunited, mercilessly exposed to the onslaughts of the mainstream, was emerging for the first time ever as human beings. The tribals needed, and still need, these supervisors. They are easily cowed, easily thwarted, guileless people who play into the hands of exploiters. Fear of others is deeply ingrained in the Lodha.

In 1985 the picture was different. In this year 3 of the contingent posts of village welfare supervisors which were established in 1983 were abolished, and 3 boys, Krishnaprasad Bhukta, Tarun Bhukta and Jadunath Mallik, were without a job. The villagers are dumb spectators. An advisory committee on Lodha development does not have a single Lodha among its members. If an employee from the Lodha cell does get included, it cannot help the Lodhas, as such a member will not have any voice. Thus the Lodha sees things being done in his name, but he has no voice to say what he needs. He cannot even say how haphazardly Lodha development projects are being implemented. It is time that an outside agency is entrusted with the task of seeing and evaluating whether such projects are helping the beneficiaries to the intended extent. And to conclude the Medinipur Savara story, has the Lodha Savara Samaj Kalyan Samiti or, for that matter, any grassroots-level organization been recognized as a responsible agency? The answer is 'no'.

What is the solution to the Lodha problem? Definitely not 'big money' projects. I do not think that big-budget projects will help the Lodha. His first requirement is love and trust. Trust him with responsibilities, and let him work for his own development. I know that it can be done. The Kherias of Purulia, for example, are very similar to the Lodhas of Medinipur. They, too, are hounded by the forest and police guards and penalized whenever there is a theft, although there is less Kheria killing in Purulia and the social milieu is healthier. The Santhals of Purulia are also generally sympathetic to the lesser tribes like the Kheria, Paharia and Birhor. The officer-in-charge of the District Science Centre, Amalendu Roy, is literally making science serve the rural poor. Even during a prolonged drought, he has made the Kherias of Garasagma village dig wells within the compound and grow vegetables. I saw wells only 10–11 feet deep yielding water. Roy has made simple, realistic and intelligent low-budget projects for the Kherias and Birhors. Since the aim is to see the beneficiaries get maximum financial benefit, the Kherias and Birhors do all the work themselves.

In the case of the lesser tribals of Purulia, an enterprising officer formed these projects. In the case of the Medinipur Lodhas, many of them are capable enough to chalk out similar low-budget projects for themselves with a little help and guidance, and even execute them. Small schemes, vegetable and fruit cultivation, fishing, wells dug by them for paddy cultivation, goat and poultry rearing, these are the types of schemes they understand and can handle.

I have heard that after much persuasion and discussion, the West Bengal Government is going to settle some Lodha families in vast conserved areas of Brindabanpur/Jhargram on barren dry land which is supposed to be converted into a cashewnut plantation. If it is true, then it is a sheer folly. The money budgeted for such a project can be better used with tangible results. Cashew may be a cash crop, but will take years to grow; how are the Lodhas to survive till then? Small-budget projects are more useful to a minority tribe; it is folly to go in for big projects.

The policy pursued by the central and state governments towards the minority tribes, that of keeping them in the role of recipients alone, is wrong. They must be active participants in any scheme meant for them. If you do not trust a Lodha, a Birhor, a Kheria or a Paharia enough to give him responsibility, he will not become self-confident and responsible. He must be involved in planning and implementing the schemes meant for his good. Usually the schemes are made by people ignorant of, or insensitive to, the needs of the tribals. The plan is then, after the usual procedures, left to the contractor. I leave it to the readers to assess who benefits from such schemes. Why cannot the Lodhas be asked what they need? Why cannot need-based low-budget plans be made? Why can't there be small labour cooperatives to execute the plans? The educated Lodhas can handle the plans with the help of Lodha labourers. I have seen what contractors make for Lodhas under government specifications. It is better to make spacious earthen huts. With a structure of cement, brick, and sand, the inevitable contractor is bound to enter the scene. To whose benefit? Not the Lodhas'.

Over 3 decades, huge sums have been spent in the name of the Lodhas, yet the community has descended much below the poverty line. During the Siddhartha Sankar Ray ministry, in the villages of Satyadihi, Pitalkanthi and Porhati, 2 rows of flimsy huts were built for the Lodhas and the doms, after spending huge sums of money. The Chief Minister was annoyed, everyone connected with it acted shocked, and there the matter ended. In 1982 I had approached someone very high-up in the West Bengal Government to involve the Lodhas in making and implementing small-budget plans. While he agreed with me, another told me point-blank that Lodhas were thieves and robbers and could not be trusted with any money. I pointed out to him that wily contractors were usurping huge sums allotted for the Lodhas, with the connivance of government officials, panchayat people and political worthies.

After centuries of living in close association with the mainstream, the Lodha has learnt to accept reality. He knows that there is no forest to sustain him; that he can only survive by fishing, cultivating, goat-rearing and the like.

But no one wants to know what he knows. The Lodha, being a tribal, must be kept at the receiving end alone. Pundits will make plans and contractors will execute them. This, and the occasional killing, have been the Lodha story till now. But the Lodhas want to change the story, they want it to be written anew.

But no, there must be big-budget projects (what does a Lodha know?); there must be contractors (who else?); the Lodhas cannot have any say in their own welfare (do the Lodhas have a mind? What does the anthropologist say?) and must accept whatever we do for them. This underestimation of an entire people, an intelligent and suffering people, has, underlying it, a supreme contempt for the minority tribe. Had they been numerically strong, they would have succeeded in getting a better deal. Which government would neglect a tribe commanding lakhs of votes? And the only chance of ultimate survival for a Lodha, Birhor, Kheria, or Paharia is as part of an integrated tribal entity. Only the Santhals, Mundas and Oraons can help them achieve this. Perhaps they will one day. I know that the Lodhas need the help of their more advanced brethren.

Compiled from articles in *Economic and Political Weekly*, 28 May 1983, 4 June 1983, and 31 August 1985.

The Kherias of West Bengal

The Kheria–Savaras are mainly concentrated in Purulia, but they are to be found in the forest areas of Medinipur and Bankura too. The Kherias of Purulia are over 10,000 in number. The literacy rate is abominably low. I do not know if there is a single Kheria with a secondary school-leaving certificate or not.

I came to know of the Kherias first when Gomastaprasad Soren of Udalbani (Bandwan) sent me a book written by him on the plight of the Kherias. His very sensible suggestions of how to improve life for the Kherias, and the fantastic life-story of Kanuram Savara, an old Kheria who received a political pension but lived in utter poverty, interested me a lot. *Bortika* printed Kanuram's life-story. I became interested in the Kherias and went to Purulia to attend a 'little magazine' conference, but spent most of the time with 2 extraordinary persons.

One of these was Subodh Basuroy, who edited an outstanding journal, *Chhatrak*, on Purulia's folk culture. He was, perhaps, the only person who had covered the entire district on foot in search of folklore. Basuroy's ex-pupil, Gopiballav Singhdeo, was also dedicated to the Kheria cause. The second person was the District Science Centre officer, Amalendu Roy, who showed me the good work he was doing at the Centre and took me to various villages.

I took Subodh and Amalendu to Bandwan. In order to reach Bandwan you have to cross a 7-mile strip belonging to Singbhum district in Bihar, and pass Kamalpur on the way. The road from

Purulia to Bandwan in January 1983 was a nightmare and from
Bandwan to Jamtoria it was just stones and pebbles. I have heard
for years and years that a proper road is being built. Purulia is the
poorest and most neglected district in West Bengal. From
Bandwan onwards, the state of affairs is hard to describe. Anyway,
that day's journey to the back of beyond inspired Roy to help the
Kherias.

The Kherias are even more primitive than the Lodhas. The
curse of being a 'criminal' tribe haunts their existence. Often I
would receive letters when Kherias were evicted from forest land
or arrested by the district or Singbhum police. In fact, no one
knows how many Kherias are rotting in Bihar jails. No one
bothers. In one instance, in October 1983, 6 Kherias—Haripada
Savara and Kahnu Savara of village Latpada, Khori Savara and
Shuku Savara of village Dumurdi, Joginda Savara of Hijla and
Uddhab Savara of Sindri—were arrested in Barabazar town by
Barabazar police and were tried and convicted at Seraikela court,
Singbhum, for 10 years. What was their offence? Nobody knew.
They were just arrested somewhere in Purulia and sent to
Singbhum. I know that till 1983, few Kherias entered Purulia
town as free citizens. Whenever they did, they were handcuffed
and dragged by a rope round the waist.

The Purulia district police is just as vindictive as the Singbhum
police and no one knows why tribals of one West Bengal district
are regularly arrested by the district police and sent to Bihar for
trial and conviction.

It is also true of the Kherias that till November 1983, every
political party used them as musclemen. Another feature of the
district is that the Santhals are not at all hostile to the minority
tribes like the Kherias, Paharias, or Birhors. They are sympathetic
to them. In November 1983, at Maldi village (Purulia), the
Kheria–Savara Kalyan Samiti was born. When I mention any
village in the Kheria context, please understand that in each
village the Kherias live in a *toli* at a distance from the people of
other castes and tribes. Maldi was no different. About two or
three thousand Kherias attended from different *thanas*, and they
came walking. The grand old man Kanuram Savara walked 18
miles, and after a freezingly cold night's Chhou dance and song,
he left in the early morning, bidding me a polite goodbye. Not
long after, the forest guards burnt his hut and confiscated his

spade and axe. The Maldi Kherias too had a Chhou troupe of their own. In Maldi a Kheria child offered me a live snake for lunch, delicious when cooked with spices, he promised. Basically a hunting tribe like the Lodha, the Kheria will eat anything and survive.

I came to know at first hand that in 13 Kheria villages there was no well for drinking water. Some of them cultivated forest land, some worked for meagre wages; their main sustenance was from the forests. Others engaged them in felling trees, thieving, robbery and had them arrested with chronic regularity to keep them in hand. The Kheria existence was abominable. The CPI(M) allegedly demanded their allegiance but did nothing for them. It did not seem that either panchayats or the tribal office existed as far as the Kherias were concerned, for nothing was done for them. The Kheria hostel at Chirudi was dismal. In bitter winter, scantily-clothed Kheria children slept on the floor. No furniture, nothing. It was cruel to ask how many meals they ate a day and what they ate. The contractor-built hostel defies description.

Anyway, the District Science Centre came forward and a new Kheria story began. To make the Kherias self-sufficient, the Centre concentrated first upon maximum utilization of available resources. The Kheria hutments have a little more adjoining land than those of the Lodhas of Medinipur. The Centre encouraged the Kherias to dig *kutcha* wells and cultivate vegetables. The myth that Purulia soil is dry was exploded when water was found within 10–15 feet. The Maldi Kherias proudly showed us the well they had dug without blasting the rock. For the first time ever, the Kherias cultivated vegetables, planted trees and eked out a living from agriculture.

What has been achieved by the joint endeavour of the Centre and the *samiti* to date? The Rural Development Consortium gave the Centre Rs 44,100 for wells. Out of this amount 11 wells and a tank have been dug. There are wells at Maldi (Purulia), Konapara (Puncha), Turang, Kuda, Barjora, Durku, Damda (Manbazar) and a tank at Jahanabad (Barabazar). Through the good offices of a concerned Planning Commission official, Rs 404,000 was granted. The District Science Centre is under the Birla Science and Technological Museum and every amount is received by the latter first and released to the Centre phase by phase. The amount sanctioned by the Planning Commission came to the Science and Technological Museum through the state government.

How is the Centre working? The Centre's science and technology programme for Kheria tribal women has generated 19 training-cum-producing centres in 12 villages under 3 police stations. Kheria women are building stone blocks for making houses and pillars. From natural fibres like jute, *mesta*, hessian and *seesal*, they make coasters, glass and cup holders, bags, hats, ropes, etc. From bamboo they make table mats, trays, folding fruit-bowls, ashtrays, penstands. About 60 women are employed. Between June and August, Manjusha, a marketing outlet under the Government of West Bengal, has purchased goods worth Rs 3000 and the local sale has been worth more than Rs 1000. The Planning Commission money received through the state government is being used to finance different projects. For the women's project mentioned above, hitherto Rs 1,78,700 has been sanctioned and Rs 24,150 has been received out of which the above-mentioned 19 projects are running. This money is released phase by phase.

The centre is working on ITDP projects, too, with that money. The first programme was an improvised agricultural-implement training programme. Ten villages are to be included. Between May and August, in 3 such centres, Jahanabad, Kuda (Manbazar) and Damodarpur (Puncha), 51 Kherias have already undergone training and made dry-farming agricultural implements for cultivation.

In the second programme, there were 30 target villages. In these villages, seeds for maize, pulses, beans, *raggi*, *gundlu*, tomato, lady's finger, pumpkin, gourd, *karela*, cauliflower, plus fertilizer and manure, have been distributed.

The third programme included water reservoirs for 30 villages. Two small tanks and a well have already been dug at Damodarpur, a tank at Garashagma (Barabazar) and a well at Akharbandh (Purulia). Work is going on at Balakdi and Kultanr (Puncha) and Boro (Manbazar). In all the tanks, the Kherias are cultivating fish as well. Another project is installing *seesal* extraction machines. Two have been installed at Damodarpur, where *seesal* is available. Training and production are going on.

In the fourth programme, an exhibition (film and slide show) on how to fight malaria was first held at the Centre and then taken to the villages. Now it is in the custody of a government organization at Ayodhyapahar. Their enthusiastic reports say that where earlier even 10 per cent homesteads refused to sprinkle DDT powder, 80 per cent are now using it. Now the stricken villagers are coming to the hospitals for medicine. The organization is showing this exhibition in both Kheria and non-Kheria villages.

In the fifth programme, the Centre undertook programmes on health–occupation–mother and child care with colourful plastic slides and explanations on cassettes. These have been given to 6 Kheria non-formal schools, functioning in huts built by the Kherias, with Kheria teachers. These schools have been given transistor sets and are now attracting non-Kheria children as well. The schools are at Akarbaid, Damodarpur, Kuda and Babuijor (Manbazar) and Latpada and Barjora (Barabazar).

With finance from Adim Jatti Sangstha, and cooperation from the Centre, the Kheria Samiti is efficiently running 2 baby and child creches at Kuda and Latpada. Each creche has a Kheria teacher and a Kheria helper, all women. The target is 25 but the creches cater to 30–35 children. The children get one meal a day. A doctor comes once a week and medicines are given. The creches have almirahs, weighing machines, toys, scientific toys, transistors, etc. For the first time, about 60 mothers can go to work for the day without having to worry about their children.

How are the neighbouring society, the political cadres, the police-cum-administration, reacting?

While digging the tank at Garashagma, 5 Kherias were arrested from Barourma *hat*. Why? No explanation, but they were *samiti* workers. Perhaps some have been bailed out, perhaps not. From Jahanabad, Singbhum, the police arrested 2 teenage Kheria boys. I wrote to the secretary, Home Affairs, and they were released. But in the same village, Lachu Savara has been debarred from entering his field. The landed and political power wielders are against Lachu. Not less than 20 Savaras have been summarily arrested from Fatehpur (Barabazar), Haludboni (Bandwan), Garashagma, Jahanabad and elsewhere.

The Centre has given 6 *sal* leaf plate-making machines to Maldi, Kuda and Konapara, where *sal* forests exist. These leaf-plates have a good local market. But we hear that the Forest

Department people and the rural worthies including the panchayat are adamantly stopping the tribals from entering the forest to collect leaves. Why? They say that the Kherias cut the trees, but they have to come out with the truth. In the past they might have. But for whom? Who owns the trucks and sawmills, who comes with transistors, torchlights and cash to bribe the felling hands? But now, from 1984, the Kherias have been planting trees in hundreds. The Adibasi Birsa Club of Maligerya (Medinipur) planted 800 saplings last year. The target this year is in the hundreds. The Nayagram Lodhas, a people hitherto associated with denuding the forest, have been planting trees widely. The Chaksahapur Adibasi Club children (Lodhas, Santhals, Mundas and others) have planted more than 1000 trees and are praying for rains. The Forest Department cannot achieve what these *samitis* and clubs, with encouragement, can. But in my state, such endeavours by non-governmental rural agencies are always held in suspicion. On the one hand they pay lip-service to it, on the other, the entire machinery is out to curb people's voluntary involvement in such issues. In Purulia the ruling party panchayat *pradhans* are allegedly openly threatening the Kherias of Maldi, Damodarpur, Jahanabad and Latpada with dire consequences. Why?

After being involved in the Centre-cum-*samiti* activities, the Kherias have realized for the first time that they can help themselves. Now they refuse to work for the landholders at Rs 3 a day. They refuse now to join their meetings and rallies, for that means losing a working day. That the Kherias cannot be had for field labour in the sowing and weeding season is a threat to the middle peasantry who never touch a plough; and they are the vote controllers in the party hierarchy.

The Centre is constructing wells and tanks which cost Rs 3500–Rs 4000. The panchayat estimates are higher. A leaf plate-making machine for Rs 5000, a *seesal* extraction machine at Rs 1000, 11 wells and a tank within Rs 44,100—this kind of economic utilization of funds spells a threat to the money and power wielders.

A whispering campaign has dubbed the Centre as being CIA-financed. And the Kherias are harassed. The district head remains a spectator. The district police arrests the Kherias and hands them over to the Singbhum police.

How could the Kherias achieve what the Lodhas could not? Because they came forward. Because the implementing agency is the District Science Centre which is accountable to the Birla Science and Technological Museum, which handles the finance and has the expenses audited. Because the Kheria development was not left to the mercy of the Tribal Department and the panchayats alone.

Neither the ruling party at the district level, nor the panchayats controlled by them, ever did anything for the Kherias. That Purulia is successful in achieving something towards tribal development, in restoring their self-respect and making them feel involved, which the state government agencies failed to do in Medinipur and elsewhere, is a lesson to be learned and admired, not to be attacked with cleverly manipulated manoeuvres. Why this hostility? The basic fact is that, even in supposedly politically progressive West Bengal, the babu class cannot tolerate it when the downtrodden of their own district demand to be allowed to live like human beings. The Kherias and the Lodhas in their search for a better life would have merited more attention if they were numerically stronger.

From *Economic and Political Weekly*, 7 September 1985.

The Story of Chuni Kotal

Chuni Kotal, a 27-year-old.Lodha girl, the first woman graduate among the Lodha–Savara and Kheria–Savara of West Bengal, hanged herself on 16 August 1992 at her husband's one-room residence in Kharagpur, a railway town. Chuni's graduation had made the news. The circumstances goading her to despair have aroused public indignation. Calcutta papers have covered the incident widely. The Chief Minister has ordered a judicial inquiry to ascertain the causes that led to her death. This was expected, for West Bengal is a great state for not seeing the naked truth. The reasons that led Chuni, a unique woman, to take her own life are palpable ones and she 'became a victim of sheer injustice and callousness of the university authorities and the West Bengal government,' according to a press report (*The Statesman*, 23 August 1992).

I have written about the sorry plight of the denotified Lodha–Savaras of West Bengal more than once. The general callousness towards the Lodhas can be seen from the fact that Chuni Kotal, the first woman from a 'primitive' tribe to have passed the HS examination, remained unemployed till 1982. That was the year the last major Lodha group-killing took place and by that time I had written often about them, mostly for Bengali dailies. Chuni was appointed a Lodha social worker in 1983 at the Jhargram ITDP office. From childhood, despite starvation, working in the fields, having no money to purchase books, she doggedly continued to study. As a social worker she cycled 20–25 km a day and made an extensive survey of the Lodha villages.

All along she continued studying. She had a strong desire to prove to the rest of the world that she, too, could do as well as others, given the opportunity. In 1985 she graduated. In 1987 she was appointed superintendent of Rani Shiromoni SC and ST Girls' Hostel in Medinipur, the district town. She was directly under the district SC and ST Welfare Officer. Her working hours were 24 hours a day, 365 days a year. No holidays, no breaks. If she had to leave the hostel for a few hours or a day, she had to take prior permission from the office, which was very unsympathetic to her.

That she was a Lodha, a hated name in the district, clung to her like a stigma. Some of the hostel staff were dead against her because of her origins. On one occasion her ailing father had to come from the village and stay in her room for a few days as a hospital bed was not available. An officer at the district office accused her of entertaining men in her room. The same thing happened when her brother, who had fractured his leg, came. Once a niece suffering from food poisoning stayed with her. The hostel staff reported her to the office. The officer demanded an explanation. Chuni felt suffocated in the job. Countless times she approached the state government at Writers Building, pleading for (a) a transfer to her original job and (b) better working conditions. The department remained brutally indifferent. I call the SC and ST Department hunters. Chuni was the quarry.

Matters became worse when Chuni enrolled herself at the local Vidyasagar University as an MSc student in Anthropology. Now weird things began to happen. From the very first day, a certain male professor started abusing her as a member of a criminal tribe, a lowborn who had no right to study MSc. The university authorities, the head of the department, did nothing about it. This man was allowed to mark her absent though she was present for days. And Chuni was debarred from sitting the examination, on grounds of irregular attendance. She lost a year.

The district office made her life miserable for leaving the hostel and going to university. In West Bengal, even after so many years of Left Front rule, the first woman graduate from a very backward tribe was openly abused because of her low caste and birth, and nothing was done about it. No one was ashamed and no one cared. Only Chuni suffered. The university authorities, too, are hunters. These anthropologists, *nritatva vijnani* in Bengali, are head-hunters or *nrimunda shikari* in Bengali. The second time Chuni sat for her examination, the same male professor gave her low marks. Thus she lost 2 years.

In desperation she complained and complained and, in 1991, the Education Minister constituted an inquiry commission which consisted of 3 principals from 3 district colleges. Throughout, the male faculty member was allowed to refer to the criminal nature of her tribe and to abuse her. The commission just went to sleep.

Chuni felt increasingly desperate and cornered. A tribal girl, she was ill-equipped to fight the enemy, whose ambitions and gameplans she was unfamiliar with. Now she also became a victim of the inner politics between the members of the faculty. She did not know the ways of the hunters. The last pressure came from a woman faculty member holding a position of top authority within the department. She had her own axe to grind. She saw an opportunity in the situation and relentlessly pressed Chuni to file a case against the offending male professor. This lady knew that Chuni's relations with the office were bad, that the government had already ordered an inquiry commission, and that it would be disastrous for Chuni to file a case at this stage. But she pressed on. This was the ultimate harassment.

In September, the examination was due, and Chuni could not afford to incur the displeasure of this woman, who professed to be her well-wisher. She had been failed twice already. She felt forced to agree. This must have been the last shove to the abyss.

On 13 August there was a seminar in the university. By that time Chuni knew where she stood. Her working conditions remained the same. She had no hope that the inquiry commision would do justice to her. Now she would have to file a case which would make a further mess of her career. If she did not, the woman faculty member might create problems. She went to the university. Thereafter she weepingly told a few co-students (according to a letter published in a Bengali daily, *Bartaman*, on 25 August 1992) that the male professor had referred to the Lodhas as thieves and robbers, completely out of context. She said that he had threatened her, saying that he would ensure that she not be allowed to sit the examination in September. She felt that she had wasted 2 years attending classes without being allowed to sit for the examination, and that, being a Lodha, she should never have dreamt of higher studies. She also said that even though she had made formal complaints to the university authorities, the offenders remained untouched.

One can only imagine what was going on in her mind. By 13 August she had made up her mind. Death was the only way to escape the hunters. On the 14th she went to her husband. They had married in a court in 1990, but due to her job had not been able to stay together. Her husband is a Lodha youth who had passed the HS examination and worked in the railway workshop. That Chuni was a graduate and he was not, had never created any friction between them. They had been in love with each other from 1981. Manmatha Savar, the husband, is a simple tribal boy. This time he found Chuni very relaxed, free of tension. They were to leave for Chuni's village, Gohaldihi, on the 16th to talk about a formal reception, a post-marriage community feast. On the 16th, Manmatha left for the workshop at 6:15 a.m. He returned at 10:45 a.m. and found Chuni hanging.

Chuni's death has revealed what West Bengal truly is. Brutal caste and class hostility and persecution has been allowed to continue. The government allowed the district babus to abuse her. Nothing was done to change her working conditions. She was kept a slave of her department. Why not? Was she not a Lodha? Was she not given a job? She should have remained eternally grateful for that. The university authorities did nothing to throw out the caste baiter. And the commission appointed by the government, apparently sleeping so far, suddenly became very active and submitted its report. Only a few days after her death, when there was a hue and cry in the media.

A new kind of hunt. West Bengal has the same caste and class hatred, but the methods are sophisticated and complex, that is the only difference with other states. Chuni's death should not be allowed to go unavenged. The tribals should realize exactly where they stand here. The curse of the babu culture runs in Bengal's veins. West Bengal forces a Chuni Kotal to commit suicide and goes ga-ga over the nauseating display of a 'Sutanuti Utsav', celebrating 300 years of the city of Calcutta.

See the face of West Bengal, now that Chuni has ripped off the mask. A judicial inquiry? Surely not. We know that judicial inquiries in West Bengal get lost in a desert of inertia. I think all democratic organizations and people should protest against this naked caste and class oppression and demand a CBI inquiry. Is not Chuni's death a pointer to the tribal in India? Well, Bengal has shown its true face.

[Post Script: The university inquiry committee submitted its report in a hurry 8 days after Chuni committed suicide. Its finding was that all allegations of harassment made by her were correct.

The Ganguly Commission set up to inquire into her suicide found that she committed suicide 'for personal reasons'.]

From *Economic and Political Weekly*, 29 August 1992.

Organizations
of the Rural
Poor

Samitis: Change through Participation

I was 21 in 1947. With many others, I tried to believe that India's independence would not totally fail the poor of the country. In 1984 I can say that for the poor of India, national independence, with its many plans, programmes, projects and acts in parliament, have come to nothing. The question is, have we reached a point of no return, or is there any hope?

I have also found that the poor of India may be mostly illiterate but they are no fools. Perhaps now they realize that keeping them in eternal poverty is very much a part of the design. People's poverty is the basis on which projects can be made, plans sanctioned, pundits enter as consultants and money inflow be guaranteed, all with an eye to see that nothing reaches the target beneficiary. They tell me so in their language, which is often unsavoury but true.

Those in power must have realized that nothing was really happening. The administrative machinery had failed, though well-meaning administrative officers can still be found. However, they are usually treated like untrustworthies and transferred at the first chance. Perhaps in desperation, the panchayati system was revived and in West Bengal, at least, the panchayats are the most powerful bodies in a district. I should say, in all honesty, that the panchayati system in my state has, perhaps, shown better performances here and there in fragments compared to other states. Knowing the situation here at the grassroots level, I shudder to think of the situation in other states. This panchayati system, in our state, too, has become an extension of the administrative hierarchy, a strong nucleus of rural power.

I should make it clear here that I have not been close to any voluntary agency or organization working among the poor for the simple reason that I have been in direct contact with the poor and the tribals, mainly of Medinipur and Purulia. I am also connected with many organizations at the grassroots level, but in order to elaborate my point I will dwell upon only a few.

Since my contact is mostly at the grassroots level, I will talk of that only. First, it has to be understood why minority tribes like the Lodha–Savara and Kheria–Savara of West Bengal have formed organizations of their own. These are minority tribes, and though in the census the Lodha–Kheria names go together, the Kherias are even more neglected than the Lodhas. Because, in West Bengal, for reasons beyond our comprehension, the Lodhas, Birhors and Totos are classified as specially protected tribes. The Kherias are denied this privilege, which exists on paper alone. One thing the Lodhas and Kherias have in common with the Birhors and Paharias is that their life-pattern has remained forest-centred for longer and they took to cultivation later than the majority tribes. Also, they have led a parallel existence with the mainstream while the majority tribes have been more exposed to the wily and devious ways of the mainstream.

The Lodhas of Medinipur and the Kherias of Purulia, though denotified, are still treated by the society, administration and the police, as criminals. No one has cared to check how many Kherias are perishing in the prisons of West Bengal and Bihar for crimes they are unaware of. Needless to say, the tribals, especially those belonging to the minority groups, have long been denied their basic human rights. Moreover, the Lodhas and Kherias lead a precarious existence since influential village and town worthies keep a section of them engaged in thievery and robbery. The Lodhas become news when they are killed and are soon forgotten. Till today no one has ever touched the rich and powerful receivers of stolen goods. The core of the problem has been allowed to remain.

It is very much like the declared forest policy of the government. The hand that fells the tree does not destroy the fast-dwindling forest belts. It is the timber merchants and forest contractors, mostly with the connivance of the forest personnel, who destroy forests and smuggle out timber and forest produce. They are allowed to function and flourish at the cost of national wealth. Yet the abominable forest law which is soon to be enforced ensures that only the poor who fell the trees are punished, and that the real marauders enjoy immunity.

This state of affairs has forced the people to form their own organizations at the grassroots level. The total apathy of society, government and others has driven them to despair; they feel their very existence is threatened. The bonded labourers of Palamau, in despair, have formed their own *samiti.* The same is true of the Lodhas and Kherias of West Bengal. What can these organizations give to the people who form them? Well, they do not have names like Nilambar and Pitambar (of Palamau), or Sidhu and Kanhu (of Santhal Parganas), or Birsa Munda (of Ranchi), based on which they can try to regain their lost identity. These *samitis* give them a sense of dignity, they cling to them as something of their very own—they feel like human beings. This has been my experience. I have seen it with my own eyes.

Let me first tell you how some of them came to be born, and when. Then I will tell you what work they can do and the threats they face; then why I think that poverty at the grassroots level can still be alleviated if these *samitis* are taken seriously.

The Palamau Zilla Bandhua Mukti Morcha was founded at Semra village on 1 May 1981, mainly through the efforts of the bonded labourers of many villages, the participation of a local journalist, Rameshwaram, and a few like me, who were spectators. I think that this was the first time that those bonded in the agricultural sector took such an initiative in this country.

It awes me to think that the Lodhas of West Bengal had felt desperate enough to form a *samiti* and have it registered in 1982. It could not function properly, due to the heavy odds against it. Between 1979 and 1982 alone, 37 Lodhas were killed. The Lodhas, in desperation, revived their *samiti* and rallied round it. After the July 1982 Lodha killing, the Lodha *samiti* organized a meeting at the village of Gopali. Speakers from villages under 9 police stations spoke. They sent me a very well-drafted memorandum with many thumbprints and some signatures. The copy of their open letter to the Chief Minister clearly stated that they refused to live like animals after 35 years of independence.

The Kheria–Savara *samiti* was founded in November 1983, in Maldi village in Purulia. For the first time ever, Kherias from faraway villages assembled in thousands. Their demands were very clear. They wanted to live like human beings.

The West Bengal Munda Samaj Sugar Ganthra, a social *samiti* of the Mundas, was formed in the 60s, but registered in 1981.

What work can these *samitis* do, and what have they done? I should make it clear that the poor non-bonded of Palamau consider the *zilla morcha* their organization, too. Since abysmal poverty is the bond of unity, the *zilla samiti* has *mukhias* or representatives in the villages. Over the years, they have collected detailed information about those in bondage and the landlords under whom they are in bondage. They have also collected information about the original debt and the original borrower, the sum demanded by the landlords for their release. This information can be of great help to the government, if it is actually interested in doing something for them. But what is worth mentioning is that they haven't stopped at that. The *samiti* has also collected information systematically regarding landlessness, irrigation needs and possibilities, support needed for small cultivators and the drinking water situation in the villages.

The Lodha–Savaras have been most forthcoming. They have, with little guidance, made detailed lists about land, income, help received from the government, the number of children attending schools, the number of Lodhas mutilated by angry mobs, everything. The Kherias have been making similar lists including cases of eviction from forest land. The Munda Ganthra has made lists of the places where irrigation facilities are needed. And, of course, all these *samitis* have made lists of the educated unemployed whose names are registered at the employment exchanges. I have hundreds of names from other tribes, castes and organizations too. Space doesn't permit me to include them all.

In each and every case, the *samitis* are doing what should have been done by the governments.

In the case of Palamau, the district administration has totally failed in recognizing the helpful role the *samiti* can play and, with the exception of a few kind officials, administrative attitude is openly hostile. So much so that the *bandhuas* are threatened with dire consequences for joining the *samiti*. They are being forced to declare that they did not volunteer any information, that the *samiti* people made them give incorrect information. The bonded labourers of Palamau and the rural poor can only be helped if the role of the *samiti* is recognized and information supplied by it is acted upon.

I do not know what is meant by rehabilitation of bonded labour, either. Even identification work has made little progress. What comes first, identification or rehabilitation? And what is the good of saying that there is no dearth of money for the bonded?

In the case of the Lodha *samiti*, relentless effort on their part has yielded some results. Some Lodhas have found employment. Their one demand was the abolition of the contractor-system in development work, with responsibility being given to the *samiti*. This has not happened. But the West Bengal Government has at least recognized that the Lodhas are not all criminals and that they need development.

In the case of the Kheria *samiti*, the Kherias have responded with laudable vigour. The Kherias of Purulia have been lucky in having the District Science Centre officer helping them with low-budget schemes and initiating them into cultivation. With help and guidance from this dedicated officer, they have dug wells, earth-dammed streams, slowly gone in for cultivation, with seeds and agricultural implements received from the Centre. Today, it is true that the Kherias are being less persecuted and hounded. This, in itself, is the greatest achievement of the Savara *samitis*. They have been partially successful in imparting the message to the mainstream that they will not tolerate being killed, maimed, hounded, exploited and used for other people's gain.

What difficulties do these *samitis* generally face? Tribal organizations are generally held in suspicion, mainly by the local non-tribals and the rulers who think they might be secessionists. Even the observance of Birsa Munda Day by the Mundas was at first suspected by the political parties. The tribal social welfare organization meetings are usually attended by the police. But slowly these hostilities are lessening. Then, the articulation of their needs for irrigation, drinking water, residential schools, restoration of alienated tribal land, employment according to the declared quota, is received with apathy by the panchayats, from whom these local demands should come. It is very difficult for tribals to get caste certificates, for instance.

Only these *samitis* can supply the correct data about themselves. They are fully capable of making low-budget schemes, as the Lodhas have done, repeatedly giving them to the relevant departments, without any result so far.

I know that the basis of confusions and weaknesses regarding all poverty-related programmes lies in the attitude of the people who are in charge of planning and executing them. The poor of India may lack literacy or formal education, but they are neither unintelligent nor unrealistic. They know the limit of their capabilities and are perfectly capable of saying just what would benefit them. But in West Bengal, as in India in general, the persons for whom plans are made, programme beneficiaries, as the government likes to label them, are never involved in planning and implementing projects made for them. They are not even consulted. The plans are made by pundits who do not have firsthand knowledge of the people they are trying to help, and once the plan or the scheme is made, it is implemented in a manner that leaves the intended beneficiary as deprived as ever.

The approach should be maximum utilization of available resources. It is no use thinking that any government will give enough cultivable land to the landless. But homestead land is a must. The Lodhas have often told me, 'Give us a few fruit, timber and fodder yielding trees, like *mowa*, *kendu*, papaya, guava, jackfruit etc. and a few goats.' In fact, even today, low-budget schemes in consultation with the beneficiary, and implementation through the *samitis* with guidance, might help. The crying need of the times is a radical change of outlook. The people must be made involved. How can they become responsible if they are never entrusted with responsibility? What the Lodhas suggest themselves is surprisingly not very different from the low-budget schemes made by the District Science Centre of Purulia. The Kherias have shown that they, with their labour, can get more wells dug than thought possible within the allotted sum. With a few fruit trees, a fair number of goats purchased from the local traders (goats given by the panchayat often die alarmingly fast) to generate rural economy, fishing tanks and support towards cottage industries, the drifting poor can still manage to eat and survive. It might, eventually, control migration in search of work round the year. Exactly what is needed where can only be ascertained from these *samitis.*

I believe that the time has come to recognize the role these grassroots-level *samitis* can play in helping the poor. As far as possible, development work should be entrusted to them. The panchayats should allow them to work for their own development. India lives in its villages, not in its cities. Why should they be in perpetual darkness?

From *Yojana,* November 1984, titled, 'You just can't do without them!'

Organizing Unorganized Rural Labour

For the last several years, I have had the opportunity of closely observing how the various programmes which exist for the rural people, the poor in general and the tribals in particular, fail to achieve their goals. I have seen, in many parts of West Bengal and Bihar, how those below the poverty level are being systematically and continuously cheated. Peoples' poverty is being ruthlessly capitalized on (see 'Samitis: Change through Participation'). That is why it is very necessary for the system to keep the poor in a state of poverty. If an area is not declared to be in dire need, how can the flow of money be ensured?

After years of probing, I have come to the conclusion that development can only be ensured if people are involved at every stage, from planning to implementation. Surveys have to be conducted, low-budget schemes formulated, with the idea of maximum utilization of available resources. Above all, in the task of implementation, the people themselves should be involved. But let me share with you the experience of some of the societies I am involved with.

I will not speak in detail about the West Bengal Lodha Savara Kalyan Samiti and Palamau Bandhua Mukti Morcha, as they have been discussed elsewhere. The Lodha Samiti was registered in 1962 but it had gone out of action. It is interesting to note that the Lodhas, a tribe often alleged to be crime-prone, had founded a *samiti* 2 decades ago, out of desperation. This *samiti* was revived in 1982 and has been most active in making a detailed survey of the Lodha villages and habitats.

The Palamau *samiti*, founded on 1 May 1981, has thousands of members, formal and otherwise. *Choupals* or seminars are organized and conducted by the *bandhuas* themselves. The *samiti* has conducted detailed surveys of blocks, villages and *tolis*. Information is collected about how many *bandhuas* there are, amount of debt taken, generations of bondage, name of the present *bandhua* owner, amount demanded for release and the like. Our estimate is that Palamau has at least 2 lakhs of *bandhuas*. Identification is conducted by the *bandhuas* themselves, and their information is reliable. The Bihar Government or the Palamau district administration has neither the will, nor the means, to identify *bandhuas*, obtain their release and get them help. The same is true of the people in distress in my state too, though they are not *seokias* or *kamias*. The *samitis* make detailed surveys, send them to me and I try to make my state government listen and take action. Anyway, let me give you some facts.

Village Gangnapur, Police Station Ranaghat, District Nadia. My informant is Ranjan Dhar, who is associated with the village welfare society. The SC and ST population constitutes 50 per cent and 25 per cent of the total population, respectively. A non-industrial area, the marginal peasants and the landless are totally dependent on agriculture-oriented jobs. The scheduled tribe people are mostly landless. About 25 per cent of the scheduled tribes have some land, which they cannot cultivate for want of irrigation, seeds, bullocks etc. Shallow tubewells installed with help from the banks have not benefited the small peasant. Chronic power shortage leaves the pumps idle. The economic condition of most of the scheduled caste and scheduled tribe people is so bad that rice is a luxury to them. They survive on roots, tubers, leaves and small game which is fast becoming extinct. Road and rail connections are in poor condition. Only 2 buses ply between Chakdah and Aishmali on a *pucca* road, which merges with National Highway No. 34. All other roads covering an area of 36 sq. miles are mud roads. The plight of the people during the rainy season can be imagined. The village is situated on the Ranaghat–Bongaon railway line. Old, discarded engines pull unwilling trains which do not run on schedule and are often stranded due to coal theft. The 4 km-long mud road between the tribal village Pandepara and Debagram needs immediate repair and conversion into a *pucca* road. The tribals remain cut off from

Debagram. The postal service is managed by poorly paid extra-departmental workers. Gangnapur is very close to Calcutta and yet it takes 7 days for a letter from Calcutta to reach. Debagram and the neighbouring areas have only 1 health centre, at Gangnapur, which is in a deplorable condition. Critical cases, especially snake-bite cases, always end in fatality. Debagram, a small town, needs a hospital immediately. The area needs primary schools. The 3 existing schools are in a dilapidated condition. Unemployment among the scheduled tribes is very high.

The findings of Gomastaprasad Soren, a keen social worker and a primary school teacher in Bandwan, Purulia district, about the tribals—especially the Santhals—are grim indeed. The Santhal girls of south Purulia are in a state of despair. Educated upto the secondary level or higher, they cannot work as daily labour like the uneducated tribal women, nor do they have any employment opportunities. I have seen, with my own eyes, the deplorable condition of the primary schools in the tribal areas of Bandwan and south Purulia. Many are non-functioning, as teachers attend irregularly. In south Bandwan, as elsewhere, persons with political pull have been employed as primary school teachers. It is not unusual to find non-tribal primary teachers in the scheduled tribe belts while hundreds of tribals with the necessary qualifications have not been considered for the posts at all. The teacher in charge of Senkebasa primary school is often absent. The hostel-cum-school built at Rithegora village under the ITDP scheme is almost nonfunctional. Padmabati Tudu of Cheredungri, Bandwan, had her name empanelled in the district Health Department. Her case was ignored and others were considered. The Santhals think that Padmabati was ignored because she was a tribal. Ashanpani, a tribal village bordering Singbhum, is so cut-off from Purulia that one has to walk a day to reach Bandwan, a Block town, spend the night there and go to Purulia the next day. Surrounded by hills, this village has a flowing stream, Satgurum, nearby. Another stream, Haramrapa Jor, flows between isolated Lukapani and Pachapani villages. A building of *jorbandhs* or check dams made of available rocks and mud could help store water and help the villagers. There are no ITDP schemes for these villages. The Santhals of Purulia are treated as Jharkhandis and rejected as expendable. The same is true of the Kherias, Mahali, Mudi, Kora, Badia, Bhumij, Birhor, Sahish, tribals and poor non-tribals.

The Santhal village Makapali is in no better condition. The case of Anil Kumar Besra, an organizer-teacher of Amghutu primary school, is true of many other tribals. They work as organizer-teachers for decades but are seldom absorbed as permanent. I ask the central government to send inquiry teams to the villages of West Bengal to ascertain how many SC-ST teachers are employed in the SC and ST areas; what is the role of the district employment exchanges in giving employment opportunities to SC-ST candidates? I take this opportunity to state that the central government's so-called reservation quotas for the ST is a cruel joke. Look at the matter from a realistic angle. The tribal boys seldom finish primary-level schooling and when they go for secondary, higher secondary or university education, in 99 per cent cases they opt for the arts or the humanities, almost never for science or commerce. So you see that though all sorts of jobs from the highly salaried ones to clerical-grade ones have ST quotas, non-tribals are employed because 'a tribal candidate was not available'. Educated Santhals, Mundas, Oraons, Bhumijs and in rare cases Lodhas or Mahalis do not get the jobs they are fit for, such as schoolteachers, clerks etc. That is so because there is a big racket in West Bengal in recruitments at these levels. The tribals are mostly registered with the district exchanges. Calcutta has the maximum number of vacancies. There is no co-ordination between Calcutta and the district exchanges. For the district quotas, people in charge of the exchanges have to be bribed and the price is often too high for a poor SC or ST candidate. The unemployment problem is very acute in West Bengal. So there is deep resentment against the SC and ST in general—the uninformed generally think that they are being pampered and getting all the benefits. An inquiry commission should find out how many ST candidates have been given jobs within the last 10 years.

The STs hire out their children from the age of 7 as cattlegrazers or *bhatuas*, for the parents are too poor to forgo the meagre income of the child. All the assistance meant for students seldom reach them and it is not possible for parents living below the poverty level to buy books and garments for a schoolgoing child. And I know from my experience in Medinipur, Purulia, 24

Parganas and Nadia that the non-tribal teachers generally hate to teach tribal children. The Lodhas of Lengamara, Keshiari, told me that they had withdrawn their children because they had not been taught even the alphabet after 4 years at the school. The Lodhas and others begged me to see that Santhal or other tribal teachers were appointed to the primary schools. Outside this state there is a highly glorified image of the government; we do not kill or harass tribals and harijans here. And yet Lodhas and Kherias get beaten up, put into jail, harassed and hated for being born Lodha or Kheria. The mainstream considers them uncivilized. What is the definition of civilization? In tribal societies, traditionally there is no dowry, no *sati*, divorce and widow remarriage are sanctioned, no child is an orphan even if he or she loses both the parents—the neighbours will rear the child and look after it. Often people tell me that the tribals are fast changing. If so, we have corrupted them. I go to them all the time, and come back recharged with hope.

In November I went to Purulia to reactivate the Kheria Savara Kalyan Samiti. All I do is to get them to form a *samiti* or society and press their demands in a peaceful and democratic but persistent manner, for inducing government schemes for the tribals, such as irrigation and drinking water etc.

The state government has slowly started to realize that Lodhas too are human beings; and something is being done for them. But there is a huge difference between what is being done and what needs to be done. Many tribals and scheduled castes are best suited for class IV jobs as forest watchers and guards, railway apprentices, peons, messengers etc. The Railway Minister has received, from me alone, lists of hundreds of names of tribals and scheduled castes. I think it is time the workings of the district and Calcutta employment exchanges were enquired into. Anyway, when some reporters from small papers in Calcutta went to Purulia to attend the Kheria Sammelan, they were apparently told by the SDO that it was dangerous to visit the Kherias as they were no better than animals and would kill outsiders at the first chance. I have been told the same thing about the Lodhas too.

To go back to Gomastaprasad Soren's report, Bandwan's first problem is communication. The *pucca* road connecting it to Manbazar-II block or to Purulia has been under construction now for ages, but is still not complete. Singbhum is just across the border, in Bihar. The Kherias are relentlessly hounded, tortured, killed and put into prison by the Purulia and Singbhum police. The Kherias are a hunting ground for the police.

If you think that being a supporter of the CPI(M) will give you the right to protest and take a justified stand, you are very wrong. For the last few months, CPI(M) cadres of Jaipur and Pratappur villages, Medinipur, are being oppressed by their own partymen. Reports to me confirm that the oppressed ones beg mercy from the ruling party, professing their loyalty to the party, and want the government to take action against arson, torture and looting of paddy and property. There are tribals on both the sides. What were the demands of the oppressed ones? They want the area to come under ITDP schemes, they wanted irrigation and drinking water, recovery of *benam* land from the rich and its redistribution to the landless.

Kherias who took part in the freedom struggle rarely receive any pensions. The same, of course, is true of the luckless peasants of West Bengal, who participated, suffered and were even imprisoned in the famous Tebhaga movement of the 40s. I have found them in Kantatala and Makaltala under Bhangar police station of 24 Parganas and know that there are thousands of them in the Sundarbans and Kakdwip area. Tebhaga, a movement of the sharecroppers for two-thirds share of the produce, has been glorified in government-sponsored literature, *jatra*, songs and plays.

Illegal brick kilns are cropping up every day in the state of West Bengal. Even the state government operates the state-owned kilns through butcher-like agents and contractors and there, too, the workers are cheated of their wages, as in any other privately owned kiln. The rapid increase of the kilns is causing great damage to the areas under cultivation. Environment and social hazards are many. In almost each kiln you will find political and mercenary *mastans* who molest and rape the working women, run liquor *addas* and help the owners to keep the workers terrorized.

In 1982, the West Bengal Harijan Kalyan Samiti of Kanchrapara, a laudable organization working for the economic and social development of thousands of harijans of the area, organized a crusade against illegal and licensed liquor shops in the heart of the harijans' *tolis*. Rajendra Bansfor, a young boy who once was an addict, but who reformed himself and became a social worker fighting to put a stop to this, was killed. Criminals, even killers, go scot-free if they have the right political connections. In Kanchrapara, the harijans are treated worse than pigs. Sanitation, tubewells, lights, living quarters, road repair, are all denied to them. Non-harijans are given jobs as sweepers and cleaners, but refuse to do any scavenging. So the handful of harijan sweepers are forced to do their work. The upper-caste sweepers and cleaners are steadily absorbed into non-scavenging office jobs which are denied to harijans, despite seniority and experience. This *samiti* has a primary school in the *toli*. Bharat Ker Adim Jati, an Oraon organization, has another in Subhaspalli, Madhyamgram. In order to repair these 2, they have approached the panchayats and relevant government departments, all in vain. In the case of the latter school, the state government refuses to recognize and regularize it though it has been running for 13 years and has 250 Hindi-speaking children every year. The government refuses to absorb the 2 or 3 teachers who are qualified and have been teaching for several years. Government recognition of the school is stalled over the question of absorbing these teachers. Here, the unwritten law is that the current teachers will have to go and others favoured by the ruling party taken on.

Everywhere in West Bengal, political party pressure is the deciding factor, from the gram panchayats to the upper levels. The district administration has been made powerless because the Zilla Parishad reigns supreme.

It is absolutely necesary to do away with the role of the inevitable contractor supplying the tribals of West Bengal with half-dead goats under government schemes for goat rearing. Whether it is goats or cows or pigs, the picture is the same all over India. This has been revealed in most evaluation studies conducted so far. The poor must be made self-sufficient. The village trader supplying goats to the local markets can be the supplier. Thus local trade would receive a boost and healthy animals would be supplied, as the supplier would have to answer to the receiver in the case of default.

Go for low-budget schemes, to start with. Focus on the maximum utilization of available resources. Before you formulate an income-generation scheme, establish backward and forward linkage. But, first of all, put your trust in the people for whom these programmes are meant. The District Science Centre of Purulia has shown, in the face of difficulties, how to do it. Since Purulia soil is not that good for paddy because it cannot retain rainwater, the Kherias, with the Centre's guidance, have dammed the streams, cultivating wheat, *kurthi* and *bajra* on their home area. The Kherias of Maldi have dug a well by hand, refusing to use the blasting technique, and have raised 3 crops in a year. True, it was possible because of the support of the District Science Centre in the initial phase. But now, after forming the *samiti*, the Kherias themselves are damming up small streams and cultivating wheat.

It is a matter of great shame that the Kheria villages of West Bengal are almost entirely dependent upon rivers or streams for water, as few irrigation projects have been undertaken for them.

In the above-mentioned Science Centre, tribals and non-tribals are being taught to make agricultural tools and implements. That Purulia has a low water-level is a partial myth. The Kherias and Santhals today dig *kutcha* wells for irrigation. Water is available at 10–20 feet depth.

The *samitis* I have in mind are grassroots-level organizations and not city-based NGOs run by intermediaries. These *samitis* should be entrusted with the task of undertaking surveys, and drawing up schemes which should, as far as possible, be low-budget ones. Then money must be sanctioned by the government. The educated ones should be allowed to keep accounts etc. and the uneducated ones can deal with the manual work and implementation of the schemes. But everyone must have total access to information and control over the organization and its decisions. Often, the poor tribals have told me that they can survive on a few fruit trees and some goats. With a little support of the type provided by the District Science Centre of Purulia, they can be initiated into cottage industries based on native resources, and form small cooperatives.

The name Sonali Tea Gardens is well known today. The tea-garden labourers there have proved that they can run a tea plantation profitably on a cooperative basis. The tribal labourers there have also, absolutely on their own, formed a cooperative dairy and it is doing quite well.

My earnest plea to the central government is, if you really want to 'help the poor', then please recognize these *samitis*. Get them involved in development work meant for them. No government machinery can achieve what these grassroots-level organizations can. They know what they need, what they can handle, and how to go about it. With a few fruit trees, some goats, ducks or poultry, fish tanks and cottage industries, the poor will be able to survive. If it checks their forced migration to other places in search of work for 8 months a year, their language and culture will revive and take roots. And most of all, they will regain their self-respect.

Discard the hoax that goes on in the name of SC and ST job reservation quotas. Ascertain from Calcutta and the district exchanges what is happening there. The exchanges should keep a list of these *samitis*, and let them know whenever a quota-vacancy occurs. And, every year, investigative studies should be made into the areas under ITDP and IRDP schemes. In West Bengal, wherever I have been to, I have seen that nothing has really reached the people. Money alone will not solve problems. Contractors, corrupt officials and the rural neo-rich will reap the harvest.

Today, towards the end of my life, I have realized that development can be ensured even at this stage, if the vital role these societies can play is officially recognized. While providing concrete services like irrigation, credit, health and education facilities is important, no less important is the role of communication. In fact, a great deal can be done in this area. The Chamtagerya Adivasi Mahila Samiti's secretary says that audio-visual means should be used to teach the villagers the necessity of health and hygienic practices and to help them overcome superstitious beliefs such as in witches.

Cressida, a research institute of Calcutta, has a keen and dedicated audio-visual unit, which has made low-cost tape and slide audio-visuals on food and health facilities. It has also made audio-visuals on the problems of artisans in rural areas and the need for them to change their design and marketing to cope with a changing environment. I would request the central government to encourage and finance such units. Communication can be an important tool for ushering in change.

A few areas where the need for communication is urgent in rural areas are:

Identification of poisonous and non-poisonous snakes; snake-bite and cure; basic science knowledge; functions of the human body, especially childbearing; health education; herbal medicines and economic uses of trees and plants. And in discussing any scheme for the poor, the forest is important. While there is a great deal to learn from the storehouse of traditional knowledge about trees and plants, we must not underestimate modern science and technology. Any other country would have nurtured and maintained natural forestry and would have made more effective and economical use of the trees, plants and herbs which we have.

The word 'tribal' always goes with the forest in India; both are closely associated. I am not concerned about people who can afford to plant eucalyptus on spare land and wait for 7–8 years. My concern is the landless poor. A mixed forest sustains both the tribal and non-tribal poor living in the vicinity. Plantation and rearing of a natural forest with varieties of trees will help them survive. Then again, I think that the time has come to take a clear stand about India's tribals. The tribal question is a national question because the tribals belong to the Indian nation and their home territory is very much a part of India. The tribals are treated as if they are not a part of the nation. Conditions for the poor, tribal and non-tribal, are the same. The tribals get a rawer deal because there is a special budget for them which they never receive. In West Bengal today, if ITDP schemes were implemented in the tribal zones, irrigation and drinking water facilities were provided, diabolically manoeuvred tribal land alienation was stopped, the tribals would not be so embittered. If the Lodhas are getting a slightly better deal today, it is because of their samiti which has given them an identification and self-respect.

The scientists should try to see things from the angle of the poorest of the poor. If damming up shallow streams with rocks can help the Kherias in growing new crops, why not build *jorbandhs* everywhere in India in the rainy season? Two monsoons will eventually silt up the floor and water will stay. It has been successful in Purulia, why not elsewhere?

Then, I ask, on behalf of my people, the poor of India, how is it that acts are made for *bandhuas*, migratory tribal labourers, landed tribals etc. and no publicity is ever given to these matters? On family planning the government spends crores. How much on the *bandhuas*? One *bandhua* of Palamau asked me, 'You say that keeping a *bandhua* is illegal. But does my *malik* know this? If he does not know, how can I be liberated?'

If the aim of this seminar is to search for a solution to the problem of the rural poor in the unorganized rural sector, then the first task is to make the people conscious of their constitutional rights through audio-visuals, documentaries, radio broadcasts and other media. Recognize these grassroots-level *samitis* as participants in the development programme, not merely as recipients of whatever trickles down to them.

In every case, for every area, the grassroots organizations should be consulted about the requirements of the people concerned. Trust them in formulating schemes, help them with technical knowledge and, finally, convince the state government not to create obstacles in the implementation of the schemes. People are surprised when I tell them that I do not preach politics to the poor. I tell them, if they want to enter politics, in that, too, the decision should be theirs, not mine. I have full respect for, and faith in, the people and I think that they will learn to regain their rights in a democratic manner through these *samitis* and will choose their political paths for themselves. My concern is to see them getting their meals, a roof overhead and working for their own development. If there is a fire, it is their huts that will burn. They must learn to put the fire out. And when they begin, they move forward fast. Take a look at the Purulia Kherias today, you will understand what I mean. The Lodhas, Mundas, Kherias, Santhals—all are resolved to work for their own welfare.

The tribals who want irrigation, tubewells, roadways, quota-reserved jobs, schools, cottage industries, are dubbed Jharkhandis! When will the central and state governments pause a little and start wondering why there is unrest amongst the rural poor everywhere in India? Why are they taking to violent protest? I do not think that we have reached a point of no return. But remember, the poor of India are desperate.

From *'Organizing Unorganized Rural Labour for Social Justice: Strategy and Methodology—Proceedings of a National Seminar,'* 5–8 January 1984, New Delhi. Organized by the Ministry of Labour, Government of India.

Superstition,
Casteism and
Communalism

June 1987

Witch-Hunting in West Bengal: In Whose Interest?

Superstitious belief is a terrible age-old malady. It exists in the dark lives of the deprived tribals of Purulia, Maldah and elsewhere. It has survived in other societies as well. The present-day urban people, including the frequently Europe-travelled rich, the middle class, the lower-middle class, the poor—all are increasingly falling prey to antiquated beliefs in fortune-telling and the supernatural. In the last decade-and-a-half, people have sought out novel gods and demons, religious gurus, astrologers and clairvoyants. The daily newspapers regularly publish what the stars foretell—this leads to a dependence on astrology and destiny instead of confidence in one's own abilities. Indian godmen, soothsayers and *tantra*, plus all sorts of hocus-pocus, are flourishing in the US and Europe.

Perhaps the residents of cities like Calcutta read stories about witch-baiting among the tribals and think how hopelessly ignorant and superstitious these people are. On the other hand, many people in Europe and the US do think that India is the land of gods, yogis, hermits and the supernatural! In India, politicians run after astrologers. What I see clearly is that the belief in the supernatural has turned into a big business in the circles of the wealthy and the educated. When the privileged sections of the country become obsessed with superstition and the supernatural, and obscurantist ideas spread unbridled among the deprived sections of the country, it seems that something unholy is behind the apparent. Could it be that there are interested quarters who want this country to remain immersed in the depths of darkness?

A highly educated couple have lost their only son—the boy contracted tetanus. Instead of giving him urgent medical help, the parents, residents of a city high-rise, were waiting for the divine ash of grace to fall from the framed photograph of a godman. A wife in a similar family had died from smallpox. They were rich and highly educated. They did not believe in vaccines since they were brahmins. They diligently worshipped their gods and did not belong to the so-called lower castes. Many such examples could be given. The other day I came across a book stating that witch-circles have, of late, become very popular among Europeans, especially women. According to a very largely circulated Bengali newspaper, one Mr Premcharan Roy came to Jalpaiguri from Bangladesh to have his wife treated, and stayed with one Kulin Roy. Premcharan was lynched in the same house on being suspected as a 'witch'. Certainly the deceased did not belong to the tribals.

Faith in witch-cults used to exist in tribal society. Suddenly it seems to have acquired a shot in the arm. I have my own explanation about their strong faith in witch-cults. The tribals are losing whatever they had due to overwhelming socio-economic changes and all-devouring political pressures, over which they have little control. They are the hapless prey who the wily hunters have been after for a long, long time. They are losing their land. They are deprived of education and are forced to work as migrant workers. Their culture is threatened by the vulgar onslaught of *jatra*, films and video parlours. The political process has created an exploitative class within them, who flex their muscles as mafia dons. Ancient social mores are being eroded. The dowry system, earlier non-existent, has entered tribal life. Their languages are denied recognition. In numerous written histories of India, there is no reference to the countless tribal uprisings against the British imperialists. Neither the centre nor the state gives any award for tribal language and literature. They have been kept as museum pieces. In such a dismal scenario, it is natural for them to think that the witch-cult is something which truly belongs to them, something of their own. Why should they have to lose everything? That is why they have embraced the cult with a new vigour, to preserve their identity.

This explanation is entirely mine. At the same time I know it's very easy to arouse the tribals by saying that something is 'purely a tribal matter'. Then one can see that it's not merely a matter of superstition. It's something entirely different. At the very sound of the term 'witch', the tribals forget all political differences and act in a frenzy, even victimizing one of their own.

The money collected through fines or from the land of those declared witches, is not spent to benefit the person whose disease or death triggered off the search for the 'witch'. A part of it is pocketed by the *janguru*, the person who actually identifies someone as a witch, and the rest goes on liquor and meat.

Laru Jonko, a tribal woman activist of Singbhum, sent me a short list in 1982. The list showed that 37 persons had been killed among the Ho tribals on suspicion of being witches, within a short span of time, most of them women. In each case, the design was to grab the land of the lynched. Laro also wrote that in order to stop witch killing, health centres should be established, medical treatment arranged to tackle infant mortality and diseases and a propaganda offensive launched to drive home the message that it is disease and not witch-craft that is responsible for death. After each and every killing, the concerned police stations were informed in Singbhum. But the police simply refused to come.

In this connection, the role of the police needs attention. In the books *Witch Killing among Santhals* and *Santhal Samaje Daini O Bartaman Samaskriti* (The Witch and Contemporary Culture in Santhal Society) by A. B. Chaudhuri, an officer of the West Bengal Police Department who has wide experience in the subject, it is clear that in the district of Maldah alone, during the period 1951–79, altogether 96 witch killings took place. Almost in every case, the police were informed and they took the necessary steps. During 1976–81, timely police interventions prevented 56 such killings.

Here I would like to draw the attention of the reader to the role of the police. Those who organized the anti-witch-cult movement in Purulia in 1983–84, had to flee from their villages because of the wrath of zealots and political parties. The prompt setting up of police pickets helped them to return to their villages. The books by A. B. Chaudhuri inform us that whenever the police received information, action followed without fail. The administration had taken measures against witch-enthusiasts in Islampur of West Dinajpur, and it worked. Once I wrote on the problem in a popular Bengali journal. After reading my article, a police officer, Prasanta Kumar Aich, wrote to me from West Dinajpur, a district in north Bengal. This letter, from a person who deals with the problem at the grassroots level, is quite revealing:

I work in the West Bengal Police. From 1983-85, I worked as a Sub-Inspector in the Kanki Check-post under Chakulia Police Station in the Islampore sub-division of West Dinajpur. In 1981 I was the Officer-in-Charge of this police station. During this period I kept a keen watch on the problems and troubles affecting the Santhal society. Because of this I, in my personal capacity, used to be in touch with the tribal quarters of Islampur and sought their co-operation in solution of their various problems. I came across your article entitled 'Tribal Society and Witch Cult' in the journal *Paribartan* and liked it. But what saddens me is that there is no reference to the role of the police in this matter. In your article, you have mentioned the incident of Sundar Tudu. Through Mohan Hansda, I came to know about the incident, while I was posted at Kanki. The victim sought my protection. I summoned the people who had branded him a witch. I also asked Mohan Hansda to protect the family of the victim from assaults. I also sent a radio message to the SDO and requested him to send an officer of the tribal department. In front of the officer and invited Santhal leaders, I explained everything and solved the problem. The restive Santhals gave me a written assurance that they would not create any trouble whatsoever. I do not seek any compliments but do feel that the incident would inspire my colleagues in the police, if publicized.

After joining the Kanki Police Post I studied the typical problems of the tribal areas which lead to trouble, and decided on a strategy. Accordingly, I trained a Santhal home guard, and I used to ask Mohan Hansda and other Santhal leaders to come to the police post and solve problems amicably through discussions. Frequently I sought the assistance of officers from the tribal department. With the help of the above-mentioned well-meaning Santhals, I effectively neutralized the battle-cry of 'Bitlaha' which was raised in Jangatuli village by the Santhals. Otherwise many lives would have been lost. My experience shows that in most cases, witch killing could be prevented by adopting early measures, including meetings and discussions, which should be done, of course, with a certain tact. In the same way, the problem of the Bongaon witch case was amicably solved by the police in 1985. This year, the Hasan village witch case was also tackled similarly. In fact, a large number of cases have been tackled this way in the recent past. In each and every case, we invariably get the assistance of Pargana Mohan Hansda.

Behind these incidents are the religious beliefs of the Santhals, as well as personal enmity and disputes. I hold the same view as you that lack of education and scientific awareness, dearth of education among women, absence of adequate health facilities—all these are major causes. In conclusion I would like to add that a very good understanding and rapport exists between the tribal department and the police administration.

In the above cases, the role of the police is praiseworthy and I shall discuss this later. In fact, administrative initiatives in this regard started long ago. It becomes clear from the accounts of various tribal authors who have written in *Bortika* and elsewhere, that a few of them believe that witches are born with supernatural capabilities. Some others believe that they are specially initiated, and not born with supernatural powers. There are specific norms and ritual hymns for the witches. Usually childless women, widows, older women or those with exceptionally ugly faces were considered witches in the Chhotanagpur division. *Jangurus* or shamans, known as Sokha, Mati, Deonra or Bhagat, used to find out the witches, who had to admit their guilt before panchayats and pay fines. Refusal to do so would lead to punitive beating, confiscation of land and, occasionally, expulsion from the villages.

Witches had their own tradition, with attendant norms. Similarly, witch-hunting also had its tradition, rules, trials and punishments. These were parts of the social structure. We find in the Palamau District Gazetteer (1961) that the authorities are fully aware about its influence, especially about the witch-hunting Sokhas, but they are not doing anything to declare it illegal. It says that the Sokhas in the past had received the patronage of lower-level government staff, specially the police. It recommends that :

1) In schools in tribal areas and hostels for tribal students, teachers should take special care to explain to the students the real causes of illness and diseases. The teachers should also inform the students that in the developed areas of the country, belief in witches does not exist.

2) If any person is assaulted on suspicion of being a witch, then the assaulter should be punished legally.

3) The tribals blame the witches for their diseases. This attitude could be changed by making modern medical facilities available to the tribals.

We know that these have not been translated into reality. The virtues of electric light vis-a-vis the glow of the kerosene lamp can only be trumpeted if electricity is amply available. What is the use of tall claims in support of electricity where only fireflies light up dark dungeons? People will continue to believe in witches where modern medical facilities are not available. Moreover, we should keep in mind that the belief is nurtured by strong vested interests.

Reverend P. O. Bodding has an explanation for faith in witchcraft in his *Taboo Customs among the Santhals* (1898). According to him, the Santhal religion is mainly centred on the male. The women can only reach the gods through the men. They are debarred from approaching the gods directly. The Santhal man and woman do not have mutual trust in their relationship. This is even true in their day-to-day lives. This leads the woman, for good or bad, to crave supernatural powers. They cannot do it openly, since the males do not approve. That is why they secretly study the witch-cult. Bodding goes on to state that the shamans are criminals to the core. They have their sleuths who smell out information and may proclaim anyone as a witch. Often they are lynched to death. Previously they were dishonoured and hounded out.

When the administration turned a blind eye, personal

initiatives were undertaken to stop witch-killing. Bodding has narrated the exploits of one Assistant Commissioner of the Santhal Parganas who used a galvanic battery in a case where a woman had been branded a witch. When the woman touched the battery, the connecting wire was kept disconnected and she was spared a shock. But the witch-hunters suffered shocks, and finally admitted their guilt.

Wilkinson said about Singbhum in 1838 that, 'Education should spread to fight the witch-cult and Sokha practice. It is the Sokhas who make the occult calculations and detect the witch which leads to the death of the ·cursed woman. These practices have not stopped and lead to numerous killings annually.' Even towards the end of the 19th century, some writers had noticed that the *jangurus* had become mercenary and persons with vested interests had taken over the cult and led to its misuse. Dalton, the Commissioner of Singbhum, took measures to stop the Sokha system in 1860. He wanted both the Sokha and the person seeking his services to be proclaimed legal offenders.

Numerous incidents could be cited showing that those branded 'witches' or 'possessed' accept the charge and abide by the social pressures. Even in non-tribal societies, if someone is reared up on the belief that the 'possessed' will flee from a bed strewn with the leaves of a particular fruit, s/he is bound to get a shock on finding such a leaf on the bed because of the power of 'auto suggestion'. Such a person would inevitably be declared 'possessed'.

In Dalton's *Ethnology of Bengal*, we come across an incident when a Sokha accuses an elderly Ho woman of eating up someone's cow. The accused admitted that the cow had died because of her occult powers. This also proved, in turn, her occult prowess! The owner of the cow forgave her crime, but warned her that further evil offences would not be tolerated. Afterwards, the cow-owner's son died. The Sokha, as usual, blamed the old woman. She said that apart from her, 3 other women were also guilty of the crime. The dead son's father beheaded the 4 women, who did not try to escape. The father went to the police station on his own and confessed to everything during the trial.

Witch and Sokha, both are intractable truths. If this belief continues through generations, the inevitable is bound to happen. An ancient tradition has transmuted into a changed form. My information about Islampur shows that the agents of the *jangurus* keep track of local feuds, the landholdings of those involved, and secretly instigate one against the other. When the case reaches the *janguru*, he at once asks for a hefty sum of money. These *jangurus* are neither wise nor equal to the medicine-men of ancient times. They are nothing but mercenaries. Those branded witches are also not the occult-loving women of yore—they are victims of feuds, political vendetta, clan-hatred, greed and conspiracies. The sad fact is that previously the tribal could cope with disease and natural vagaries, with the help of his indigenous knowledge. His world was comprehensible to him. All that has gone. With his arsenal of ancient herbal medicines, he cannot fight the onslaught of numerous diseases, as the medicinal herbs have vanished together with the receding forests. Nor does he have access to modern medicine. He does not know that various mysteries can be explained by science and reason. In such a situation it is natural for him to seek the aid of the *janguru.*

I remember certain incidents. A Muslim bus driver of Maharashtra ran over a python and killed it. His children, since birth, had skin covered with scales like that of a snake. People called it the curse of the dead python and the children were ostracized. But a doctor diagnosed this as an incurable skin disease which is a result of frequent inter-marriage within the family. The disease, identified in 1881, still has no known cause. A girl in southern India had a nest of flying insects in her ears, but the reason is unknown. A young man of Bangladesh is afflicted with a strange malady. Stone-like objects resembling grains of rice come out of his eyes. All these cases are serious challenges for modern medical science. But if such an incident occurs in an area bereft of electricity, health-care, science and education, it is quite natural to accept it as a curse of the evil powers.

Two cases were published in the journal *Suchetana*, edited and published by Prakash Samanta. Instead of milk, blood and pus were oozing from the udder of a cow in Dhadika village. The village heads thought that a witch had possessed the cow and called in a *janguru* to exorcize the evil. Nothing happened. But a veterinary doctor diagnosed the disease and explained to the people, that if one sticks to the view that the cow is under an evil spell and refuses to seek the aid of a vet, then the cow loses its capacity to produce milk, which in turn would be a big loss for the owner. The same journal reports that in Brahmardiha village of south Bankura, a widow named Manada Patra had been branded a witch by the neighbouring Sinha family, and she had been beaten up. Neither the woman nor those who beat her up were tribals. All this was done only to usurp a small plot of land owned by her. The local panchayat and the police station took no steps despite complaints. The same thing happened in the case of Kaminibala Singh, an old Munda widow of Gopiballhavpur, Medinipur, West Bengal. The aim was clear—to get hold of the land owned by her.

Witch-cults and the dependence on the *janguru* originated in the distant past. They were prevalent all over the world, not confined to the tribals. In developed countries, the beliefs have died out because of science, advancements in industry, and growing prosperity. India is still languishing in the mire of underdevelopment and antiquated feudal land relations. The tribals are entangled in the cobwebs of backwardness and poverty. India is not the glamorous face which is shown on state-owned television. In the real India there is lack of drinking water and water for irrigation. In the real India famine continuously stalks the countryside. In Kalahandi, a perpetual famine situation exists for the poor tribals and they are often driven to suicide by relentless starvation. In Madhya Pradesh, thousands of poor tribals and non-tribals are turned into slaves by moneylenders, and silently work the farms owned by them. Contractors use them as slave-labourers all over India. India is the land of massacres like Arwal, Banjhi and Kansara. And there is a planned strategy to keep the real India in a state of perpetual deprivation. Millions are allocated for the development of the underdeveloped and tribal areas. If these areas attain real development, the wheel of the money game would come to a halt.

The tribals are victims of this tragedy. In view of this, is there any meaning in clinging to the witch-cult in the name of keeping tribal identity and tradition alive? Everything traditional is not supportable. If the practice of *sati*, infanticide and the like were not abolished by law, what sort of society would we have today?

The present-day witch-cult is a complex game. Many

unfortunate incidents have taken place in Purulia in the period 1982–84. When the famous poet Saradaprasad Kisku and others organized a movement against witch-hunts, they immediately became targets of vicious attacks. When a recent witch-killing took place, the 2 influential political parties claimed that the victim belonged to them and that the other party was responsible for the killing. These parties did not mount a campaign against the witch-cult, did not demand punishment for the killers. They did not ask for adequate police steps. Behind the incidents of witch-killing in Purulia and Singbhum are the presence of greed, political hatred, motivations of land-grabbing and extortion of money.

Nowadays, it is not only the women who are killed as witches. In *Witch Killing among Santhals*, A. B. Chaudhuri writes that between 1951–81, 96 witches were killed in Malda district, several of them men. In Habibpur police station area alone, 31 women and a man were branded as witches but the police saved them. The book has the names and addresses of 15 *jangurus*. Regarding the killing of the 96 witches, the facts given below deserve attention. The information was brought to the police by 18 policemen, 4 *chowkidars*, 2 non-tribals, 1 panchayat president and 68 tribals; and 209 persons were convicted for the killings. But the book does not refer to punitive sentences. What is noteworthy here is the prompt action taken by the police. This has also encouraged the tribals.

From the same book, we find that a majority of the Santhals live in the Barinda area of Maldah. According to the 1981 census, the total population of Barinda is 5,01,317 of which 1,24,452 are tribals—85.35 per cent of the tribals of the district live in Barinda. During 1976–77, the per capita annual income of the tribals was Rs 555, that is Rs 34.28 per month. The per capita annual income of the district was Rs 1047. Facilities for education are non-existent. Of the 1,30,715 tribals of Maldah, only 985 have received secondary-level education. Barinda is inaccessible during the rains and its area is 3,31,937.22 acres. The area has 4 primary and 10 subsidiary health centres. This means that 88,889 tribals have to depend on each centre. Apart from that, there are non-tribals. The tribals suffer from malnutrition, respiratory problems and infectious diseases. There are numerous patients of leprosy, tuberculosis, and sexually transmitted diseases.

The Santhals have to survive in this cruel one-crop land. There is no irrigation, crop productivity is poor. Lack of potable water and medical facilities add to his woes. The fear of losing his land haunts him relentlessly. He cannot grasp the intricacies of the legal system and he is hounded by heartless non-tribals. This has turned the Santhals of Barinda into myopic introverts. According to law, it is forbidden to buy the land of a tribal but this law has been defeated by the *khai khalasi* custom. Using this custom the non-tribals grab tribal land by paying money in exchange for handwritten chits. The 1951 census shows that Santhals have lost 25,000 acres of land. The process is continuing unabated. When official records show that a Santhal owns 15 acres of land, in reality he may own only 2 acres. Official records fail to give the true picture since illegal land transactions are never recorded. This process is forcing the Santhal to withdraw as far away as possible from all contact with the mainstream. It is no coincidence that places where the witches are killed are generally inaccessible and cannot be reached during the rains. It is the same everywhere in West Bengal—the same life and environment. The tribals are facing increasing pressure and exploitation from the non-tribal world. Their racial identity is at stake.

In these muddy waters, the crafty sharks do everything within their means to take advantage of the ignorance of the tribals— the process of witch identification, community trial of the identified witch, fines imposed on the person and even the killing itself. In a majority of cases, the objective is to mark someone as a witch and then grab his or her land, cattle, money and even life. The political parties are afraid to take a clear stand and demand in unison—stop this damned custom! They are afraid of alienating the Santhal vote. The police also keep quiet, saying that this is an internal affair of the community.

Does the West Bengal Government really want an end to this practice? One doubts their intentions and honesty of purpose. Since positive measures have been taken by the police in West Dinajpur, the least that the government could have done is to widely publicize the measures. But that has not been done. Why? Would the entire Santhal society turn away from the ruling parties if the government took determined steps to put a stop to this ghastly practice? Certainly not. Many Santhals, the largest tribal group in this part, are fighting against this practice as they have realized that witches are killed for the personal or political gains of a few, including the *jangurus.*

Let the government provide the tribals with specific programmes—both social and cultural. Santhals are culturally very alive. The tribal areas must be provided with roads, water, electricity, educational infrastructure for women etc. Moreover, medical and natural phenomena like disease, deformed children, cattle epidemics, drought, famine should be scientifically explained through documentary films and slide lectures. Socio-economic security and spread of scientific awareness through education—both should be done simultaneously. Then you would see the Santhals coming forward to help the government.

The government should issue strict instructions to the Tribal Department and the police. Till 1981 witch-killings in Maldah were treated as man-slaughter. The same should be done for the rest of West Bengal. Moreover, the government must work in league with the village heads like *majhis, deshmajhis, hadams, nayakes* and *parganas.* And when the *jangurus* are up to any tricks, strict measures should be taken against them. Why is not a list of known *jangurus* being prepared and publicized, asking the people and law-enforcing agencies to keep a strict vigil on them? Change the laws, if necessary. Aren't they changed all the time to suit the interests of the ruling power and the dominant sections of the society?

Places like Maldah and Islampur, where the witch-cult has been partly checked by the police, Tribal Department and well-meaning tribals, are also areas where the Left Front has a strong base. But it is not utilizing the bold examples set by a section of its own administration and giving them adequate publicity. If the government fails to adopt bold policies, then who will do the job? The government should come to the aid of those who are fighting the cult. They should appoint tribals in the Tribal Department, police and homeguards in larger numbers, especially in the affected areas. The government should seek the cooperation of social development organizations working in tribal areas and also of the district newspapers.

And a lot needs to be done on the cultural front. A section of Santhal society has become vocal in support of their language and literature. This educated vanguard is fighting the witch-cult.

The rest of the Santhal society must also come to understand that witch-craft has mutated into something new, unlike the past—it has become the oppression of the weak by the strong and hence should be stopped. Like dowry killings, witch-hunting is also an inhuman crime. The tribals need to learn that as long as they cling to it, only the vested interests will continue to reap the benefits. The tribals are becoming victims of mainstream political conflicts and they are unaware of the funds allotted for their development by both the centre and the state. There is no awareness generation system.

There is also the question of tribal unity. Before independence and the politics of votes, the tribals used to have their own law and court, and their community was much more cohesive than it is today. After the hunting festival they would hold their community trials. They rarely went to the police and the courts. But that unity has broken down. They must now unite and demand that funds allocated for their development are actually spent for their benefit. I am speaking for the majority of tribals who are landless day-labourers, unemployed and jobless. Foodgrain, electricity, education, child health, medical facilities, reservation of jobs, forest preservation and afforestation, awareness about government projects—are not these more important than clinging to the leftovers of a witch-cult?

I am quoting from a song which was sung during Birsa Munda's *ulgulan*. Replace the words 'country' and 'land' by 'tribals' and you will get the correct picture.

My country is being destroyed.
My land is floating away
Like turtles floating in water
The country is in the clutches of crimson fire
Like red leaves blooming on the tree
My country is going to its destruction
Land is flying away
Like dust kicked up on the road.

I am imploring the tribals to dispassionately think about their society. I want them to question themselves—will their society progress if they keep alive the witch-cult? They are being destroyed, they are floating away, they are burning like red coals in an unequal battle. In the darkness of a dust-storm they are walking like ghostly slaves, walking behind the contractors, agents and touts, going to their end. They are being blown away like dust kicked up on the road. They are losing their lives, nationhood, language and culture, identity—all that there is to lose. Those who are privileged among the tribals should also think about this.

The tribals should think about who actually causes them the greater harm—those who deprive them of medicines, health, education, jobs, right to land, human rights in a free country, roads, water, irrigation—or those innocent women and men whom they brand as witches and kill? If this goes on unabated, it would be suicidal for the society.

I am quoting verbatim from a leaflet issued by a group of tribal activists against witch-cult activity in Purulia—

LAW AGAINST WITCH HUNT IS NEEDED

Even the Indian Constitution has been referring to special measures for the all-round development of the tribals, since they are backward. Santhals are numerically the majority tribals in West Bengal. The witch-cult is the first among other customs which are hindering their progress.

There is no written or unwritten evidence about when and how this cult originated among the Santhals. But for a very long time, this blood-sucking unit has been crippling the Santhal society like the proverbial octopus, as a result of which the Santhal society is becoming gradually weaker. In fact, there is no such inhuman, merciless rite among the Santhals as the witch-custom. Each year countless innocent and simple lives are lost, numerous hapless families are driven to destitution, many face barbaric tortures.

Countless crimes are being committed by believing the words of the hypocrite *jangurus*. In fact, the cult is nothing but a dark belief, a cursed superstition. It has no scientific basis whatsoever, and neither can it benefit anyone directly or indirectly. And its roots are so deep that its immediate eradication is not possible. It is a mindboggling question how such a barbaric rite exists in a welfare state like India, even after so many years of attaining independence. For eradication of the custom, the government should enact laws. The rite can be stopped if the *janguru* activity is declared illegal. We implore the state and the central

government to sympathetically look at the matter and request them to enact anti-witch custom laws without delay.
Saradaprasad Kisku, President, Santhali Sahitya Parishad, Purulia.
Mahadeb Hansda, Editor, Tetre, *Santhali monthly.*
Kalendranath Mandi, Editor, Sili, *bi-monthly.*
Gurudas Murmu, Editor, Kherwal Jharpa.
Baliswar Saren, Editor, Jirihiri.

Age-old beliefs cannot vanish in a second. A lot of work has to be done for this. And when the beliefs go, the resultant vacuum should be filled in by education and health care for all. The social attitude to the status of women needs to be changed and an overall scientific outlook has to be developed. We must revive the bonds of love and amity, long lost, which we have replaced with hatred, greed and political violence.

The country and society have undergone big changes but our minds are still imprisoned in age-old darkness. Meaningful steps from the centre and state administrations could, perhaps, make it difficult for the cult to exist in its present form, at least. I am asking the tribals to think anew about their customs, which are hindering their development. When everywhere you are already at the receiving end, why should you yourselves kill each other? Take a look at the world at large—all the misery and crises are due to a lack of love and understanding between man and his fellow-beings. Would you like to move forward or backward? If you fail, it is you who would suffer while the vested interests would have a happy time. These forces want you to remain in darkness and fight an internecine battle over the witch issue. Will you still remain a passive victim of their evil designs?

From *Bortika,* June 1987.
Translated from the original Bengali by Nabarun Bhattacharya.

Death of a Crusader

It is now 11 in the evening. A short while ago, I got the news that Saradaprasad Kisku was no more. For me, this is the death of a man larger than life. Experts say that if a *sal* tree is planted today and protected for 50 years, it would still not grow as massive in size as trees of the same age of the past. The soil, the water, the environment—nothing helps the tree to grow to that stature any more.

The social environment, the all-embracing love and passion for fellow people, the sense of commitment that had nurtured Saradaprasad and made him what he was, no longer exist. This is as much true of the tribal society as it is of the mainstream.

Sarada was certainly a distinguished poet in the Santhali language, his mother tongue. But as a brave man, committed to the goal of freeing his own community from superstition and obscurantism, he was even more remarkable. With his going, I feel an all-pervading sense of emptiness. He was a man of numerous qualities. Does the younger generation of even the Santhali community of his area know how many trees he had planted there with the mission of making the area green? I doubt it.

How many knew about his personal life? He was a teacher in a primary school. After retirement, it took years for him to get his pension from the government. Why are such delays so inevitable in the case of the Saradas of this society? And all this because he simply wouldn't approach the powers that be to speed up the movement of his own file.

His life was full of misfortunes. His daughter's husband was also a teacher in a school in Bankura. One day, when he was taking a class, a gang of political opponents entered the classroom and killed him. The daughter Jastimani didn't have any option. She came back to her father with her child. Jastimani had passed the HS examination and, under the existing government norms, she should have got a job in the Education Department. But it was not to be. Not even after I ran from pillar to post requesting everyone who mattered in the state for a job for Jastimani.

In 1989, when I went to their place, Jastimani was not at home. After some time, she returned from the fields with a bundle of paddy on her head. She was working as an agricultural labourer. By that time Sarada's right side had become paralysed. His speech had been affected. He could not hold a pen in his right hand. And he had such wonderful handwriting.

But within a few months I started receiving letters from him. 'Trying to write with my left hand. Not doing too badly, as you can see,' he wrote.

When I was there in 1989, the drinking water for his house had to be drawn from holes dug in the ground, locally called *denr*. No one thought of installing a tubewell near the house for a man who was a source of pride for the country and the people.

Dhurmal, his son, graduated from the Bankura Medical College. That year, the Public Service Commission had announced that 100 tribal doctors would be recruited. Only about 30 tribal doctors took the examination with Dhurmal. He even got called for an interview, but only 22 tribals were taken. He was told that his marks in the test were not 'up to the mark'. So much for reservation of posts for the scheduled tribes! Dhurmal is probably still practising in the village.

Such misfortunes and disappointments were a part of Sarada's life. But Sarada would never speak of his problems, so strong was his self-respect.

He started writing to me about 16–18 years ago, on his own. In his first letter he wrote how his elder son had died because of the delay in taking him to a hospital. The delay was due to water from the Kangshabati dam flooding the road to the hospital in Purulia. The same old story. Why must development for a few inevitably mean devastation in the lives of many?

It is easy, from the safe distance of Calcutta, to speak against the system of witches. There is no personal risk involved. But it is not so easy when one lives where Sarada lived, in a remote village in Purulia. The greatest achievement of Sarada's life is that he started a struggle against the system and gradually developed a group of activists for the cause. And this was a struggle which he kept up till the last. He used to live in one corner of a village that was totally neglected in terms of electric power, medical facilities, drinking water, roads and communication. So many times, he and his volunteers were threatened with dire consequences, even attacked physically, because they dared to question the dark superstitious beliefs of their own community. He was the recipient of the President's medal as a teacher. He was respected as a writer. Even then, his house used to be stoned regularly, trees in his garden chopped down, his family threatened, all because of his fight against the belief in witches. He was, of course, unmoved, and continued with his battle against the deadly superstition.

Once, news came that Sarada was in grave danger, that he might even be killed. His crusade against superstition, his mobilization of a group of activists for the cause, threatened a section of his own community who had a vested interest in perpetuating the age-old ghastly practice. It was, I think, in 1987. I rushed to the house of the Chief Secretary of the state, requesting police protection for Sarada and his group. The police swung into action. Only then could Sarada and his boys return home. A police camp was set up in his village, near his house, and remained there for several months, before it was withdrawn. But the very fact of setting up the police camp sent a signal, loud and clear, to those who had tried to harm him, that the government was firm in taking action, if necessary. From then on, no one tried to harm him openly.

I remember seeing him in 1988, in village Chakadoba, in Bankura district. The Santhals of the area had organized an all-night programme of plays to generate social awareness, and to mobilize public opinion against superstitions and the custom of witches. Sarada was transported in a jeep, from a distance of 75 miles. This was after he had become partially paralysed. I still remember him, walking across the long courtyard supported, by a stick, letting no one help him. A towering personality.

Once Sarada reported how 2 of his volunteers, Sudhir Tudu and Milan Tudu, were falsely implicated in a murder case. After getting the details, I wrote about it in some newspapers. There was a tremendous response from the readers. There were remittances of money to Sarada to meet the legal expenses. Madal, a theatre group of Ghatshila in Bihar and Nabanna, a group in Calcutta, staged plays to raise money. At the book fair at Berhampur, I remember, an organization of agricultural labourers gave me money for Sarada. People volunteered to do the running around. The lawyers of Purulia treated it as a public interest litigation and did not charge fees. I also went to Sarada with a bundle full of money in small denominations, donated by a large number of people. Ultimately, the evil design of the local police station was foiled and the state government lost the case. When Sudhir and Milan were released, the tribals gave them a hero's welcome.

Sarada knew that the public killing of those declared witches might decrease, but branding people as witches and forcing their families to pay exorbitant fines would continue. He was correct. In Purulia, this is still continuing in the most brutal fashion, in complete secrecy and, it seems, will continue unabated in the future. In the last 7 years, I have received information about a large number of such cases. The police administration of Purulia has been informed of these occurrences, and has also taken timely action in many such cases.

In Bihar, the government has declared, without thinking of the possible impact on the tribal vote bank, that declaring someone a witch, seeking the help of a *janguru* or a witch *ojha*, or practising as a *janguru*, are all criminal offences. The Government of West Bengal should also have such a tough legislation. For how much longer will the soil of Purulia grow wet with the blood and tears of hapless tribal women? From my long experience I can confidently say that the tribals are law-abiding. That has been proved time and again. Then why is such a legislation not being made in a state known as the most progressive state in the country?

There is alarming news in a newspaper today, which should be immediately investigated. Lakshmi Devi, wife of a sweeper of the Calcutta Municipal Corporation, has been declared a 'witch' in the heart of the city. Those who have declared her a witch include a woman *tantrik* of Howrah, 6 *maulvis* of Park Circus and Anarbaba of Tollygunge. They have all declared that she should be killed. I know there is an election round the corner. But still, the Calcutta police should immediately arrest these criminals. All the rationalist organizations should go to the area, create a noise and barricade the roads, if necessary. Every step taken in support of the cause would be a recognition of Sarada and all that he stood for, and provide courage to others fighting for the same objective.

A journalist was wondering why Sarada should not be awarded the title 'Man of the Year'? I don't know. If it were within my power, I would have done so. His biography should become a part of the school syllabus. He was a full-statured man, in a world of midgets.

From *Aajkal*, 24 March 1996.
Translated from the original Bengali by Maitreya Ghatak.

Beyond Communalism

Often non-residential Indians and non-Indians write to me, 'What is happening in India? Why this business of communal trouble all of a sudden?'

How to explain to someone who does not live in India, that the fundamentalists have been trying to influence India's politics for the last few years, and that V. P. Singh's government and its allies admitted them to national politics? And from that time the wheels of the *ratha* are on a bloodpath.

The hapless victims of communal vengeance, and the non-communal majority of India's populace, will not remember V. P. Singh for his vow to implement the recommendations of the Mandal Commission, but for the long rope he has given to the Hindu fundamentalist forces to create havoc in a country which is reeling under poverty, injustice to the poor, unemployment, widespread closure of industries, illiteracy, a feudally exploitative land system and a thousand more onslaughts. This well-planned fundamentalist upsurge has served the rulers well. They have unleashed war on the poor and the struggling, by their determination to continue with various anti-people projects such as Baliapal, Tehri Dam and Narmada Dam. All over India an entire generation has been raised cut off from the real causes of suffering in India. Thus the water has been muddied and the fundamentalists are taking full advantage of the situation.

That they have not been very successful in West Bengal is because people in this state are, generally speaking, non-communal, and the authorities have always been very alert to take strong steps whenever a communal situation threatens. West

Bengal once had a tradition of democratic struggles, and stress on communal harmony has always been a part of those struggles. But that fundamentalists can hold open meetings, supporting the *rath yatra*, is due to an unsavoury fact. In recent years, democratic movements have been almost absent from the state and the Left Front government is very repressive towards such movements. In Andhra and other pockets of India, the fundamentalists have not succeeded in creating and generating a communal situation as there have always been genuine people's movements in these areas.

Were post-independence politics ever non-communal? With electoral politics, it was decided that only Muslim candidates should represent Muslim belts, and the same was followed for the SC and ST zones. Thus, the idea was injected into people's thinking that only a representative of their own religion or community or tribe would represent them best. It should have been seen to that the entire educationally and economically disadvantaged populace, irrespective of religion or caste or tribe were so developed that people felt equal. That has not been done. And the fundamentalists are reaping the harvest.

We are totally ignorant of the strong non-communal folk religion and culture that maintains harmony at the grassroots level in rural Bengal. The *bauls*, *fakirs*, scroll painters and cultivators in Nadia, Burdwan, Murshidabad, Medinipur, Bankura and Purulia, follow a religious belief which says that there is no caste or creed. God created 2 castes—the male and the female. The others are man-made. These people bury or burn their dead. They do not go to temples and mosques. When a Hindu follower died in Nadia, the Muslims carried the dead, cremated him and did the after-rites. It was not something unusual to them, for the liberal religion they follow permits them to intermix in all social functions. The Left Front government and the people who want to fight communalism would do well to highlight the culture and customs of these people. They achieved a cultural revolution some 300 years ago. I think that the people who have achieved total communal harmony, after heavy attacks from the Muslim and Hindu fundamentalists, should be asked about this terrible crisis, for they have proved victorious, though their weapons were culture and trust in the people, not cudgels.

From *Frontier*, 26 January 1991.

The Chains of Untouchability

By 9 in the morning the heat was almost unbearable. We reached Daltonganj at noon on 30 April. The same evening Rameshwaram, my host, took me to the *domtoli* at the river side. The Koel was dry. Thin streams of water here and there. Men, women and children washing, cleaning utensils and filling earthen pitchers. I want to describe my experience of the *domtoli* in some detail as, according to me, this experience is a mirror to Palamau. Crossing Shivaji Maidan, a very prominent place of the small district headquarter town, we turn right, pass Shivala Ghat and the temple, and enter an area of darkness. This is the *domtoli*.

I saw that the surrounding area had electricity, but the *domtoli*, even the road before it, had not a single electric lamp-post. The dwellers of the *toli* came in ones and twos to meet us, and an old woman, Tetri *mausi*, greeted us with a string of abusive words, 'Now they have come for votes. No, we are not interested. Please leave us in peace.' Rameshwaram, in vigorous local dialect, silenced her. Oh, so it was Rameshwaram who had come. Well, he was okay because he had no power, nor had he ever promised them anything. He could be trusted. But people who promised them succour from eternal misery could not be trusted. Not any more. A *khatia* was dragged out, *bidis* and *khaini* changed hands. We drank water. Talks began.

The *domtoli* is situated on government land secured for them by Kamala Prasad Vakil, a former member of parliament, long ago. Idris Khan and Laksman Babu Khainiwala have usurped their land and raised buildings on it. A civil case is going on. A government-appointed pleader is handling their case. No, they do not know the name of the pleader, nor anything about the development of the case. Why? Because none of them are literate. Are there not schools? Yes, why not? There was Madhya Vidyalaya on Shivala Ghat, a primary school, and Girivar High School on Shivaji Maidan, both very near. But harijan children are not allowed there. Once the daughter of a headmaster visited the *toli* urging them to send their children to school. Her father first wanted Rs 10 for each student. This they were ready to pay. But then the headmaster refused to admit them. So the children remain illiterate.

The *toli* has 50 to 60 huts and 200 residents. The doms are municipal employees. They sweep the streets, carry night soil and remove dead animals from the streets, for which they receive Rs 2 per animal. Their salary on paper is Rs 227 a month but they only get Rs 100. 'What to do, mataji? Everyone wants and demands bribes.' They are allowed only 15 days leave a year. The women get maternity leave not for 3 months, as per rule, but for a month and 10 days. Previously maternity leave was granted for a month and 15 days. They have to pay a bribe if they are absent. How do they manage to survive on Rs 100? Why, there are moneylenders to oblige them. The rate of interest is very high. The town of Daltonganj has 5 police stations and 600 municipal employees who are doms.

Yes, the municipality issues uniforms in their names, but they never receive them. Only once during the floods were they given Rs 55 per head, a sari or a *dhoti* each and some *sattu* or *khichri* for 2 or 3 days. Yes, they are untouchables. During election-campaign time, often the candidates do not come to them. They have to go to the various candidates before sunrise or after sunset. To see an untouchable face to face would be inauspicious indeed. One kaiti, and a mochi, rich persons both, have failed them too. The mochi took the 4 big bundles of clothes, rice and *atta* issued in their names for himself. Once his sister beat Tetri *mausi*.

Despite repeated appeals and promises they still have not been given electricity. During a wedding they borrow it from their upper-caste neighbours. No drinking water for them. The river bed is their latrine, river water their drinking water. During the monsoons, they purify the muddy Koel water with alum and drink it. There are 5 prostitute centres nearby. The women of the *toli* are molested, too. Urmila's mother Dhanmania was killed by 2 local toughs who entered her hut demanding women. Tetri's sister was run over by a tractor and killed. But the person concerned gave a bribe of Rs 1000 and nothing came of the police case. Of course, they are not allowed inside the temples. Usually they do *puja* inside their huts. On special occasions they go to the temple priests and place money on the earth, which the priest purifies with Ganga water before accepting.

The *toli* has 5 castes living there. I have spoken about the doms. The bhuiya men carry loads and their women break rocks at Rs 3 for 8 hours' labour. The chamars make shoes. Their women sever the naval cord of the newly born, give oil massages to the infant and the mother as long as they remain 'impure' owing to *janmashoucha* and receive 50 paise per day.They get some *bakshish* after the 'unclean' period is over. Kaharas work where they can; kurmi men sell gram; their women clean utensils.

The ostracized existence of the *domtoli* reveals the pulse of the place. Daltonganj is a small town and these social injustices go on openly there, and no one is concerned. Dr Ambedkar's birthday celebration takes place somewhere, official institutions for the upliftment of harijans exist, but the untouchables are left untouched. The idea that scheduled caste and tribe people are meant to serve the upper castes has entered the bones of the landowners, forest contractors and bureaucracy. The 2 all-India Communist Party offices are present in Daltonganj, but they, too, remain uninterested. This explains why the downtrodden never stand up and fight for their legitimate rights. They have learnt that in order to survive, it is safer to suffer silently, because no one is bothered about them. We can take part in international affairs, our Aryabhattas and other satellites may reach outer space, but no one in India can raise the untouchables of the innumerable *domtolis* of Palamau to the status of free individuals.

Why independence? Why say we are a free nation ? What right have we to do so? After so many years of this independence, we see Tagore's words come true. Our untouchables have made us untouchables too, for we have allowed this curse of untouchability to flourish and stay.

From *Business Standard*, 20 May 1981.

Untouchability in West Bengal

According to several district newspapers, caste hatred is taking root in Jangipur of Murshidabad district. Several newspapers are published regularly from every district of West Bengal and some are quite good. They publish investigative reports of social and political importance. As I am close to the small newspapers federation, I use material from these reports for my weekly, column in a Bengali daily. In 1989 I was alarmed to find that in a prosperous and densely populated village under Jangipur police station, the upper castes did not allow the scheduled caste people into the community Durga Puja funded by the scheduled and upper-caste people. Leaders of this ostracism were a local CPI(M) leader and a local Congress(I) leader, both brahmins. A village-born local journalist took the lead.

The SDO was informed, police were posted. The scheduled caste people took courage, united, and managed to break the caste barrier. But Jangipur is a place from where the BJP secured a fair number of votes and Hindu fundamentalism is on the rise there. The 1989 incident was clearly between the upper castes and the scheduled caste people. This year caste hatred has struck deep roots and the non-upper-castes are at war with the cobblers or muchis.

On 13 April 1991, Unnati Das, a local cobbler, went to have his hair cut at the local barber's saloon. The barber, Rajen Pramanik, refused to defile his hands by touching an unclean muchi. He threw him out, cursing and calling him names. And this 'muchi boycott' programme spread in the neighbouring villages. The rajbanshis (SC) and the kumbhkars or potters (listed under both advanced and backward classes) and the other scheduled caste and backward class people, happily joined hands in boycotting the muchis as untouchables. The muchis not only repair and make shoes, they beat the drums during festive occasions and their women work as midwives. Constant clashes with the untouchables were reported to the police station. This happened in today's West Bengal, in 1991, at Harwa, a big, sprawling village. The muchis submitted a report to the District Magistrate of Murshidabad, a great one for never doing anything without receiving the signal from the political worthies. I have had personal experience of having to fight with him as the president of the Berhampur Municipal Sweeper Worker's Union. Ours is a strong union and we have been fighting against the nefarious practices of the Congress(I) chairman of the municipality, but that is another story. The muchis prayed for security. The DM did nothing. The muchis sent appeals to the DM, the SDO, the SP, the police station OC, the Chief Minister and the political leaders. No one cared to help them. Even the local CPI(M) panchayat supported this boycott of the muchis.

Now the muchis are living in terror. They are threatened with verbal eviction notices, they can't go to the market or shops. No one will sell them a handful of rice. Meagre sources of income have dried up. Parents are afraid to send their children to the village school, fearing they might be heckled and thrown out.

Murshidabad district is a strong base of the Revolutionary Socialist Party (RSP). One RSP panchayat member of Harwa village, muchi by caste, approached the RSP leaders who refused to do anything because of the coming elections.

The village panchayat of Harwa, which supports the boycott, is a CPI(M) panchayat. One can see the state of affairs in West Bengal after 3 terms of Left Front rule.

The muchis are despondent. Now they know that the Chief Minister, the district administration, the village panchayat (the supreme court in rural Bengal), the political leaders—no one will come to their help. Forty muchi families will either have to leave, or have to commit mass suicide. While talking to the district newspaper reporter, they broke down and wept.

Jaydeb Das, a muchi of Harwa, has passed the HS

examination. I do not know whether he could obtain a job or not. In West Bengal, the Mandal Commission report recommending job reservations for 'other backward castes' is meaningless, as the weaker section, especially the tribals, never get the benefit of the already existing reservation quota jobs. The hitherto existing quota benefit has never been fully implemented. There have been cases of upper-caste students availing of the admission quota for scheduled tribes on the basis of false certificates in the Medical College of Calcutta. Protests from tribal students and a few like me did not yield any results. The story of tribal unemployment is very complex and it needs a powerful political movement to expose the game.

Jaydeb asked the reporters, 'Is there no redress in supposedly politically-conscious West Bengal for this naked and brutal caste oppression, even after 40 years of independence?' The reporters had no answer. Persons who should come forward with answers, choose to remain silent. Till the date of writing this report, the situation remains unchanged.

How to treat the cancer eating into us? The big newspapers remain conspicuously silent. When I reported this in my weekly Bengali column, I appealed to the city media and the political party organs to investigate, write and demand redress. Naturally no one is interested in 40 muchi families in an unknown village in Murshidabad district. I put forward some questions, too:

1. Why are the district members and supporters of the Left Front government silent watchers of this abominable phenomenon of caste hatred?

2. The District Magistrate is the administrative head. Why should he not be brought to task to account for his inaction and tacit support of the boycott?

3. The SP and the SDO of Jangipur, and other administrative officers—how do they account for their conduct in the affair ?

4. What step will the panchayat minister take against the Harwa village panchayat?

5. Why should not the caste-proud barber Rajen Pramanik be brought to justice ?

6. Why should children be afraid to go to school in West Bengal, a state which enjoys a progressive image in the rest of India?

7. Our Chief Minister is mainly to be blamed. These muchis wrote to him in April requesting intervention and his office just ignored it.

I think that this evil should be fought on a war-footing, for caste oppression instigated by Hindu fundamentalism is spreading in Murshidabad.

Left ideology seems to have failed here. Else how could such incidents happen with brazen effrontery? Or is West Bengal on the march to join hands with states where caste and class war goes on unabated? These muchis would not have faced ostracism had they been rich and powerful. And such political apathy is the reason why the BJP is gaining ground here.

From *Frontier*, 12–26 October 1991.

A Tribute

Remembering Asoke Bose
1920–1983

The well-known trade union leader of Rajnandgaon of Madhya Pradesh, Prakash Roy, died in Bhilai Hospital on 3 September 1983. For over 30 years, he was known as Prakash Roy, and few knew that his real name was Asoke Bose, a fugitive from the law since 1949. The name Asoke Bose and its aliases Bidyut and Nikunja are renowned in the context of the 1948–50 peasant insurrection in the Sundarban–Kakdwip area of the South 24 Parganas district of West Bengal. But, from 1952, he had to live under an assumed name and adopt a new personality—that of Prakash Roy.

The difference was not merely one of name. The two were, it would seem, entirely different persons. While the Prakash Roy we met had a great fondness for Asoke Bose, he was also critical of many of Asoke's misadventures. For over a decade Prakash Roy of Madhya Pradesh had taken deliberate and carefully planned steps to wipe out every trace of his past identity. He had a very hectic political life as a trade union leader of Madhya Pradesh. He even beame a member of the National Council of the CPI for several years. Yet, for a person whose real life was stranger than fiction, all the chapters of the past cannot be wiped out completely.

With due respect for Prakash Roy, about whom we know very little, here we pay our homage to Asoke Bose and, through him,

A Tribute

movements in the country. For us, Asoke is a symbol of that chapter.

His past had, so far, remained an untold story to the general public, shrouded in mystery. Within his own Party, the Communist Party of India (CPI), only a few high-ups knew that Asoke Bose and Prakash Roy were the same person. For most people even inside the Party, Asoke Bose was missing since 1951–52. Those who joined the Party later in Madhya Pradesh knew nothing about Prakash Roy's past, except that he and his wife were refugees from erstwhile East Pakistan. They did not know that for 13 long years there was a warrant of arrest against him in West Bengal on charges that were enough to get him hanged. The warrant was withdrawn as part of a special amnesty on the Independence Day of 1962, granted by the government at the intervention of Prime Minister Nehru.

Born into a landlord family in Nadia district of West Bengal in 1920, Asoke lost his mother when he was 2 years old and was brought up by his grandmother Mrinalini Bose. Her maternal uncles were Swami Vivekananda and Bhupendranath Datta. Influenced by such people, Asoke's grandmother was a well-read and patriotic woman and she left a deep impression on Asoke.

But his father had different plans for his son. He wanted Asoke to take care of the property in due course. He did not understand his son's sentiments, empathy for the poor and love of literature. He remarried after his wife's death.

In 1940, while in college, Asoke came into contact with the CPI. The Party was then operating underground, under a government ban. He was entrusted with the task of organizing an anti-landlord movement in his father's zamindari, which he did quite efficiently. Alarmed, his father promptly got him a job in the Post and Telegraph Department. There he got involved in trade union activities. He was transferred to Patna and after working there for a year, he left the job and increasingly got involved in Party activities, much to the dismay of his father. There was constant friction between the two and finally Asoke left home for good.

At the end of the war, he showed excellent organizational skill when he mobilized over 2000 peasants to harvest paddy, defying the prohibitory orders of the government in Haringhata in Nadia district.

But all this is trivial compared to his role in the militant peasant movement in the Kakdwip area of West Bengal in 1948–50.

In March 1948, after the Second Congress, the CPI opted for militant armed struggle. The Party was banned by the government and Asoke, along with many others, was imprisoned. When he was released, in June 1948, he was sent to the Sundarban–Kakdwip area as an underground organizer of the peasants. Kakdwip was specially chosen by the CPI for a militant movement because the famous Tebhaga movement of 1946–47 in the rest of West Bengal had fizzled out, but in Kakdwip–Sundarbans the peasants were in an increasingly militant mood and had refused to withdraw their struggle. For over the next 2 years, his own name as well as his aliases, Bidyut and Nikunja, used to strike terror in the minds of the police, landlord-*jotedars* and their allies.

This certainly does not mean that Asoke was the first or most important leader to mobilize the peasants in that area. The area had a history of peasant protests from the 30s and there were a number of local leaders who had been working there for many years. Among them were Kangsari Haldar, Manik Hazra, Hemanta Ghosal and Rash Behari Ghosh. There was a group of local activists under the leadership of a local leader, Jatin Maity. However, the character of the 1948–50 movement was very different from the earlier ones and Asoke played a key role in this new phase.

The land tenure system of the Sundarbans was different from the rest of Bengal, as it was kept beyond the purview of the permanent settlement system. At the top of the land tenure system were *latdars*, who were tenure holders of very large lots, sometimes of over 10,000–15,000 acres. They used to sub-let their land to people known as *chakdars*. The *chakdars* in turn would sub-let their lands to tenants and the tenants to the under-tenants. All these people extensively used sharecroppers or *bhagchashis*. According to a government estimate, half the total agriculturists of the area were sharecroppers in 1949. The sharecropper did not have any right to the land he cleared of forest cover, improved and cultivated. He was frequently shifted from one improved plot to another to prevent any accrual of rights. The sharecropper had to bear all the expenses of cultivation. There was no law fixing his share of the produce. By convention, he could get a half-share of the crop. In reality, he rarely got even one-third, as he was subjected to a large number of illegal exactions, sometimes on ridiculous grounds. These exactions, while not peculiar to the Sundarbans, were more severe there than in the rest of Bengal in those days. Taking advantage of his dependence on the landlord and his employees, the sharecropper was often subjected to extra-economic coercion and made to provide free labour. Sexual exploitation of women from poor sharecropper families was common. And all in a region barely 70 miles from Calcutta. Kakdwip was a riverine area on the fringe of dense forests, boats the only means of transportation. The villages were almost inaccessible to outsiders and, for all practical purposes, Kakdwip was several light years away from Calcutta, even in the 40s.

From the mid-30s, the Krishak Samiti of the CPI had started mobilizing the peasants in the area. In 1946–47, when the famous Tebhaga movement of the sharecroppers spread to the rest of Bengal, demanding two-third share for the sharecropper and one-third for the landlord, the sharecroppers of the Sundarbans also participated in the movement. However, in 1946–47, the sharecroppers' main demand in the Sundarbans–Kakdwip area was not so much *tebhaga* (two-third share of the crop), as refusal to pay the various illegal exactions. But once roused, there was no going back for the sharecroppers of the area for a long time to come.

In 1946–47, the very next harvesting season, the *tebhaga* call was no longer heard in the rest of Bengal. But the sharecroppers of Kakdwip not only demanded *tebhaga*, in many villages they harvested the paddy and stored it in their own *khamars* instead of in those of the landlords, in defiance of the age-old practice. This rebellious mood created severe tension and leaders of the provincial Krishak Sabha had to rush to the Sundarbans in February 1948 and plead with the local leaders and the peasants to return the paddy to the landlords before division, to avoid confrontation. The peasants refused. From the harvesting season of 1947–48, the whole of Kakdwip was 'unquiet' according to official reports. Even in the 1948–49 harvesting season, the demand for *tebhaga* was in the forefront. However, from 1949 the movement reached a new peak. It was no longer a demand for a two-third share of the crop, but for the whole crop. The battle-cry now was 'Land to the Tiller'. A movement for increased share of the crop thus turned into a militant movement for land.

The following excerpt from the appeal of the Government of West Bengal against a High Court judgement of 1962 setting aside the Third Tribunal judgement of 1960 imprisoning Kangsari Haldar for life, will show how the government viewed the movement:

> In 1947, just after independence, an agrarian movement called Tebhaga, demanding two-third share for the *bhagchashis* instead of the customary half, was launched in the Kakdwip area. It was sponsored by the local Communist Party and led by outside leaders such as Kangsari Haldar, Manik Hazra and others in collaboration with local leaders. A *kisan samiti* was formed from among the *bhagchashis* and they used to hold meetings in different villages in the area, lead processions and also distribute inflammatory leaflets and posters. In 1946 and 1947 the *bhagchashis*, at the instance of the accused and other leaders, forcibly appropriated 2/3 share of the produce. In 1948, as the movement grew, Kangsari Haldar and other leaders including one Asoke Bose who subsequently joined in the movement, started preaching violence among the *bhagchashis*, exhorting them to take away the entire produce of the land without giving any share of the crop to the *jotedars*, and inciting the peasants to exterminate and kill the *jotedars* and members of their families and their supporters, to set fire to the houses and *kachcharis* as also the school buildings in order to drive away the *jotedars* with the object of appropriating the entire land of Kakdwip area for the peasants. They also incited the *bhagchashis* to attack the police, snatch away arms from them and to kill them . . .

Though the immediate objective of the Communist Party in starting the Tebhaga movement was for the establishment of the *tebhaga* rule, the prosecution case was that between 1 January 1948 and 31 March 1950, Kangsari Haldar, Gajen Mali, Manik Hazra, Asoke Bose and others entered into a criminal conspiracy in the Kakdwip area to commit murder of the *jotedar* class, its supporters and police personnel, and also to set fire to their houses and *kachcharis* as well as school buildings, in order to achieve their objective: namely, to establish a Communist regime in Kakdwip in a bid to overthrow the government itself.

Once sent to Kakdwip in June 1948, Asoke teamed up with Kāngsari Haldar and other local leaders and began to mobilize the sharecroppers in the villages. Meetings were held in remote, inaccessible villages. The sharecroppers were told not to take the harvested paddy to the *khamars* of the landlords but to their own places. The state power decided to strike before the situation went out of control.

The first major confrontation took place in an interior village called Dakshina Chandanpinri. This was a village where Asoke's associates had held a meeting on 4 November 1948. On the 6th morning a team of armed policemen came to the village in a motor boat, as the river was the only route from the nearest police station. Asoke was in a boat carrying a very senior leader of the Party who was ill. He was going to Calcutta with the leader, and they escaped without being noticed by the police.

After reaching the village, the police searched the house where the local Party unit had its office. Paresh, an employee of one of the bigger landlords, showed the way. After some initial resistance by the villagers, the policemen went away. The angry villagers locked Paresh into a house.The police soon returned in larger numbers. This time they had come to rescue Paresh. The swelling crowd blocked their way. There was a scuffle and the police fired on the villagers, killing 4 women—Ahalya, Batashi, Sarojini, Uttami—and 4 men—Aswini, Deben, Gajen and Adhar. Ahalya was pregnant. Later, from Kakdwip to Naxalbari and beyond, her name became a symbol for the struggling peasantry. The police went away with 6 bodies. They could not trace the bodies of Ahalya and Batashi that day.

Initially stunned, and then incensed by the massacre, the villagers killed Paresh and disposed of his body in the nearby river. Despite severe repression let loose in the village over the next few weeks and largescale arrests of the village males, no one told the police about what had happened to Paresh. In official records he was mentioned as missing, believed to have been murdered.

The Chandanpinri events did not demoralize the peasants in other villages of the area. The peasant activists had a strong base in Budhakhali for several years. Despite heavy police presence in the area, it remained a nerve-centre of the movement and Asoke was in constant touch with the local activists and leaders.

The authorities decided to strike at this nerve-centre. In the afternoon of 31 December 1948, the police fired upon a group of villagers, killing 3—Surendra, Sudhir and Nilkantha—and injuring many. The police went away with the bodies of the dead. Several of the injured were hidden in the houses of the villagers.

A few hours later, when the nearby city of Calcutta was celebrating New Year's Eve, a boat came to the village in the silence of the night. In that boat was a young medical graduate from Calcutta who had come to the Kakdwip area only a few days before to train peasant activists in emergency treatment. Only a couple of days ago he had met Bidyut for the first time in a nearby village. Bidyut had explained to him that his task was to train the peasant activists in such a way that they could save the lives of their comrades with whatever resources they could find in the remote villages. He must never forget, Bidyut had told him, that they were in the middle of a battlefield. The training had to be in 'last-aid' and not 'first-aid,' as the injured activists could not be taken to hospitals. The discussion had a lasting effect on the fresh medical graduate. He didn't know then that within 2 days he would be called upon to do something which medical college had never taught him.

With the help of a kerosene lamp, a few surgical instruments, 'vocal anaesthesia' (keeping them busy in conversation), and not much else, the doctor that night extracted the bullets from the bodies of 2 of the more seriously injured. Thirty-five years later, this very doctor, Purnendu Ghosh, was traced to Bilaspur in Madhya Pradesh, not very far from Rajnandgaon. It was he who accompanied us to meet Asoke Bose, his old comrade and leader, in January 1983.

From the middle of 1949, there were sharp twists and turns in the policies of the CPI. In the urban areas, the calls for the railway and industrial strikes were not successful. In such a situation, there was pressure from above for further militancy in the rural areas. Asoke was entrusted with the task of taking the movement in Kakdwip to a higher level of militancy. On behalf of the CPI, Nripen Chakravartty was sending directives to Asoke about what needed to be done in Kakdwip. Many, many years later, Nripen Chakravartty became the Chief Minister of Tripura. But that is a different story.

The movement began to spread to surrounding police station areas. In Kakdwip, the peasant activists captured a number of *kachcharis* of the landlord-*jotedars*, confiscated their land, distributed the paddy among peasants and destroyed the papers relating to land and money-lending. For a few months, the landlord-*jotedars* and their men fled the area or were neutralized and there were even villages where the police dared not enter. The main base of the peasants was set up at Loyalgunge which was renamed 'Lalgunge' or 'Red Gunge'. Clashes between the peasant activists and the police and landlord-*jotedars*' men became intense. Kakdwip began to be described as *shishu-*Telengana, or an infant Telengana, after the region of Andhra Pradesh where a militant agrarian movement on a much larger scale, under the leadership of the CPI, was crushed by the Indian army at about the same period.

The authorities were desperate to arrest Asoke. Once, in Budhakhali, he was caught by a police team and was about to be shot by them when hundreds of peasants rushed to the area to save him and chase away the police.

Toward the end of 1949, as the harvesting season approached, the movement reached a new peak. It was now a battle for the whole crop, for the land itself. Firearms were brought into the area and activists trained in their use. During this period, there were bitter fights within the CPI along political lines. Terms like sectarian, reformist and 'ultra-left' were freely used. Kangsari Haldar, the veteran local leader, was sidetracked as 'reformist' by the Party and Asoke and his activist associates took the movement to a new level of militancy. Warnings given by Kangsari Haldar were ignored. In the judgement of the High Court, releasing Kangsari Haldar from responsibility for the conspiracy and many of the violent acts, it was observed by the judge that 'initially the accused (Kangsari Haldar) might have taken some, even prominent, part in the Tebhaga movement, but with the advent of Asoke Bose, chronologically speaking, he seems to have completely faded out.'

But this level of militancy could only be maintained for about a month. Between 15 December 1949 and 15 January 1950, there were 25 incidents where the *kachcharis* of landlords and possible police shelters were set on fire. The technique was described to us by Asoke years later. There were several tribal peasants in the core group of activists. Among them, Bhushan Kamila was an expert at shooting *agnibans* or fiery arrows. The trick was to wrap kerosene-soaked cloth around the point of an arrow and light it just before shooting.

In 8 incidents, the peasant activists used firearms, twice on the police. Four persons were killed and 9 were injured in these firings by the peasant activists. According to prosecution witnesses in the subsequent cases, Asoke was personally present at most of these incidents. Gajen Mali, a peasant activist, became one of his closest associates, feared by the landlord-*jotedars* and the police. He used to move around with a sten-gun sent by the Party.

In practical terms, the movement did not create any major impact in the rest of West Bengal. Even within the 24 Parganas district, it was confined only to a few police station areas. During the last phase of militancy in December 1949–January 1950, while the intensity of the movement was increasing, it was becoming confined to fewer villages. But the political implications of the movement were far greater than its geographical extent. This was a period when the People's Liberation Army had entered Beijing and Communist forces were struggling for national liberation in a number of countries in the region. In such a situation, the authorities could not take a chance. In the biography of Sardar Patel, the then Home Minister of the country, Kakdwip has been mentioned as a place that was a matter of serious worry for the government for a year. The Territorial Army was sent to Kakdwip. Police camps were set up in many places. Combing operations started in one village after another. Hundreds of peasants and activists were arrested and their houses demolished. Severe repression was unleashed by the police and the landlord-*jotedars*' men. Innocent peasants were made to sit near police camps for the whole day without being allowed to go to work. People could not move without identity cards provided by the police. The CPI had been banned in 1948. Now the Krishak Sabha, the peasants' organization, was also banned.

The whole movement was in disarray. Most of the activists were arrested one by one. The surviving ones and their leaders no longer had any base or shelter left in the villages and had to spend most of their time in boats. Within the Party, there was bitter in-fighting, blame and counterblame. Also, unknown to the peasants and the activists in the remote villages of Kakdwip, decisions determining their fate and their future were being taken thousands of miles away, in another country. On 27 January 1951, an international directive from the Soviet Union called for a major policy-shift in the form of an editorial in the journal *For a Lasting Peace, For a People's Democracy*. The call was for unity among all classes, all parties and all organizations. Armed revolution did not have any place in the new line of thinking. Soon, the CPI line of 1948–50 was branded as 'adventurist and juvenile'.

The confused, fragmented and embittered leadership of the Party in West Bengal welcomed the editorial and began preparations for participation in electoral politics.

Most of the activists were already under arrest. Arrangements were made to prosecute them in the famous Kakdwip Conspiracy Case. There were 7 separate cases of conspiracy and treason against 36 peasant activists, as well as Kangsari Haldar and Asoke Bose. In fact, Asoke was cited as the main accused in each of the 7 cases, along with Gajen Mali. In 1953, 9 of the activists were sent to prison for life by the Third Tribunal, a special court. Many other peasants were implicated in a large number of other cases and had to spend long periods in jail. Six of those wanted could not be arrested. Among them were Kangsari Haldar and Asoke Bose alias Bidyut, alias Nikunja.

Kangsari Haldar avoided arrest till 1957 when, still absconding, he contested the parliamentary elections from Kakdwip itself and won, getting more votes than even Nehru got in his own constituency that year. This only showed the massive support the movement had among the peasantry. That year he surrendered himself to the police after attending his first Lok Sabha meeting, evading the eyes of the police contingent from West Bengal. Then he was also tried and imprisoned for life. He finally came out of jail in 1962.

After the collapse of the movement, Asoke was totally isolated and on his own. He was ostracized by many of his Party leaders as a 'Trotskyite agent of the most dangerous type'. The lawyers of the CPI who were defending the other activists sent word to him that he must evade arrest, otherwise not only would he be hanged, but several others would face capital punishment. This was corroborated by the tribunal judge himself when he delivered the judgement sentencing the others:

The criminal conspiracy established in this case is a most heinous offence. It has become doubly aggravated and all the more heinous by reason of the fact that a number of murders and mischief by setting fire to a number of dwelling houses and kutchery houses were committed by some of the conspirators. Ordinarily, such an offence calls for capital sentence. But, in the present case, a departure from it, in my opinion, is warranted by the extraneous circumstances that these accused are unsophisticated sharecroppers driven to a wrong course and initiated to the cult of violence by Asoke Bose, a young man belonging to the middle class who has gone underground, leaving them in the lurch and thus evading for the time being, if not for all time to come, the hands of justice, and that they have been languishing in jail custody for an abnormally long period of time, that is, four years (*The Statesman,*12 December 1953).

For about 2 years after the collapse of the movement, Asoke stayed in hiding. In June 1951, he prepared a document criticizing the line followed in Kakdwip, which was also full of self-criticism. This was not a document prepared by a theoretician out of touch with ground reality. It was prepared by someone who, along with his associates, had to implement in action the difficult, daring, but adventurist theories imposed by the Party from above. In doing so, he and his associates realized the theoretical and organizational limitations, as well as their own shortcomings. And, above all, he admitted that he himself was greatly responsible for many of the mistakes.

The document admitted that due to wrong policies, the rich and even the middle-level peasants were alienated and became hostile to the movement. Mass organizations were completely neglected. Instead of narrowing down the enemy front, 'we helped broaden it'. The movement could not broaden its geographical base and became an easy target for state repression. The advanced sections of the peasantry had repeatedly asked for proper defence arrangements and training in armed resistance. Instead, in the name of mass resistance, unprepared masses were thrown into frontal clashes with the police. 'We exaggerated our own strength and minimized the strength of the enemy.' He also admitted that terms like 'liberated territory' and 'liberation army' were freely used and 'we acted as contractors to an imaginary revolution'. A higher form of struggle was imposed on a backward mass with low consciousness and very little experience of a mass movement. 'This did not help us to extend the armed struggle; rather, it stabbed Kakdwip, so to say, in the back.'

The document also provided an outline of a suggested course of action in the changed context. Among other points, it suggested participation in the coming general elections with a separate election manifesto for the Sundarbans, with the slogan for *tebhaga,* demand for land and a stand against the eviction of sharecroppers. Despite all the mistakes of the past, he felt that the struggle must be continued, avoiding both right reformism and left sectarianism.

We consider this to be a very valuable document because only those involved in practice really understand mistakes and limitations and can provide direction, for the future. We do not know what was the ultimate fate of the document. If it had been widely circulated and publicized, many mistakes and aberrations committed during the subsequent Naxalite movements would, probably, have been avoided. Yet, there was a sort of conspiracy of silence about his report for many years. He wrote it while he was underground. We came across it while working on the Kakdwip movement in the archives of the CPI headquarters in Delhi. It reached the hands of Dr Gangadhar Adhikari, a founder-member of the CPI. After the document came to his notice in 1975, Dr Adhikari wrote to Prakash Roy of Rajnandgaon, who was then a member of the National Council of the CPI. Highly moved at seeing his own document after so many years, Prakash Roy wrote to Dr Adhikari:

Rajnandgaon, 30.7.75

To
Comrade G. Adhikari.

Dear Comrade Adhikari,
    . . . The news that the typed report in English of the Kakdwip peasant struggle has come to your hand as mentioned in your postcard has again switched on my emotion. This report was written by me. Nikunja was one of my tech names in those days . . . I wrote this on the eve of the extraordinary Party conference held in 1951 when the international guideline was there and the conference was called to

review the left sectarian adventurist line of the 1948–50 period as well as to adopt a correct path. In our field, we had, at that time, withdrawn from all fronts. Late Comrade Muzaffar Ahmed, Jyoti Basu and all others came out of jail. Inside the Party they also had begun guiltifying individuals as war criminals. Campaigns went on inside the party to isolate and brand me as a 'Trotskyite agent of dangerous category' and then [came the turn of] Comrade Kangsari Haldar, Naren Guha and a few others. There was no comradeship or human touch . . . On the other hand, from the government side, vigorous hunting went on. Zamindars and the government declared rewards of thousands of rupees to find us, dead or alive. At this stage, I got a letter from Comrade Krishnabinode Roy: 'Survive (escape arrest) anyhow else none (arrested Kakdwip activists) can be saved from the gallows.'

. . . I got information about the conference and decided to send my opinion in writing. It was originally written in Bengali and sent to Comrade Nikhil Chakraborty, requesting him to translate it into English, maintaining the spirit and letters. He was kind enough to do that and send it to me. Then, by his arrangement, the typed copy was sent to the leadership. The original Bengali and the hand-written English translation were sent to me, but at the time of leaving West Bengal in January 1952, I destroyed them. I also destroyed many other important papers, under compulsion. Amongst them was a letter from the late Comrade Abdul Halim, who acknowledged my honesty in dealing with huge party funds. About Rs 40,000 in cash and other valuable things of several thousand more came to me and I deposited every penny with him. He was the Provincial Treasurer of the Party in those days. But in the most difficult days of 1950–51, when we, along with other underground comrades starved, when a big sum was required to save a comrade who had met with a dangerous accident, we got nothing. On the contrary, they campaigned in Kakdwip area to establish me as a traitor, saying that I had misappropriated money for my personal ends . . . But in 1973, when I visited Kakdwip after a long gap of 20 years, I found the people there had not forgotten me.

Prakash Roy

The last few months of 1951 were very cruel for those involved in the movement. The movement was crushed. The peasant comrades were in jail. Shelters were becoming scarce. There was no money. Asoke was isolated, forsaken by many of his earlier comrades and, above all, always haunted by the feeling that if he was arrested, several of his closest associates might be hanged along with him. While still in Calcutta, in hiding, he contracted tuberculosis. During this time, Madhabi, his wife, stood by him. She had also joined the CPI in 1948 and used to work as a nurse. She sold off whatever ornaments she had to pay for his treatment. Asoke's father also gave her some money for his son's treatment. Then, one cold January evening, he and Madhabi left Calcutta for Madhya Pradesh.

In January 1952, a young Bengali refugee from East Pakistan called Prakash Roy, and his wife Madhabi, arrived in Rajnandgaon and started living in a *bustee* of textile workers. They did not have any money, and he started teaching the workers and their children for Re 1 per head per month. He lived in the same house till his death in 1983.

In 1957—58, the intelligence wing of the central government suspected that he could be Asoke Bose. They even planned to bring officials from the Special Branch in Calcutta to check on him. Getting inside information, Prakash Roy, by then a trade union leader among the textile and *bidi* workers, organized a peaceful protest of the workers, a *satyagraha* in the Gandhian style. He was even sent to prison for a month-and-a-half for this. After this incident, the police stopped checking on him because Calcutta informed them that if he really was Asoke Bose, he would not have organized a peaceful protest and tamely let himself be imprisoned.

On 15 August 1962, at the intervention of Prime Minister Nehru, a special Independence Day pardon was granted for the 10 Kakdwip activists who were in jail at that time. Pardon was also granted for 53 others involved in various radical movements in West Bengal, Kerala, Bihar and Punjab. Warrants of arrests pending against 6 persons were also withdrawn. Five of them were from Punjab and 1 from West Bengal—Asoke Bose.

By that time Prakash Roy was a well-known CPI trade unionist in Madhya Pradesh. A few years later he even became a member of the National Council of the CPI, but as Prakash Roy. His wife Madhabi was also involved in the activities of a number of social welfare organizations. They lived in the same house where they had taken shelter on their first arrival in Rajnandgaon. One of the old comrades who knew the truth throughout, and who kept in touch with Prakash Roy till the last, was Kangsari Haldar. In

1973 Asoke came to West Bengal for a short visit, without telling anyone. He went straight to Kakdwip and met a few of the surviving peasant comrades. He came with a lot of apprehension over his reception. He went to Chandanpinri where Ahalya and 7 others had been killed, and could not hold back his tears. He was deeply moved when he found that the peasants of Kakdwip still loved him dearly. That was his only visit to West Bengal after 1952.

In 1975, Madhabi died. Their son Amit had left Rajnandgaon for a few years to study. Prakash continued his organizational activities without taking any care of himself. We went to meet him in January 1983. With us was Purnendu Ghosh. For a short while Asoke took cover under the mask of Prakash Roy, but not for long. For 2 days, both Asoke and Purnendu were back in their Kakdwip days, exchanging notes, reminiscing about people, places and events; sometimes sad, sometimes laughing at the top of their voices. Asoke asked about all his old Kakdwip comrades. From both of them we heard many untold stories of the Kakdwip movement. He looked heartbroken when he narrated that during his 1973 visit to Kadwip, he had found that Gajen Mali, his close associate in the movement, had died in abject poverty after his release from the jail, and that his wife was reduced to begging.

The movement in Kakdwip had not taken place because of the leaders. It had its roots in the exploitation of the landless agricultural labourer, peasant and sharecropper and their demand for a just share of the produce and, above all, for land. It left a mark on history because of the courageous struggle of a large number of struggling peasants, many of whom remain nameless and have passed into obscurity. Many of the peasant activists had to sell off whatever little land they had to meet the legal expenses of the cases in which they were implicated. What has happened to them? Has their situation improved? How many of them today have land? Among those who suffered or were sent to jail, how many have any compensation or pension or any other support or even recognition for what they had done?

Asoke continues to live in the hearts of the people. Years ago we read a poem in Bengali in a certain magazine,

In Kakdwip and Dubir Bheri
The eyes of the old peasants gleam

When they tell their grandchildren,
Tales of Asoke Bose.

We don't know about that; but, in 1976, when one of us was in Budhakhali where old peasants from faraway villages assemble every year on 31 December to remember comrades who had died on that day in 1948, an old woman came forward and asked about Asoke Bose. She was Nityabala Jana, a very brave peasant activist of the movement. Seeing the outsider, she asked with deep affection, 'Son, do you know where Asoke Bose lives nowadays?' At that time the whereabouts of Asoke were not known to us. Hearing this, the old woman muttered, 'Wherever he is, may he live long . . .'

Years later, in January 1983, when we were looking for his house in Rajnandgaon, a rickshaw puller told us, 'Prakash Roy? He works for us and also lives in the same *bustee* where we live.' About how many leaders, leftist, rightist or centrist, can this be said today?

We don't know whether the news of his death has reached those who knew him in Chandanpinri, Budhakhali, Bera's Lat, Loyalgunje or other places in Kakdwip–Sundarbans, or whether any flag will fly at half-mast when the news reaches them. Does it matter? The struggles of that period, with all their achievements and shortcomings, continue to live in the minds of the people of the area. And there, we know, along with all his other comrades and associates, Asoke will live for ever.

For us, Asoke Bose is not a mere leader of a shortlived movement that failed years ago. It has been proved time and again in the history of peasant struggles in this country, that failure can be more glorious than victory. Who remembers the names of the victors of these struggles? Or of those who defeated Birsa Munda and Sidhu–Kanhu? It's the defeated who continue to live in our minds. The name of Kakdwip has become a part of this history and has provided inspiration to movements of later periods and will continue to do so. Regimes change, but the struggle continues.

Written in Bengali with Maitreya Ghatak.
Earlier versions were published in *Samaskriti O Samaj*, 1984, and *Bortika*, Kakdwip–Tebhaga Special Number, July–September 1986.
Translated from the original Bengali by Maitreya Ghatak.

A Brief Note on the
Rural Administrative Structure

The district is the most important unit of the administrative system introduced by the British in India.

The administrative head of a district is the District Magistrate (DM). In some districts (for example, Palamau district) where the DM has special responsibilities, he is called the Deputy Commissioner (DC).

The next administrative unit within the district is called a subdivision in West Bengal, and a *tehsil* in other states. The head of the subdivision is known as the Subdivisional Officer (SDO). In West Bengal today, there are 17 districts other than the city of Calcutta. These have 47 subdivisions.

For rural areas, at the next level are Community Development Blocks, which were set up in the 50s. These are commonly called Block Offices and the officer-in-charge is the Block Development Officer (BDO). Traditionally, the BDO's office is the nodal agency for all development activities and a focal point of various administrative functionaries; all development resources are routed through this office. So, after the introduction of the system, the BDO became the most powerful official in his area. The number of Blocks in a district, depending on its size, ranges from 12 to 54 in West Bengal. There are now 343 Blocks for the 17 districts of West Bengal.

A police station, or *thana*, generally (not always), covers the same area covered by the Block. At present, in West Bengal, there are 390 police stations—excluding Calcutta—while there are 342 Blocks in the state. At the head of the police administration in the district is the Superintendent of Police (SP). For each subdivision, there is a Subdivisional Police Officer (SDPO). At the next level, that is, the police station or *thana* level, there is an Officer-in-Charge (OC).

At the lowest level are the *moujas*. This is a 'revenue village' or a unit for the collection of land revenue. The census books deal with the *mouja* as the lowest unit in the rural areas. Depending on its size, a *mouja* may be composed of one or more actual villages. There are now 40911 *moujas* in West Bengal, 37910 of which are inhabited villages.

These administrative divisions are common all over the country. In the rural areas of India, there is a local self-government system called the panchayat. While, technically, more or less the same panchayat system operates in all parts of the country, it is particularly active in West Bengal, where panchayat elections are contested by political parties and the panchayats have a very high degree of effective control over the administration and resource distribution, unlike most other states.

At the lowest level, a cluster of villages constitutes a Gram Panchayat. There are 3325 Gram Panchayats in West Bengal, that is, about 11 inhabited villages constitute one Gram Panchayat. For every 600–1200 rural voters, there is provision for one elected representative to the Gram Panchayat. The head of the Gram Panchayat is called the *pradhan*.

At the next higher level is the Panchayat Samiti, which, roughly, approximates the area of a Development Block. There are 332 Panchayat Samitis in rural West Bengal, while there are 343 Blocks. The head of the Panchayat Samiti is called the *sabhapati*. Under the panchayat system in West Bengal, the once all-powerful BDO has to serve as the Executive Officer to the Panchayat Samiti.

The apex body of the district level panchayat is called the Zilla Parishad, and its head the *sabhadhipati*. The previously powerful DM is now the Executive Officer of the Zilla Parishad. Thus, at all levels, the superiority of the elected representatives of the people over administrative officials has been well established in West Bengal.

The panchayats, at their respective levels, are the nodal agencies for the distribution and expenditure of development resources, and are, therefore, immensely influential.

Glossary

abad. Cultivated, inhabited
adda. Gossip session
adivasi. Indigenous peoples, tribals
amaltas. Kind of tree
amla. Kind of tree
arjun. Kind of tree
atta. Coarse flour from wheat
aurat. Woman
babu. Cooloquial usage indicating a higher class gentleman
bajra. Millet
bakshish. Reward
bandhua majdoors. Bonded labourers
bandobasti. Arrangement
bania. Upper caste, trader/merchant
banjhara. Arid land
bargadars. Sharecroppers
bauhinis. Kind of tree
benam land. Land owned in someone else's name to conceal
    real ownership
bhadralok.. Gentleman
bhatta maliks. Owners of brickfields
bhatta. Brickfield
bhendi. Kind of tree
bhuiya. Low caste, landless poor
bidi. Indigenous cigarette

brahmin. Highest, priestly, caste
bustee: Slum, hamlet, ghetto
chamar. Low caste, leather and hide worker
charwaha. Type of bonded labour
chiranji. Type of edible fruit
choupal. Meeting
chowkidar. Low ranking security guard
churriatoli. Name of a colony
cottah. Unit of land
crore. 10 million
DA. Dearness Allowance
dada. Local political party boss
dalal. Agent, tout
dhamsa. Percussion instrument used by tribals
dharmasabha. Religious congregation
dharumaru. A type of bonded labour
dhobi. Low caste, washerman
dholak. Percussion instrument
diku. Term used by tribals for non-tribal intruders
dom. Low caste, scavengers
gheraoed. Surrounded, cordoned off
ghooral. Mountain goat
gothi. Form of bondage in Orissa
gramsevak. Government extension worker at village level
gundlu. Wild edible tuber
gur. Molasses
gwala. Low caste, milkman
hajam. Lower caste, barber
harijan. Lit. 'son of god'. Term adopted by Gandhi for
    'untouchable' or low castes.
harwaha. Type of bonded labour
hat masul. Tax collected from weekly village market
hat. Village market
hawa. Lit. 'wind'; Trend
hul. Santal (tribal) uprising of 1855–56
ilaka. Area
izzat. Honour (in connection with women: chastity)
jagir. Area unit for revenue collection in pre-British times
jagirdar. Owner of jagir
jamun. Fruit-bearing tree

janguru. Witch doctor
janmashoucha. Post-natal seclusion of mother
jati bhrasht. Outcaste
jatra. Local theatre
jawan. Indian army soldier
jeetha. Bonded labour in Andhra Pradesh
jhopri. Hovel
jonwar. Type of bonded labour
jotedar. Tenant with secure, heritable tenancy rights over
    substantial amounts of land. Mainly employs
    sharecroppers for cultivation, who traditionally bear all
    the costs of cultivation and pay a half-share to the
    jotedar.
juloos. Procession
kachhari. Office of landlord
kahara. Low caste, porter
kamias. Bonded labourers
kamiauti-seokia. Bonded labour
karamchari. Employee
karbinda. Local berry
karela. Bitter gourd
kendu. Leaf used to make *bidis*
khadan majdoor. Mine labour
khaini. Chewing tobacco
khalasi. Helper
khamar. Storage for grains
khana. Food
khas jamin. Government land
khata. Register
khatia. Indigenous string cot
khetmajdoor. Agricultural labour
khichri. Gruel made of rice and lentils
khoraki. Daily meal
kisan. Peasant
kumbhkar. Low caste, potter
kurmi. Low caste, landless poor
kurthi. Cheap food grain
kusum. Kind of tree
kutcha. Rough, unfinished. Also, informal unit of
    measurement, less than a standard unit; e.g., a *kutcha* kg

will weigh approximately 700 gm.

lakh. 100,000

lathi. Staff

lota. Metal pitcher

lukma. Watery gruel

lungi. Wraparound sarong-like male dress

madal. Percussion instrument used by tribals

mahua. A tree. Part of tribal life in south Bihar, Madhya
 Pradesh, Orissa and West Bengal. The dried flowers are
 used to make roasted cakes, the fruits to make wine, and
 the seeds oil.

majdoor. Labourer

malik. Owner, master

manki. Village head

mastan. Rowdy, tough, muscleman

maulvi. Muslim religious preacher

mausi. Maternal aunt

mesta. Kind of tree. The fruit is eaten, and the fibre used to
 make rope.

mochi. Low caste, cobbler

morcha. Front, alliance

mouja. Administrative unit—a revenue village

mowa. Same as mahua

muchi. Same as mochi.

mukhia. Village head

mukti morcha. Liberation Front

mulkui. Uprising for land led by Munda (tribal) chieftains

munshi. Accouns-keeper

nagara. Percussion instrument of tribals

namkari aur jankari. Well-known

ojha. Faith healer and medicine man

paan. Edible betel leaf

palhatu. Land given to a bonded labourer strictly for the
 duration of the bondage period

pancharangi. Colourful, varied

panchayat. Rural local self-government

parcha. Land-owning record

patta. Ownership right for land received from government

piasal. Kind of tree

pran pratistha. Imbuing an inanimate object with life or

divinity

prasad. Food offerings to an idol, which are blessed and then
    distributed to the devotees

pucca. Permanent

puja. Worship

puris. Deep-fried bread

raggi. Coarse grain eaten by the poor

rajbanshi. Low caste, poor peasant

rakshasa. Monster

Ramnavami. A Hindu festival

ratha yatra. Chariot festival

ratha. Chariot

reja. Women labourer in brick kilns

sabha. Meeting

sahityasabha. Literary conference

sal. Kind of tree—integral part of tribal life

samiti. Organization

sammelan. Meeting

sarkar. Government

sarpanch. Head of local self-government unit

sati. Woman who is burnt alive on the same funeral pyre as
    her dead husband

sattu. Flour of gram, millets etc.

sattu-pani. Sattu mixed with water

satyagraha. Non-violent protest

seesal. Tree

semul. Silk cotton tree

seokia. Bonded labour

sevak. Field-level government workers

shisham. Kind of tree

shivir. Camp

sidha. Kind of tree.

tajjub. Amazing

tamasha. Farce, spectacle

tanr. Dry, rocky land

tantra. Stream of religious practice associated with the
    supernatural

tantrik. One who practices tantra

tech. Technical/assumed name

tehsildar. Land revenue collector

tendu. Same as *kendu*
thana. Police station
thekedar. Contractor
thik hai. Okay
tikli. Token
toli. Hamlet, quarter, ghetto
toon. Kind of tree
ulgulan. The famous Munda tribal rebellion of 1895–1900
zamindar. Landlord, landowner
zilla morcha. District Front
zilla samiti. District level organization
zilla. District
zulum. Oppression